To Highlands
Best Regards -
Judge Janice Law
Houston, Tx.

WITHDRAWN

Presented to

### Stratford Branch Library

By

### Highlands Rotary
### Courtesy of the Author

# What People Are Saying About *Sex Appealed*:

When you have to put *Sex Appealed* down, you don't want to!

—*Louis Macey*, Houston civic leader,
former Houston City Council member

I found *Sex Appealed* so interesting that I read it from cover to cover in one day! Congratulations on an excellent book!

—*Reagan Simpson, esq.*,
prominent Houston appellate attorney
(listed in *Texas Monthly*'s Super Lawyers)

When I began reading *Sex Appealed*, I couldn't put it down even through Hurricane Rita warnings!

—*Robert J. Young, esq.*, Houston,
former corporate counsel

*Sex Appealed* is phenomenal! Great subject. The extensive research is remarkable. Beautifully packaged. Has all the ingredients of a good movie.

—*Dr. Hiley Ward*, Warrington, Pennsylvania,
former Chair, Journalism Department,
Temple University

What a wonderful book! Judge Law is a great writer whose investigative reporting background rings loud and clear. Like a mystery novel, the ending of *Sex Appealed* sheds light on all the issues raised. And, like the television show "Law and Order," both the police and attorneys are showcased. *Sex Appealed* makes fascinating reading for both lawyers and non-lawyers.

—*Joel S. Berman, esq.*, General Counsel,
Nova Southeastern University School of Law,
Fort Lauderdale, Florida

*Sex Appealed* is a fabulous book! Judge Law's account is dead on correct. It is unfathomable to me how the prosecution in Harris County, Texas, failed to investigate any facts. Judge Law unearths the whole story. And she writes with great humor! I wish Liberty Legal had had her facts in *Sex Appealed* to include in our *Lawrence v. Texas* amicus brief to the U.S. Supreme Court!

—*Hiram Sasser, esq.* Director of Litigation,
Liberty Legal, Plano, Texas

(Judge Law) nailed what happened because of her dogged search for the truth . . . Judge Law is to be commended for her hard work.

—*Gary Polland, esq.*, attorney,
Houston radio and television personality

I always knew . . . Janice was a crackerjack reporter and writer. With *Sex Appealed*, she has outdone herself.

—*George McEvoy*, columnist,
Palm Beach (Florida) Post

# SEX
## APPEALED

**Was the
U.S. Supreme Court
Fooled?**

## Judge Janice Law

EAKIN PRESS    Austin, Texas

FIRST EDITION
Copyright © 2005
By Janice Law
Published in the United States of America
By Eakin Press
A Division of Sunbelt Media, Inc.
P.O. Drawer 90159 ⬢ Austin, Texas 78709-0159
email: sales@eakinpress.com
💻 website: www.eakinpress.com 💻
ALL RIGHTS RESERVED.
1 2 3 4 5 6 7 8 9
ISBN 978-1-57168-888-0
ISBN 1-57168-888-9
Library of Congress Control Number: 2005926679

Dedicated with grateful thanks...

To my court coordinator, Debra Ann Griffin, of Madison, Georgia, a genuine southern lady whose incandescent smile lit the Harris County, Texas, criminal courthouse, whose loyalty is absolute, and whose spiritual strength sustained us all.

To law professor, Joel Stuart Berman, of Nova Southeastern University, Fort Lauderdale, Florida, without whom I would never be an attorney.

And to Charles L. "Chip" Babcock, of Jackson Walker, Houston, Texas, who is the best and brightest media lawyer in America.

# Contents

# Introduction

Texas Penal Code Section 21.06 (a): A person commits an offense if he engages in deviate sexual intercourse with another individual of the same sex. Deviate sexual intercourse is: A) any contact between any part of the genitals of one person and the mouth or anus of another person, or B) the penetration of the genitals or the anus of another person with an object.

This book is about sex.

This book is about the institutional power to grant or deny sex.

This book details how far human beings are willing to go to achieve a goal.

This is a book about the extremes of every passion, including murder.

When Deputy Joseph Richard Quinn and three other veteran Harris County sheriff's deputies with guns drawn, burst into a southeast Houston apartment the night of September 17, 1998, searching for a black male with a gun, their shocking discovery in the back bedroom triggered a chain of events resulting in a June 26, 2003, U.S. Supreme Court decision in *Lawrence v. Texas*—that state laws criminalizing consensual, adult sodomy are unconstitutional.

*Sex Appealed* is an intriguing portrayal of the events

surrounding that September night, and the aftermath. It is a nonfiction narrative of jealousy, risk, betrayal, ambition, political maneuvering, and murder. *Sex Appealed* recounts the passionate devotion of an elite Ivy League team fielded by a New York-based, national homosexual rights organization, whose legal skill resulted in the high court's controversial 6-3 decision favoring *Lawrence*, and over-turning a 17-year Supreme Court precedent to the contrary.

The six justices voting in favor of striking down Texas' law were Stephen G. Breyer, Sandra Day O'Connor, Ruth Bader Ginsburg, Anthony M. Kennedy, David Hackett Souter, and John Paul Stevens. Justice Kennedy authored the majority opinion. The three justices voting to uphold Texas' sodomy law were Chief Justice William H. Rehnquist, and Justices Antonin Scalia and Clarence Thomas.

The 2003 *Lawrence* ruling is significant because it is the trigger event kicking away roadblocks to gay marriage.

As long as consensual adult sodomy remained a criminal act in some states, homosexuals could not legitimately seek same-sex marriage, because the sexual acts implicit in marriage were, until the *Lawrence* decision—illegal.

Without marriage, employer benefits often eluded gays. Nor, as implicit criminals, could homosexuals comfortably present themselves to authorities as proper parents to adopt children.

If you open a newspaper or watch television on any day you are reading this book, you probably will encounter an article or program based on *Lawrence*. A recent case brought by military personnel challenging the Don't Ask, Don't Tell policy is based on the *Lawrence* decision.

*Lawrence* has elongated coattails.

Some observers have opined that the 2004 presidential election was decided indirectly on the basis of *Lawrence*, which motivated conservatives and the religious right to the polls to vote on reverberant issues.

*Sex Appealed*'s unraveling of *Lawrence* suggests that the dramatic events of the internationally publicized case probably were based on a pre-arranged, orchestrated arrest. Such a setup, if known at the time, could have abruptly halted the case's climb up the appeal ladder to the U.S. Supreme Court.

Is the *Lawrence* ruling based on arrests that were a brilliant deception?

Absolutely yes, says one Texas appeal court justice who ruled on *Lawrence* and is now speaking out publicly for the first time. He is not alone. Even the non-attorney justice of the peace in the lowly court where the sodomy cases first began, has lingering concerns about red-flag inconsistencies in the events of the arrests.

In an America where academic cheating is at epidemic levels, where television entertainment is about millionaires who weren't, and where even the previously unassailable *New York Times* and *Washington Post* printed fake articles—did the culture of smoke and mirrors infect even a case brought to the Supreme Court of the United States?

A grandiose, legal-world intellectual heist equivalent to the Great Train Robbery?

Was the highest court in America fooled big time?

Was this high court bastion, revered by attorneys and the public as the "real deal"—the real dupe?

Constitutional scholars say they do not know what would be the legal effect of disclosure that a case already decided by the U.S. Supreme Court was based on events *manufactured* for litigation. As far as any scholar knows, such a stunning event has never happened in the history of that court.

*Sex Appealed*'s controversial themes will stimulate argument for years from all factions.

Lawrence, Garner, and their Houston and New York attorneys have always maintained that the arrests were pure happenstance—not manufactured. But, inviting further scrutiny, Lawrence, Garner, and their Houston attorneys, in 2004, strongly implied that Lawrence and Garner were not engaged in sexual conduct when they were arrested.

If they weren't having sex, there was no factual basis for the case.

*Sex Appealed*'s detailed account is based on my original research through personal interviews with both key and behind-the-scenes personalities—many of whom have never spoken publicly—the arresting officers, the defendants, attorneys, judges, and Republican Party leaders in Harris County who pressured Texas judges they felt strayed from the party line: that consensual, same-sex adult sodomy should remain criminal.

Because defendants Lawrence and Garner pled no contest at every trial stage, the Supreme Court based its landmark ruling solely on the facts in the 69-word probable cause affidavit, handwritten by the arresting deputy sheriff.

I have constructed the misdemeanor trial, uncovering facts and inconsistencies never considered by any court. This "trial" lacks sworn testimony under penalty of perjury, and there is no scrutinizing cross-examination by the opposing side.

Information gaps remain. Some persons with knowledge declined to be interviewed. Lacking subpoena power, neither statements nor records could be compelled. Tantalizing new puzzles arise—some original, some created by the passage of time.

Incomplete as it is, *Sex Appealed* is an historical record of this culture-altering case.

If the arrest was a setup, then one or more people involved with the *Lawrence* case would have had to keep that explosive secret for more than five years, and continue to keep it.

Or be dead.

But until recently, the homosexual community worldwide has survived by secrecy for thousands of years. A secrecy inviolate by even close family members or coworkers. The secret closet was a way of life. Sometimes homosexuals' very lives depended on their skill at concealing information about themselves—their skill at pretense.

If ever there were experts at lifelong secret keeping, homosexuals have no peers.

And yes, there *was* a mysterious homicide in October 2000. Still unsolved.

There is no statute of limitations on homicide.

"I'm glad you're writing about *Lawrence*," exclaimed one of my judicial colleagues on the Texas state appeal court through which the case traveled. "That case has a cast of characters more fascinating than a novel."

*Sex Appealed*'s nonfiction account introduces the *Lawrence v. Texas* cast of characters, and poses the question: Was the U.S. Supreme Court *fooled*?

# Après Moi, Le Deluge
# (After Me, the Ruin)

Deputy Sheriff Joseph Richard Quinn shifted his six foot two, 245-pound bulk behind the wheel of his marked patrol car, reaching down in front of his right knee to unhook the microphone after he heard the broadcast about 11 P.M. He could feel the straps on his stiff bulletproof vest cut slightly into his right side as he leaned forward.

"Unit 4361 is en route," he responded after dispatch broadcast the location.

"4361 show you en route. Reportee advised there is a man with a gun going crazy inside the apartment. Possible shots fired," a disembodied voice acknowledged from the speaker.

"Clear," he told the dispatcher, signaling he understood the information.

At night in the cramped front seat of his patrol car, it was not always easy reuniting the mike with the round metal hook nearly underneath the dashboard. His Kevlar vest—called "Second Chance"—is the kind purchased for officers by the local 100 Club, a police charity to which citizens donate money to assist law enforcement.

Muscular, nearly bald, with waist-thick arms and a rumbling, resonant bass voice, Deputy Quinn is the kind of guy you'd hope would be on your side when a chair-bustin', whiskey-fueled, pool-table fistfight broke out in one of the icehouse bars in the blue-collar, working-class neighborhoods of sprawling southeast Harris County, Texas where he patrolled on night shift. Houston, the fourth largest city in the United States, comprises most of Harris County.

Hundreds of round, white petroleum storage tanks the size of football fields, intermingled with acres of shiny oil-refinery pipes entwined in intricate serpentine patterns, coil over the flat landscape near the Ship Channel and Port of Houston. A few cattle and horses graze in open fields off the freeways.

Alone in his patrol vehicle, Deputy Quinn had been on duty about an hour on Thursday, September 17, 1998, answering minor disturbance calls at other locations when the weapons disturbance call was broadcast to all sheriff's units in the area.

Simultaneously with the broadcast, the call and location popped on the blue screen of the Mobile Data Terminal glowing at his right, joining the "calls pending" column. He could use the MDT keyboard to trace license plates, criminal records, stolen guns and property, and "wanted" descriptions. The equipment could be a lifesaver, especially at night when stopping a vehicle with tinted windows and unknown occupants.

From the address—794 Normandy, Apartment 833—Deputy Quinn realized he was the closest officer, and could make the scene quickest. Priority One.

Reaching between the seats, he punched the flat, red button activating his siren, then flipped each of the small, metallic switches setting all his emergency lights spinning, side and top. He drove quickly toward the Colorado Club apartments.

The report of weapon disturbance was one of thousands of similar calls to which he had responded during his 13 years as a deputy sheriff in Harris County—including nine years on street patrol.

Although Deputy Quinn, 39, was a veteran street deputy, he still felt that bit of extra caution officers sense when responding to a call where a gun may be involved. Guns, combined with the possibility of a domestic or residential location, are the most potentially lethal calls officers answer. Like a simple traffic stop, such a call can turn deadly in a terrifying instant. The chafe of the bullet-proof vest now felt reassuring.

The area around 794 Normandy borders an enormous sprawling petrochemical complex where, even from miles away, massive security lights almost transform night-sky horizon into day. Some days an acrid chemical odor drifts on the wind.

That portion of southeast Harris County is a racially mixed area of abandoned buildings, seedy motels and downscale bars commingled with residential neighborhoods of well-kept, middle-class brick homes and attractive, new strip centers—a typically discordant example of Harris County's lack of zoning laws.

For Deputy Quinn, who moved to Houston when he was three years old, southeast Harris County was familiar ground. Graduating from nearby Channelview High School in 1978, he enlisted in the army, then went directly to the police academy. A family tradition. His uncle attained the rank of Major with the sheriff's department, and his sister-in-law was the first female Captain in the Harris County sheriff's office. His other sister-in-law, Elizabeth Watson, was Houston's first female Chief of Police from 1990-1992. Deputy Quinn's family is well-known law enforcement royalty.

Honorably discharged from the army with the rank of Chief Warrant Officer, the highest non-officer rank obtainable, Deputy Quinn served as a helicopter pilot in Germany, and studied for a couple of semesters in college. His wife is a nurse.

A treeless, wide grassy band separated the multi-building Colorado Club apartment complex from Normandy Street. Deputy Quinn turned down the half-block entrance street into the complex. The apartments are built of beige wood and pale red brick in Cape Cod-style architecture, with outside staircases.

From prior experience answering calls at the complex, Deputy Quinn knew that the apartment specified on the radio broadcast was around back. He was the first officer to arrive.

As he turned right, circling around the three-story apartment buildings, he could clearly hear distant sirens of his fellow deputies' vehicles moving closer and closer toward the Colorado Club. They would soon join him.

He turned off his patrol lights and siren as he neared apartment 833.

He lowered the cover of his MDT, extinguishing the electronic glow that otherwise would have illuminated him inside his vehicle.

"I went completely black. It's standard practice for anything like that." Quinn said, recounting that night. "You don't know where this person [with a gun] is. You don't know if they have exited [the area].

"I'm just creeping through, making sure I have a safe approach.

"I parked, shut off the engine."

"4361 out," he advised the police dispatcher, meaning the officer is exiting out of his vehicle. The dispatcher immediately restricted the channel.

"4361 show you out. All units hold your traffic. Emergency traffic only," the dispatcher broadcast.

The channel went silent. That means no talking on the radio unless it is an emergency—a safety measure to protect the officer so that he can call for assistance in case of life-threatening events.

Out of the patrol car.

In those moments, Deputy Quinn was standing in uniform in southeast Harris County, Texas, alone in the shadowy parking area next to his marked vehicle. A Thursday night, relatively quiet.

"In that section of the county, people tend to vanish when they hear police sirens," Deputy Quinn explained.

The reported man with a gun could have been anywhere: four feet away in the bushes, watching from a balcony, crouching next to a nearby car, waiting unseen in the darkness with the gun, aiming.

"I could hear the other police units pulling in the [apartment complex] gate. You don't mistake their [engine] rev. When they come in they are punching the accelerators. You can hear it. They are trying to get back here as quickly as they can."

Deputy Quinn began walking through the complex, eyeing the buildings for markings to indicate where the 800-numbered apartments were. Passing through an arch into a breezeway, "That's when I saw Robert Royce Eubanks," he said. "Eubanks was probably 100 feet away from me at the opposite end of the building, at the eastern end. He began waving his hands, yelling at me 'Over here! Over here!'"

So intensely focused on locating the man with a gun, Deputy Quinn was barely aware that Deputy William Darnell Lilly, 36, came through the breezeway just as Eubanks yelled.

"I know the other deputies are arriving, but I'm focused on Eubanks. As we approached Eubanks, he was shaking. He kept saying over and over: 'Over here! Over here!'

"Did you report a man with a gun?" Deputy Quinn immediately demanded of the 40-year-old, slightly built Caucasian male with ear-lobe-length unkempt brown hair, and who could easily pass for a decade or more younger.

"Yes! Yes!"

"Where is he?"

"He's up there!" Eubanks exclaimed, pointing to the stairway up the side of a nearby building.

"Are you saying that apartment up there?" Deputy Quinn pressed, pointing directly at an apartment on the second level.

"Yes! Yes!" Eubanks, who wore a T-shirt and denim jeans, was sobbing and appeared to be emotionally hysterical, Quinn remembered.

Deputy Quinn gestured silently to arriving deputies Kenny Landry and Donnie Tipps, indicating that they should follow him and Deputy Lilly up the concrete steps of the outside stairway as quietly as they could.

They ordered Eubanks to remain at the bottom of the stairs.

Deputy Quinn un-holstered his .45 caliber semiautomatic. The other uniformed officers un-holstered their weapons, and began moving single file up the outside stairs, weapons fully drawn.

"We were trying to be quiet. Those stairs kind of make noise as you are going up there. With the wrought iron railing, I was worried about our weight making a vibrating sound.

"I'm standing at the door of apartment 833 trying to listen to see if I can hear any kind of sounds of disturbance or anything going on. The apartment door was pushed to, but not fully secured. If you were to look at it, you would think the door was closed. But you could tell it was just pushed to.

"I wasn't actually touching the front door. I'm just kind of leaning up toward it because the doorway is what we refer to as the 'fatal funnel.' Everything funnels to that point. If I am in a room, I funnel toward the doorway. That's the Dead Man Zone, the doorway. That's why when you enter in that kind of situation, you move away from the door because it silhouettes you.

"I'm at the edge of the [front] door with my right shoulder against the [outside] wall."

Deputies Lilly, Tipps and Landry were right behind Deputy Quinn.

"I didn't hear anything inside the apartment. I looked down at the doorknob. When I touched it, it twisted slightly in my hand. The door gave way. That's when I popped it open just a little bit so I could scan into the room to see if I could see anything.

"I opened it maybe an inch. I don't see anything. The room was lighted. That's when I looked back at Lilly, Tipps and Landry. I told them: 'I'm fixin' to go in.' I mouth my words silently to them. I use silent gestures. We dedicate again [Deputy Quinn pointing to himself]: I'm going left, you go right, you cover center. I took left because it was the blind spot as I went in the door. We are body-to-body as we are going in.

"Lilly was [then] to come in behind me and go clear to the right. As the [front] door opens, I'm making a quick scan to see there's nobody there in my blind spot. Then I'm going left into the blind area of the room. The blind area is to my right. I want to make sure that nobody is waiting there—waiting for me to enter.

"We go in that way, because a suspect could be hiding in a closet."

Deputy Quinn screamed "Sheriff's Department!" into the living room just before he and deputies Lilly, Tipps and Landry charged through the door. Quinn's deep bass voice could be heard a considerable distance. Announcing their presence would have awakened the dead in the small, quiet five-room apartment.

No response.

Deputy Quinn boomed out "Sheriff's Department!" a second time. The four deputies were in the living room.

"I had my right hand on my weapon, left hand on my flashlight. One arm is crossed over the other so the flashlight lights my gun path. You yell 'Sheriff's Department' one time very loud, then listen for any kind of response. Maybe they [suspects] are trying to take a defensive position. Then you yell 'Sheriff's Department' again as you enter."

It was quiet. No television playing, no radio. No one seemed to be around. Silence.

"I didn't see anything. I didn't hear anything. I gazed toward the bathroom." Communicating silently to the other officers with gestures, Deputy Quinn indicated he would look in the bathroom.

There was nothing there.

❈

Deputies Lilly, Tipps and Landry head toward the kitchen where they made a surprising discovery.

"Unbeknownst to us, there is a male in the kitchen. There is an opening across the kitchen countertop [under] the cabinets. He is talking on the telephone. He never responded at all when I shouted 'Sheriff's Department!' He's standing next to the refrigerator talking on a wallmounted phone. He sees our guns pointed at him."

He drops the phone after Quinn, Lilly, Tipps and Landry, in uniform, guns drawn, scream: "Show us your hands! Show us your hands!"

"We didn't know if he was a suspect, or if he might have been the man with the gun. So we handcuffed him until we could determine what's going on," Quinn said.

Initially thinking the man in the kitchen might be the suspect, they yelled down to Eubanks, asking him for a better description of the man with the gun. But Eubanks continued to sob and shake, and couldn't say what the alleged gunman was wearing.

The man talking on Lawrence's kitchen phone told deputies his name was Ramon Pelayo Velez, date of birth July 2, 1962. Concluding that the male, who police identified as Hispanic, couldn't be criminally charged with anything, the officers eventually released him at the scene without photographing him, and without checking the validity of the name and date of birth he provided. The Hispanic man ultimately vanished into the night—this fourth man who said little; who seemed to police uninvolved.

While Deputies Tipps and Landry were busy handcuffing and securing the male they identified as Hispanic, Deputy Lilly turned toward the back bedroom, followed by Deputy Quinn, both with guns still fully drawn.

The back bedroom was dark. But the bedroom door was partly open, illuminating the bedroom with some indirect light from the kitchen.

Deputy Lilly inched forward first.

Deputy Quinn was so close behind Deputy Lilly that when Lilly jerked backward at the bedroom door, he bumped Deputy Quinn.

"Whatever Deputy Lilly saw in that bedroom caused him to jerk back hard and fast. From the way Lilly reeled backward, I knew Lilly had seen something shocking. Because we were responding to a report of a man with a gun, I thought Lilly was seeing an armed man in there. So I went low."

Deputy Quinn immediately crouched with his own .45 to protect both deputies from whatever threat waited in the half-light of the bedroom.

"The adrenaline was flowing. I drew down, ready to fire. I had two pounds on a three pound hammer."

Deadly force that can never be called back.

An instant to decide: Fire? Don't fire?

In the sweaty, heart-pounding nanosecond before squeezing the trigger of his .45 in what he perceived was defense of himself and his fellow officer, Deputy Quinn saw in the dim light of the back bedroom what had caused Deputy Lilly, a veteran officer, to jerk full backward in shock.

Tyron Garner, 31, a black male, was naked on a bed, on his hands and knees, doggy style, his buttocks raised near the edge of the bed, Deputy Quinn said.

John Geddes Lawrence, 55, a white male, stood naked behind Garner, his hands holding Garner's hips. Lawrence was thrusting his penis rhythmically in Garner's anus.

Lawrence and Garner looked at Deputies Quinn and Lilly blankly, emotionless.

"Lawrence and Garner did not seem at all surprised to see two uniformed sheriff's deputies with drawn guns walk into their bedroom," Deputy Quinn remembers incredulously.

Garner and Lawrence's lack of reaction to what, to most people, would be an extremely startling event, shocked Deputy Quinn almost as much as the sex act he saw in progress.

In his 13 years as a law enforcement officer, mostly on street patrol, Deputy Quinn thought he had seen everything until the night of September 17, 1998.

"You could tell me that something was happening like 'there's a guy walking down the street with his head in his hand,' and I would believe it. As a police officer, I've seen things that aren't even imagined.' But what he and Deputy Lilly saw that night ranks at the top.

Lawrence continued his sexual activity with Garner as if the two uniformed deputies with guns drawn, weren't present a few feet away. Lawrence did not stop thrusting his penis into Garner, nor did Garner pull away from Lawrence.

"Most people, in situations like that, try to cover up, hide or look embarrassed. Lawrence and Garner didn't look at all surprised to see us. They just kept doing it."

"'I don't believe this! What are you doing? Did you not hear us announce ourselves? Don't you have the common decency to stop?' I shouted at them. They just kept on having sex. So I walked up to Lawrence and pushed him back [away from Garner] with the heel of my hand on his chest. I used an open palm strike that caused Lawrence's penis to come out of Garner's anus. I mean I actually *saw* his penis coming out of Garner," Deputy Quinn remembered.

Forcibly disengaged from Lawrence, Garner then climbed off the bed.

"Since both Lawrence and Garner were naked, we knew there were no weapons. We then searched the entire apartment for weapons, finally concluding there were none," Deputy Quinn said.

According to Deputy Quinn, almost immediately, Lawrence, a medical technician at Bayshore Medical Center in Pasadena, Texas, launched a verbal torrent of legal phrases. "You have no right to be here. I want to call my lawyer. You have violated my right to privacy"—a non-stop barrage of constitutional law terminology mixed with profanities, berating the deputies.

"Motherfuckers. Jackbooted Nazi thugs. Lawrence called

us everything," Deputy Quinn said without rancor. For cops, verbal abuse often comes with the job.

Lawrence, who had two prior criminal convictions in Harris County for Driving While Intoxicated, smelled of alcoholic beverage.

Garner, unemployed and with a Harris County criminal history that included felony charges of Aggravated Assault of a Police Officer, was meek, effeminate, and compliant, according to Deputy Quinn.

"We told Garner to get dressed, and he did." Garner did not smell of alcoholic beverage.

"You can't arrest us! We are in the privacy of our own home!" Lawrence shouted.

"Oh yes I can!" Deputy Quinn countered.

Lawrence became increasingly belligerent, refusing to obey the officers' orders to put on clothes. Finally, Lawrence put on only underwear.

With quiet matter-of-factness, Deputy Quinn denied Lawrence's later allegations that the deputies refused to allow him to put on clothes. "I'll allow anybody their dignity," the deputy said.

"Sergeant Ken Adams arrived on the scene. I told Sarge that Lawrence and Garner wouldn't stop having sex even after we entered the bedroom. I phoned Ms. Williford, the assistant district attorney on desk duty that night. I told her, 'I want to verify with you this is what we had.' She said, 'Absolutely. File!'"

Quinn asked her about the Texas statute.

"It meets all the statutory elements under 21.06 for Homosexual Conduct," the prosecutor advised him. She accepted the charges, a Class C misdemeanor punishable only by a fine.

Sergeant Adams, Deputy Quinn's on-scene supervisor, concurred.

"We told Robert Eubanks he was being charged with Filing a False Police Report, because there were no weapons found." Deputy Tipps brought Eubanks upstairs. Deputies already had the Hispanic male sitting in the living room too.

With Eubanks, Garner and Lawrence in the same room, "there was tension. Eubanks said to Garner, 'How could you do this to me?' Apparently it was a lovers' triangle," Deputy Quinn speculated.

When the officers searched Lawrence's apartment to make sure there were no weapons, they found "pornography everywhere. There were 25-30 sexual videotapes, drawings depicting homosexual acts, and magazines depicting homosexual sex on the covers." The material was stacked on tables and in plain view. In the other bedroom Deputies Tipps and Landry found a big poster on the wall of actor James Dean with an exaggerated penis.

Lawrence, clad only in underwear, refused to walk downstairs, struggling violently, kicking and trying to bite Deputies Tipps and Landry as the officers strove to maintain their balance while maneuvering Lawrence down the outside stairs. Deputy Quinn calmly denied Lawrence's later allegations that officers mistreated him. To the contrary, Lawrence was combative, according to Quinn.

Garner cooperated fully with the officers' directives.

Robert Eubanks rode to the nearby Wallisville Road Sheriff's substation in Deputy Quinn's vehicle, pounding the deputy's ears with nonstop disparagement of everyone and everything. Deputy Quinn doesn't recall Eubanks' specific comments. Lawrence and Garner rode with one of the other deputies.

The five deputies all deny the defendants' later allegations that when they arrived at the jail, the deputies identified the defendants as homosexuals to other prisoners. They deny taunting the defendants in any way.

"When I told Eubanks he was being charged with False Report to a Police Officer, Eubanks smirked. He just had this smirky smile on his face. There was no doubt in my mind that Eubanks knew what he had done," Deputy Quinn said.

"I was infuriated at Lawrence and Garner. Because of their stupidity in not responding when we announced ourselves, I could have killed someone just because they were having sex," Deputy Quinn added.

For Deputy Quinn, the events of that night would not end with booking defendants John Geddes Lawrence and Tyron Garner at the nearby Wallisville substation. An hour or so later, Quinn handwrote his initial 69-word probable cause affidavits, based on the information available to him at that time. As affidavits, their purpose is not to provide exhaustive, minute detail of an arrest, but to state information sufficient for probable cause.

Thursday, September 17, 1998, was just the beginning of the Class C misdemeanor cases that would skyrocket from local to international *cause célèbre*, occupying media attention for years to follow, making legal history.

Deputy Quinn's two affidavits, the same one each for Lawrence and Garner, read:

> *"Officers dispatched to 794 Normandy #833 reference to a weapons disturbance. The reportee advised dispatch a black male was going crazy in the apartment and he was armed with a gun.*
>
> *Officers met the reportee who directed officers to the upstairs apartment. Upon entering the apartment and conducting a search for the armed suspect, officers observed the defendant engaged in deviate sexual conduct namely, anal sex, with another man."*

The probable cause affidavits constituted the sole "official" sworn record in the two cases.

Those same affidavits would be read by the nine justices of the Supreme Court of the United States.

Although Deputy Quinn did not realize it, conceptualization of the arrests may have originated about four years earlier, suggested, ironically, by Texas' highest civil court on January 12, 1994.

On that day, Texas' Supreme Court dismissed *State v. Morales*, a challenge to 21.06 filed in Austin, Texas, civil court by a group of homosexuals who said that although they had never been arrested, the mere existence of 21.06

on the statute books branded them as criminals and affected their employment.

Texas' highest court told the *Morales* litigants that it was refusing to rule on the case because it handles only *civil* matters. Therefore it lacks jurisdiction to rule on issues in 21.06 because 21.06 is a *criminal* statute.

The justices advised litigants that they needed a criminal arrest under a criminal statute such as 21.06, which then could be argued up the appellate ladder to Texas' Court of Criminal Appeals. Texas is one of a few states where jurisdiction of the highest state court is bifurcated into civil and criminal matters.

The *Morales* justices seemed to be telling the homosexuals: *"Bring in an arrest, then we'll talk."* However, in *Morales*, the Texas Attorney General stipulated that no one had ever been arrested under 21.06, and no one was likely to be arrested in the future.

A slippery slope.

Bring the judicial system an arrest for violating a statute under which no one has ever been prosecuted or ever will be prosecuted.

The court deciding *Morales*, in effect, issued a public challenge to the homosexual community.

In 1994, a gauntlet was thrown down in Texas.

It was thrown down to brilliant, creative people for whom the issues were the very core of their being. People who possessed an emotion that can almost never be defeated: passion.

A degree of passion that, for many heterosexuals, is beyond understanding.

# En Flagrante Delicto
# (In the Act of)

Deputy William Darnell Lilly, 38, a soft-spoken African American, was finishing his 3-11 shift, alone in his patrol vehicle, just leaving the Wallisville Road substation on his way home when the "weapon disturbance, man with a gun" call broadcast over his radio.

He remembered the call as specifying "a *black* man with a gun."

Born in Houston in 1962, Deputy Lilly graduated from Jack Yates High School in 1991. He began with the Galveston County, Texas, Sheriff's Department, moving to the Harris County Sheriff's Department in 1991. He has taken 76 hours of college courses at the University of Houston and Texas Southern University in Houston.

Deputy Lilly, five foot eight and of medium build, was familiar with the Colorado Club apartments from answering many previous calls there. Arriving at 794 Normandy moments after Deputy Quinn, Lilly parked his vehicle, then walked through the apartment complex breezeway where he witnessed Eubanks telling Deputy Quinn that the reported man with the gun was upstairs on the second level.

With Deputies Donnie Tipps and Ken Landry quickly arriving next, Deputy Lilly, then 36, drew his 9mm Beretta, creeping quietly behind Deputy Quinn up the outside stairs. Lilly was glad he had not yet removed his bulletproof vest prior to heading home.

They ordered Eubanks, who was crying, to stay at the bottom of the stairs.

After Deputy Quinn announced their presence by bellowing "Sheriff's Department!"—they pushed open the closed-but-unlocked front door and rushed in, surprised to find a guy in the kitchen calmly talking on the phone. Deputy Lilly describes him as slightly taller than medium height, Hispanic, medium build, full head of black hair, about 30 years of age.

"The [Hispanic] guy didn't jump or react on seeing four uniformed police officers pointing guns at him. He didn't drop the phone. But I could see both his hands. We asked him if there was anyone else in the apartment. He pointed to the bedroom."

Deputies Tipps and Landry secured the guy in the kitchen. Deputy Lilly turned toward the back bedroom, still with weapon drawn, followed by Deputy Quinn.

Deputy Lilly said he thinks the back bedroom door may have been closed—opened by Lilly.

His eyes widen. His voice intensifies, amplifies, then fades.

Describing what he saw Lawrence and Garner doing together in the back bedroom on September 17, 1998, seemed almost to re-traumatize Deputy Lilly. He recognized his own voice saying the descriptive words, but he hesitated as if he could not believe he was saying those words, or hearing himself utter them. It was as if his personal repugnance at what he saw had not yet allowed him to achieve the freedom of mental distancing.

Like a victim of forcible rape, armed robbery, or aggravated assault—or a soldier remembering mortal combat—

vocalizing the September 17 experience re-inflicted the original trauma, the original shock.

His speech pattern became hesitant.

"I walked in. I saw a black male performing what could be oral sex . . . it was oral sex on an older white male.

"He was either on the edge of the bed or on a footstool. Actually I . . . if I'm not mistaken, he was either on the edge of the bed or on a footstool . . . the white guy was on a footstool by the bed or something like that.

"The black male was on his knees on the floor, in front of the bed," Deputy Lilly remembered.

"At that point, I jumped back. I kind of jumped back when I saw it."

Did they look up?

"No! You wonder why they didn't hear us coming in!" Deputy Lilly emphasized, his face, body language and demeanor registered extreme shock even years later. Clearly, the memory was etched forever. Clearly, for him, the flashback was unpleasant, gross.

His speech pattern animated, picked up pace.

"I was very surprised at what I saw...to see two men engaged in oral sex! It surprised me! It was not what I was expecting! It was one of the most shocking things in my [police] career! The sex act itself, plus the fact that they didn't stop having sex when two uniformed deputies with drawn guns came into the room!" Deputy Lilly, a veteran street patrol officer, remembered, shaking his head in permanent disbelief.

Did the two men voluntarily stop having sex when they saw the deputies?

"No!"

When did they stop?

"I think he just finally stopped. The black guy," Deputy Lilly recalled.

"Someone behind me [probably Deputy Quinn] said to the defendants: 'Hey! What's going on?' They jumped up."

"We separated them and began looking for a gun. We asked them if there was a gun. They said no," Deputy Lilly recalled.

Deputy Lilly initially remembered the sex act as oral sex. But after studying the police report, he thinks that John Lawrence and Tyron Garner were engaged in anal sex.

"I want to say it was oral. It could have been anal. It may have been anal," he said.

If it was anal sex, who was where?

"It was definitely the black guy doing the performing. I do remember that much."

So if they were having anal sex, the white guy would have had his penis in the anus of the black guy?

"Right," Deputy Lilly said.

"The old [white] guy [Lawrence] was very uncooperative, somewhat belligerent, using a lot of profanity. I really thought he was intoxicated. We had to wrestle the white guy. The black guy [Garner] was cooperative," Deputy Lilly said.

"We charged Eubanks with Filing a False Police Report. I think [when we were able to sort it out] Eubanks was jealous of the black guy [Garner], and that Eubanks had a relationship with the white guy [Lawrence]. It was some kind of love triangle," Deputy Lilly speculated, based on the comments he heard from the group after they were placed together in the living room. He can't recall specifics of what other comments were.

"That whole apartment smelled of gay. An anal odor. Very unpleasant," Deputy Lilly recalled, shuddering slightly and squinching up his nose at the sensory memory. "There were gay magazines in the house, stacks of them."

Lilly also disputed John Lawrence's contention of being mistreated by the deputies or being forced to leave the apartment unclothed.

"Deputy Landry had to carry [Lawrence] downstairs because Lawrence refused to walk."

Deputy Lilly did not go back to the station that Thursday night. He had seen enough.

He drove home, marveling that after seven years on street patrol, he could still be as shocked by anything as he was by what he witnessed in Lawrence's back bedroom on September 17, 1998.

Lilly bears a vague resemblance to United States Supreme Court Justice Clarence Thomas, who would, about five years later, rule on the case deputy Lilly and the others made that night.

Deputy Lilly has since been promoted to the rank of Detective, working in the child-abuse section of the Harris County Sheriff's Department.

Drawing his Glock Model 23, .40 caliber revolver, Deputy Donald Wayne Tipps, 38, a thin, earnest man wearing a uniform of tan trousers and a blue-and-black shirt like his fellow deputies, followed Deputy Lilly up the outside stairs to apartment 833 at 794 Normandy, on September 17, 1998.

Eubanks, whom Deputy Tipps described as "a frantic white guy, emotionally upset, who pointed upstairs to the apartment where he said there was a black man with a gun," waited below on orders of the police.

Deputy Tipps, like Deputies Lilly and Quinn, had responded to many prior calls at the large Colorado Club apartment complex.

The front door to the apartment was unlocked, ajar. Deputy Tipps too avoided standing in the fatal funnel in the middle of the doorway. Quinn yelled out "Sheriff's Department!" as they charged in.

Deputy Tipps, on the force seven years in 1998, remembered first hearing the Hispanic guy speaking English on the phone in the kitchen. He described the Hispanic male as normal build, in his 30s.

"The [Hispanic] guy did not appear shocked to see four uniformed deputies charge into the kitchen pointing guns at him," Deputy Tipps said. Deputies Tipps and Landry got him on the kitchen floor and handcuffed him while Deputies Quinn and Lilly went toward the back bedroom.

"I heard Quinn say 'Stop!' while Quinn was standing at

the back bedroom door," Deputy Tipps remembered, verifying the statements of Deputies Quinn and Lilly that Lawrence and Garner continued having sex in the deputies' presence.

When Deputy Tipps entered the back bedroom after Quinn and Lilly, he saw the two defendants standing naked beside the bed. Deputy Quinn told Tipps the two defendants were having sex. Tipps recalled Deputy Lilly's extreme shock at finding two men actively engaged in a sex act.

"The white male [Lawrence] didn't want to follow our orders to get dressed. He kept saying, 'I want to call my lawyer.' I kept telling him, 'You'll be able to call your lawyer at the station.'" He refused to dress more than putting on underwear, profanely insulting everyone. The black defendant was cooperative with the officers.

Deputy Tipps agreed with Deputy Quinn that the defendants should be charged with Homosexual Conduct. They made a thorough search through the apartment for a gun, instead finding numerous homosexual videotapes. No gun was found.

"[Lawrence] refused to walk down the stairs. Me and Landry had to carry him."

Deputy Tipps was an Army brat, born in Germany. He and his brother, abandoned by their biological father, were provided a home at Boys Country, a Houston charitable institution, where a staff member raised them as his own sons, then formally adopted them. His biological mother was unable to take care of the children. He spoke with forgiveness and without apparent bitterness, of his biological parents, and spoke lovingly of his adoptive parents, and of Boys Country.

Deputy Tipps graduated from Scarborough High School in Houston, then went to work for the sheriff in 1991. Both his brother and his adoptive father are police officers. Deputy Tipps and his wife are parents of a son.

❧

Deputy Kenneth Paul Landry, then 34, was en route from home to the station to begin his 11 P.M. to 7 A.M. shift on September 17, 1998, when dispatch broadcast the call of a weapon disturbance/male with a gun.

"It was Priority One: Must respond if not tied up or too far away. The more the merrier. I was about a mile away from 794 Normandy. Dispatch said the caller would meet us in the common area of the apartment complex. I'd answered a lot of calls at the Colorado Club. It's a clean complex, but lots of young people live there. Lots of drug and intoxication disturbances on the weekend. I would describe the neighborhood as lower middle-class."

"I called in to say 'en route.' I turned on my lights."

Turning right into the complex, Deputy Landry used the intense spotlight on his vehicle to search the building groups for numbers indicating he was nearing apartment 833.

Like Deputy Quinn, Deputy Landry's adrenaline went up, alertness up, because a gun is reportedly involved. "You don't know. Anything could happen anytime. Your sense of attention goes up." He wore a bulletproof vest.

In remembering the reportee Eubanks' demeanor, Deputy Landry noted a disconnect between the level of emotion Eubanks displayed in front of the officers, and the events Eubanks was describing.

"Eubanks seemed upset, but not as upset as you would expect under those circumstances. He smelled of alcoholic beverages," Deputy Landry said.

After being briefed quickly by Deputy Quinn who pointed out the apartment 833 location, Deputy Landry drew his Colt .45 and joined the others creeping up the outside stairway. He remembered screaming "Sheriff's Department!" with Deputy Quinn as they entered the small, five-room apartment.

The male in the kitchen, whom Deputy Landry described as Hispanic, "in his 20s or 30s with lots of short straight hair, medium build, speaking English," was intoxicated. Deputy Landry couldn't see what the guy in the kitchen was doing when Deputy Quinn ordered the man to show his hands. Velez, the man police described as Hispanic, said almost nothing during all the events of the evening, which concluded in his release. He did speak English well, according to deputies.

After deputies subdued Eubanks, Lawrence and Garner—handcuffing them and seating them and the "Hispanic male" in the living room to try to sort out what happened—Lawrence verbally lashed out at Eubanks for contacting the police, which Eubanks initially denied.

In front of the group, Eubanks protested his innocence so vigorously, that Deputy Quinn called Sheriff's dispatch and asked from where the call to police originated?

"Dispatch has the equivalent of Caller I.D. Whenever we get a call, the number being called from flashes up on a screen. The call to the sheriff's office was made from that apartment. When Deputy Quinn confronted Eubanks with that information, Eubanks stopped claiming he didn't make the call," Deputy Landry remembered. (Deputy Quinn's recollection of checking Eubanks' remarks matches Deputy Landry's except that Deputy Quinn remembers that dispatch told him the call came from a pay phone. A copy of the call slip confirms a pay phone. However, since a tape of the call is apparently unavailable, there is no evidence of who made the phone call to law enforcement.)

Eubanks volunteered that he lived in the apartment with Lawrence. Eubanks told Deputy Landry that he brought the Hispanic and Garner to the apartment for a party after meeting them somewhere. During the evening, Lawrence became sexually interested in Garner, going to the back bedroom with Garner, which Eubanks said made him jealous. Eubanks said he phoned the police in hopes of breaking up the sexual activity between Lawrence and Garner.

Lawrence was telling the deputies he'd "have all their

jobs!" when Deputy Landry walked into the back bedroom.

"Mr. Lawrence was intoxicated, extremely belligerent, out of control. He said we didn't belong in his fuckin' house. He wanted to call his lawyer. He got on his underwear and sat on the bed. Suddenly, Mr. Lawrence dove toward the nightstand. Of course we were all on him in a moment [because the initial report had been of a gun]. We didn't let him reach the drawer. He may have been reaching for the phone, but we didn't know [what he was suddenly reaching for]. After that, [Lawrence] refused to cooperate with us in any way," Landry remembered.

Lawrence spit on Deputy Landry as he and Deputy Tipps struggled to get Lawrence down the outside stair and into Landry's vehicle. Landry remembers the spitting incident unemotionally, and without apparent bitterness. On the ride in Landry's vehicle to the Wallisville Road substation, Lawrence was quiet.

Pulling up to the sally port—a metal, cage-like secure entryway encasing the sheriff's office back door—Deputy Landry honked in a prearranged signal. The deputy on duty inside studied the driver and passenger on a closed-circuit camera. The huge, metal-screened door rattled slowly up. After Deputy Landry pulled in, the gate clattered to the cement behind his patrol vehicle.

Leaving his prisoner momentarily, Deputy Landry opened one of the gray metal boxes to the right of the satellite jail door, and un-holstered his Colt .45, placing it on the padded inside surface. He closed and locked the box, putting the key on his belt.

His prisoner, John Geddes Lawrence, refused to get out of the police vehicle.

So Deputy Landry, five foot eight and 175 pounds, dragged Lawrence into the booking area of the substation, handcuffing him to a wooden bench on the left-hand side of a small, gray-painted room.

Deputy Landry remembered that when they searched the apartment to make sure there was no weapon, there were boxes and boxes of pornographic materials everywhere. In plain view on a living-room table was a dish, with a small amount of marijuana, or a dish and a roach (the butt of a marijuana cigarette). Deputy Landry said the assistant district attorney on duty that night advised that the DA's office could not file charges involving the drugs because, since there were at least four persons in the apartment, it could not be legally determined to whom the marijuana belonged, clouding the possession requirements.

Born in Lake Charles, Louisiana, Landry joined the sheriff's department in 1993, and was assigned to work in the jail: first-floor security. He then worked the visitation area, then in emergency response. To obtain street experience, on his own time Deputy Landry rode street patrol with a veteran street deputy. Landry was assigned to street patrol in April 1998. He keeps a big wad of chewing tobacco in one cheek, spitting the juice periodically into a white Styrofoam cup.

Landry graduated from nearby Furr High School in 1981. He served as an Army Ranger for 11½ years until 1992, achieving Staff Sergeant rank before being honorably discharged.

If you contacted Central Casting requesting a quiet, benevolent police sergeant, they'd send over Sergeant Kenneth Oliver Adams. Short, with thick, curly salt-and-pepper hair, and a slow, soft Southern drawl, Sergeant Adams served four years in the navy, including service in Vietnam in 1961-62 where he attained a rank equivalent of Sergeant.

Born in Denver, Colorado, he attended Haltom City High School in Texas, but graduated in 1960 from Gillum High School in Gillum, Arkansas. Joining the Harris County Sheriff's Department in July 1977, he retired in March 2003 at 63 years of age. He served 24 years on street patrol, plus two years working in the jail. He was promoted to Sergeant in December 1993.

Adams said, "Certain calls, like weapons disturbance, it was mandated that a supervisor respond." So Sergeant Adams, then 58, and a 21-year veteran on September 17, 1998, monitored the weapons call at the station, and showed up at 794 Normandy just as, or just after, his four uniformed officers, guns drawn, were entering apartment 833. He didn't recall if he un-holstered his 9mm semiautomatic, but he did enter Lawrence's apartment after the other officers.

Now retired, Sergeant Adams' memory remains cloudy, even after reviewing the police report, on what he regarded as a routine response and arrest.

"I do remember clearly hearing Deputy Lilly gasp [loudly] in total surprise when he saw the two men in the back bedroom having sex. I could hear Lilly's gasp even from the other room. Deputy Lilly started back out of the bedroom [exclaiming] 'I don't believe it! I don't believe it!' I guess he had never seen anything like that before. When I entered the bedroom, the defendants were still in bed, but not having sex," Sergeant Adams said. "Lawrence was very verbally abusive.

"Things were a little chaotic. We tried to find out from Eubanks who made the call to police about the man with the gun. I watched the two or three males in the living room, to back up the other officers.

"Eubanks said, 'I made the call because I knew you would come. I knew weapons disturbance would get your attention.'"

"[Eubanks] said he knew that in order to get police attention, he had to report something beyond a disturbance. Eubanks knew that a report of a gun would get attention," Sergeant Adams remembered.

At first Sergeant Adams thought that Lawrence, not Eubanks, may have confessed to being the one who phoned the police. Then, with further thought, Adams recalled it may have been Eubanks confessing, since Eubanks was charged with making a False Report to a Police Officer.

Deputy Quinn phoned the attorney on duty in the district attorney's office to inquire about filing the Homosexual Conduct charges. Because Deputy Quinn was first to take the call, the case, by custom, was assigned to him.

"I was a little curious to see if the DA would take the charges, and if not, why [not]? Deputy Quinn was within the law. He is a mature deputy. He is intelligent, knows what he is doing, and knows how to do it," Sgt. Adams said of Deputy Quinn.

Sergeant Adams joins Deputies Quinn, Landry and Tipps in disputing Lawrence's claim of mistreatment by the police. "We called Emergency Medical Services. When EMS arrived, Lawrence and Garner refused treatment," the sergeant said. "Lawrence was very combative toward the deputies."

In 1998, Homosexual Conduct, under Texas law 21.06, was a Class C misdemeanor, punishable only by a fine. With a Class C, officers have the option of issuing a citation to a defendant at the scene, then releasing a defendant on a promise to show up in court on a future date—or making an arrest, and transporting the defendant to jail.

"We decided, and I agreed, that the defendants should be arrested—for the safety of the public, the safety of the other residents of that apartment complex, and the safety of the defendants themselves. If we had just issued a citation, and allowed the defendants back together, we probably would have been called back out there that night. And, we had had the report of a gun, so we were concerned about the whole situation. Someone could have been seriously hurt. It was best for everyone to get the three of them out of there and take them to jail," Sergeant Adams explained.

Adams remembers arriving on the scene as or just after the deputies went in the front door. However, all four deputies remember he arrived just as or after the man on the telephone was being subdued in the kitchen.

The police report states that on arrival at the Wallisville Road substation, Eubanks: "...had to be forcibly removed from the patrol car. Eubanks fell to the ground claiming officers assaulted him, and had to be picked up and carried a portion of the way into the station. He then began walking on his own."

The sergeant, agreeing that Velez, the male described as "Hispanic," couldn't be charged with anything, authorized his release into the night. All deputies agreed that the "Hispanic male" spoke English well. (All deputies were interviewed separately on different dates. No deputy was apprised of information provided by other deputies.)

Preplanned, orchestrated arrests were 1960s staples at lunch counters, bus stations, and schools across the South, for the purpose of mounting legal challenges to racial segregation laws. Everyone, including the courts, knew those arrests were invited.

The 2003 U.S. Supreme Court seized upon "right to privacy" as its constitutional reasoning in ruling for *Lawrence*. So the issue of whether the arrests were *invited* for the purpose of litigation, is of crucial importance. Defendants can't invite cops over to see them having sex, then complain that the responding police violated their privacy!

Only Justice Sandra Day O'Connor, although she voted with the 6-3 majority, based her decision on equal protection grounds. On *privacy* grounds, the vote was a narrow 5-4. The majority hinted that they chose privacy as a basis for their *Lawrence* ruling rather than equal protection because, had they chosen equal protection, the statute could be changed to apply equally to heterosexuals, thus creating the possibility that years down the road, the high court would again face the same controversial issues.

If the defendants or anyone admitted—before or after *Lawrence* was decided—that they *invited* the arrests by setting up the September 17, 1998, scenario, the invitation would relinquish their legal right to an expectation of privacy, undermining the very privacy grounds on which the high court granted relief.

*Lawrence* would implode legally.

Defense denials of a setup must be permanent, unwavering, resolute.

During the entire case, including its nearly five-year journey to the U.S. Supreme Court, no one, not even prosecutors, ever talked with the five arresting deputies! (Deputy Quinn said a man identifying himself as "a college professor writing a paper," phoned not long after the arrests to ask Deputy Quinn questions).

Whoever phoned September 17, 1998—the call to police, untraceable except to a pay phone, was perfect.

Since the sex act would be consensual, and would occur in private—logically, one of the participants would have to summon police to invite the arrest. But if one of the same-sex participants invited police observers (*"We're sodomizing in violation of Texas Penal Code 21.06! Come on over!"*), such a call would get nowhere. Or if complicit third parties invited observers (*"They're having sex! Come on over!"*), those *invitations* would destroy claims of an expectation of privacy, thus precluding a constitutional challenge predicated on privacy grounds.

Police would have to encounter a 21.06 violation after entering private premises for a legally defensible reason other than same-sex sodomy—and, ideally, under exigent circumstances (commission of a felony, immediate danger of death or serious bodily injury).

The factual circumstances required for an arrest under 21.06, legally sufficient to use as a vehicle for a constitutional challenge, were so narrow as to almost eliminate happenstance. Deliberately violating 21.06 required precise events, tailored exactly to the criminal misdemeanor statute.

The report of a black man going crazy with a gun perfectly complies with the exigent circumstances legally necessary to evaporate any Fourth Amendment (search and seizure) issues with the deputies' entrance into Lawrence's home. Police *have* to respond to a report of a gun, just as Eubanks told deputies.

Although all three longtime friends (Lawrence, Garner, and Eubanks) have criminal records, only Eubanks—who ran downstairs to assist arriving deputies in locating apartment 833, and incurred an almost certain arrest later for what he knew was a false report—was a convicted felon. Of the three, Eubanks was the only one for whom an arrest for false report, a misdemeanor that could involve jail punishment, would be an insignificant interlude.

By pointing, the man identifying himself as Velez, helpfully funneled deputies to Lawrence's back bedroom a few feet away, where the door, like Lawrence's front door, was conveniently unlocked, ajar. Thus Velez joined Eubanks on September 17, 1998, as the second person to helpfully channel deputies at crucial points—closer and closer toward locating Lawrence and Garner having sex.

Every possible impediment to the officers' outside entry and inside entry seemed to have been conveniently removed.

Deputies found the two old friends, Lawrence and Garner, naked, engaged in sodomy, undisturbed by the ruckus of: five heavy men navigating metal-railed stairs, booming-voiced deputies twice shouting entry, scuffling with Velez on the kitchen floor only a few feet away, searching the front bedroom, and shouting further questions to Eubanks downstairs.

Lawrence and Garner, like Velez on the phone, were unfazed by the unfolding hubbub a few feet away. The lovers exhibited neither surprise nor shock, continuing their sex act as if two uniformed deputies with drawn guns were invisible.

After being ordered to stop the sexual activity, Lawrence, a non-attorney, immediately began spewing legal phrases and concepts such as: "You have no right to invade my home! You are violating my right to privacy!"

*Invade? Violating?* It seemed Lawrence was reading

aloud from the table of contents in a constitutional law book.

Contrary to popular misconceptions, cops really don't *want* to make misdemeanor arrests. When you get to know cops, you learn this.

All four deputies were veterans. Veteran cops have seen *everything.* Despite public beliefs otherwise, cops develop tolerance for petty failings and ordinary human frailties. If for no other reason than a practical one, police are inclined to overlook minor transgressions, particularly misdemeanors like 21.06 that involve only a fine. If they make a misdemeanor arrest, they have to do the paperwork.

But if the deputies *didn't* arrest Garner and Lawrence, all the years-long hope in the national homosexual community for a 21.06 test case would be lost.

Tantalizingly close, and yet so far.

Before the cops turned to leave in disgust, it was essential that they quickly be goaded into arresting Lawrence and Garner.

Insiders familiar with cop culture know there are two classic variables that will motivate cops into making a misdemeanor arrest they wouldn't ordinarily make: 1) mouthing off, smart-assing, verbally challenging the officer's authority to arrest; and 2) continuing whatever act or transgression after the officer orders "Stop!"

Someone who had read an equal number of arrest reports seemed to have scripted Lawrence's instant mouthing off to the deputies. And that was followed by his failure to obey the deputies' routine directives. To seal the deal, Lawrence suddenly lunged toward a bedroom drawer. Significantly, Lawrence did not lunge toward the drawer when only two deputies were present. He waited until *four* officers were present, ensuring that he would annoy *more* deputies, increasing his chances of arrest.

The futility of lunging anywhere with four substantial

deputies with guns standing within six feet is obvious. Lawrence had been arrested at least twice previously. He knew the drill. He knew what would happen when he lunged.

Since the drawer was in *his* bedroom, Lawrence had to know it was empty; had to know the consequence of lunging toward it would clinch his arrest. Lawrence had to know that if the deputies hesitated to arrest him for sodomy, they would certainly arrest him for resisting their authority.

If they arrested Lawrence, they'd have to arrest Garner.

Guar-an-teed free ride to the substation.

The small amount of marijuana the cops found in plain view suggests additional "bait" to invite arrest if the officers didn't think the misdemeanor sex sufficient. In the thousands of police reports I've read about drug cases, drugs are rarely in plain view unless defendants are engaged in using or selling them at the time of the arrest. Defendants usually keep drugs hidden.

The stacks of homosexual pornographic material deputies described as in plain view throughout Lawrence's apartment, seems—like the marijuana—over-the-top. Something most people tend to keep out of sight. Was Lawrence's lure to the cops: *"If you hesitate to arrest us for this misdemeanor sex act, or my resisting arrest— look! We've got marijuana, and homosexual porn too! There must be something illegal you could combine with the sodomy that would convince you to arrest us. Please!?"*

Some of the circumstances support speculation that the arrests were choreographed in such meticulous detail that the planners may even have arranged the sexual conduct to occur on the shift of a particular deputy known to have the greatest propensity to make such an arrest.

Sheryl Roppolo, chief clerk of the JP Court nearest the arrest scene, was a high school classmate of arresting officer Deputy Joe Quinn, and graduated two years before him. In conversation, she sought every opportunity to malign him for having been, in her opinion, overly zealous in performing his duties.

Roppolo, who is not gay, is a community activist and longtime close friend of many of the homosexual participants in *Lawrence.* Her gay assistant is a longtime friend of gay activist Lane Lewis, a major participant in the events of the case. The clerk's office shares the building with the sheriff's substation where deputies' shift schedules and patrol routes are accessible.

Deputy Quinn is known as a no-nonsense guy from a family of law enforcement superstars. If any officer would know about Texas Penal Code 21.06, it would be Deputy Quinn. If any cop was likely to arrest someone under 21.06 it would probably be Deputy Quinn.

He follows the rules exactly. A quintessential cop's cop.

If a fine-only offense occurs near the end of a cop's shift, he/she is less likely to make a misdemeanor arrest, which will add a 2-hour minimum of paperwork to delay going home.

The dispatch call that drew Deputy Quinn to 794 Normandy came about 1 1/2 hours into his shift.

The call came late in the night when most working-class people at that apartment complex would have gone to bed, clearing the scene from rubberneckers as much as possible. The call came on a quiet week*day* evening, not a week*end* when the huge Colorado Club apartment complex which, according to the cops, had a reputation for raucous activities, would be teeming with partiers who might be observers, interfere with the plan, or distract the deputies.

Masterful.

The events of the arrests were absolute *genius,* flawlessly executed down to the last meticulous detail: defendant Lawrence was on a preset day off from his work on September 17, 1998, and for the following two days. He didn't even miss work.

Someone thought of everything.

# Who Is Mitchell Katine?

Mitchell Katine—short, slight, intense, with dark curly hair—had zero criminal law experience when the sodomy cases first came to him. He was 38 years old.

He is a real estate attorney who also practices employment law.

When asked at public lectures to explain his legal qualifications to handle the high-profile criminal cases, Katine jokes that the sodomy took place in an apartment, so obviously real estate was involved!

Katine, born in Miami, Florida, November 17, 1960, has an extreme fondness for Hispanics and Hispanic culture. Colorful native tapestries from Central America cover tables in his office. He enjoys dancing salsa and frequenting Latin gay bars, which is where he first met his lover and partner Walter Domingo Avila of El Salvador.

Although Katine's regular e-newsletter to a long list of recipients includes Walter Domingo Avila's complete name, Katine does not want Walter's last name, "Avila," printed in this book. Katine's reason is: "Walter is a little more private than I am." Notwithstanding, I am referencing the complete name because Katine has routinely, widely, frequently disseminated it in print previously, and for other reasons explained in later chapters.

Katine and Avila's two children are adopted from Guatemala.

Katine snaps photos of everyone and every event all the time, preserving the photos museum form, catalogued in meticulous scrapbooks, organized by volume and year.

Katine carefully documents everything about his life. *Everything.*

"I have a lot of energy. I am a very happy person. I truly appreciate things like beautiful days, nature and the world. I don't get angry very often. I believe that people are telling me the truth. I believe people are sincere. I believe that people are good. I also am very appreciative," Katine said in an April 2004 interview.

"I know that I am very lucky. I have a very fortunate life, thanks to many factors, including my parents and that I live in America, that I am male, that I am white. Things like that make my life a little easier.

"I have never thought of my sexual orientation as a hindrance or as something to overcome. I have never wished that I wasn't who I am. I think some people do. But I have never felt that way.

"I enjoy feeling a little special and a little different than the majority. I like living my life that way," Katine responded when asked to describe himself.

Katine is the son of Allen Katine, a court reporter (transcriber), and Loni Katine, an insurance agency secretary. He has two sisters.

Katine has no middle name. "Everyone else in my family has a middle name, but not me," he explained.

All other homosexuals interviewed said they knew they were homosexual at a very early age, almost from the moment they were sentient. For Katine, his sexuality ricocheted from heterosexual to homosexual until his late teens.

When at 18, and a freshman at University of South Florida, in Tampa, he finally told his mother, "Ok, you can call me 'gay,' if that is easier for you." Her response was,

"Oh! I was afraid you were going to tell me you were going to want to be a rabbi!"

"Evidently she felt not that [being homosexual] was better than that [being a rabbi], but that *that* was an extreme lifestyle also I guess," Katine interpolates.

Katine majored in Communications and Media—training that served him well in the years-long media tumult surrounding *Lawrence*.

Katine does not consider himself a practicing Jew. The Jewish faith has no role in his life, he said. "I see my Judaism as more of a cultural and historical significance for me. I'm respectful of other religions. I have some religious tenets such as being good to people, helping people who need to be helped. Kind of a moral code of honesty, of being nice.

"We celebrated the major [Jewish] holidays. I was bar mitzvahed. I went to Hebrew school. It was not an enjoyable experience," Katine recalled.

Katine decided to adopt children after a surrogacy attempt in Iowa, using Katine's sperm, failed.

According to Katine, his partner Walter Domingo Avila came to the United States from El Salvador 13 years ago, because Avila has family in Washington and Texas. Walter "worked as a cook in a restaurant for many years while getting his cosmetology license." He graduated from cosmetology school, then studied English two years at Houston Community College.

Katine has never learned to speak Spanish, but "Walter speaks excellent English," Katine said.

"We got Sebrina and Sebastian. So Walter went right to staying home and taking care of them. He is a house husband."

Walter Domingo Avila had no role with regard to *Lawrence*, Katine said.

Katine remembered meeting New York-based Lambda Legal attorney Suzanne Goldberg in the mid-1990s at a gay and lesbian "Creating Change" conference in Dallas, sponsored by the National Gay and Lesbian Task Force.

Katine said over nearly 10 years of their close friendship based on their mutual national activism for homosexual causes, he and Goldberg never discussed the homosexual community's intense longing for a criminal case to test Texas' sodomy law (21.06) through the courts.

"They, the Lambda people, the civil rights organizations discussed it. That was never discussed with me," Katine said.

In a 2004 interview, Goldberg stated that she and Katine discussed many times homosexuals' longing for a test case.

Katine keeps scrupulous, detailed records, often including photos, of his legal and personal activities—so thorough he can recite the precise time and day of the week events occurred. He said that he is unable to find the 1998 date he first phoned Suzanne Goldberg to tell her about John Lawrence and Tyron Garner's case—the test case the homosexual community had been waiting and hoping for, for years.

"I remember calling her. I don't have a date. I don't have notes of me calling. I called and spoke to [Goldberg]. By the end of that day [whatever day it was] they [Lambda] had their meeting and agreed that they would be involved [in litigating _Lawrence v. Texas_]," Katine said.

Searching his records further, Katine said he phoned Goldberg "sometime between October 12 and 21, 1998' after he met with the defendants October 12. "Here is a communication from [Goldberg] to me on October 21 at 3:58 P.M.," he said, consulting one of his meticulous, tabbed folders.

"How did [the defendants] end up with me? They were referred to me through Lane Lewis. [Lewis is a local gay activist]. They were getting lots of calls from criminal defense lawyers.

"I knew Lane Lewis through a prior legal matter. Not directly associated with him, but with someone he knew. Lane at the time was very involved with the HIV civil rights movement. We would go to gay, lesbian and HIV events. He was in his teens. He was probably 18 or 19 and was an activist, radical type person. We became friends. If

someone has a problem with the police, or they are ha-
rassed, they call him. That's the role that Lane Lewis had
at the time. He was out there. He was with ACT UP. Lane
would be the gatekeeper of where he sent people."

Katine imparts the impression of a mentor-protégé,
teacher-student dynamic with Lewis. They share the
same day and month of birth. Lewis was 31 in 1998.

Robert Royce Eubanks, whose phone call apparently
summoned police to the apartment where Lawrence and
Garner were arrested, accompanied Lawrence and Garner
to Katine's office on October 12, 1998. Did that strike
Katine as odd? Wouldn't Lawrence and Garner be angry
with Eubanks?

"I believe that they were upset with Eubanks. But they
were all still friends and they gave [Eubanks] the benefit
of the doubt that he wasn't really trying to hurt them.
[Eubanks] was upset with [Garner] wanting to stay with
[Lawrence] in [Lawrence's] apartment. They really didn't
feel [Eubanks] had done anything that terrible.

Katine expressed an immediate dislike for Eubanks. "I
took one look at that guy and said 'You have to wait in the
reception area,'" Katine said, remembering how he ordered Eubanks to leave the room. Katine can attribute no
real reason why he didn't like Eubanks on first sight.

David Jones, the veteran Houston criminal defense attorney in Katine's firm, and who attended the October 12
meeting, is even less charitable toward Eubanks.
"[Eubanks] ratted them [Lawrence and Garner] out,"
Jones said angrily.

Jones had a different perspective on the dynamic
among the three defendants. He thinks Lawrence and
Garner were not so forgiving of Eubanks.

"I definitely heard a lot about Eubanks from [Lawrence
and Garner] and it was not positive stuff. [Eubanks] was
a drunk, a troublemaker, and liar. [Lawrence and Garner]
just condemned him vigorously," Jones said.

Since Katine continued—even after the June 26, 2003,
Supreme Court ruling—closely controlling access to
Lawrence and Garner, is Katine still their attorney? Since

the case is long closed, doesn't that closing extinguish the attorney-client relationship? What is Katine's legal basis for restricting access to Lawrence and Garner?

"That's a good question. I am still their attorney as I am still trying to get the bond money back. But technically, I would imagine our attorney-client relationship has ended. I'm not advising them or representing them legally. I'm doing this more based on a relationship we have developed over five years of my being their representative and friend. They still refer to me as their attorney," Katine explained.

When did his professional [attorney] relationship with the men end?

"I presume at the end of the case."

Has the professional attorney-client relationship been extinguished?

"I have not sent [Lawrence and Garner] a letter that our relationship is over. But I presume it is. Our formal relationship."

So would ethical rules be violated if someone tried to talk to Lawrence and Garner about the case without notifying Katine? Attorneys are ethically prohibited from speaking with someone they know is represented by counsel without permission of that counsel.

"I don't think so. But I also don't think they would talk to anybody. They still get calls from media people. They say, 'Call [Katine],'" Katine said, smiling confidently.

"When you hear people speak, don't believe everything that everybody says. Don't take what one person says as the end of the conversation. Research, learn, think, figure things out," Mitchell Katine advised a local, law student audience at a February 13, 2004, Houston seminar on *Lawrence*.

Katine was cautioning Houston law students against being intellectually seduced by the conservative right. In researching *Lawrence v. Texas*, I decided to apply Katine's recommended skepticism to everyone, including Katine. That's what I had done in my approximately six years as a state and federal prosecutor, and nearly nine years as a criminal defense attorney for the indigent.

What turned out to be equally significant in my investigation was not what participants like Katine said they knew, but what they said they *didn't* know. A legal concept called "willful blindness."

The "accepted facts" on which *Lawrence* was predicated were never examined by any outsider. Inexplicably, not even by the prosecution.

Katine, who at his many public appearances, often with John Lawrence, is frequently questioned about allegations of an orchestrated setup, issues adamant denials. "Bring me one shred of evidence that this was a setup," Katine challenges his questioners.

I began my research by reading two 69-word probable cause affidavits, the same one for each defendant. Early on in the appeal process, the two sodomy cases for Lawrence and Garner were consolidated into one case: *Lawrence.*

The defense version, articulated mainly by Katine and his co-counsel David Jones, and unchallenged by the prosecution, was:

> John Lawrence and Tyron Garner were arrested in Lawrence's apartment September 17, 1998 for having sex with each other. Robert Eubanks, an acquaintance jealous of the impending sexual act between Lawrence and Garner, and wanting Garner to leave, called the Sheriff's office from a pay phone outside Lawrence's apartment, stating falsely that there was an armed intruder. The deputies physically mistreated Lawrence.
>
> One subsequent day, both defendants in a criminal case, appeared on the office doorstep of Mitchell Katine, a Houston real estate attorney and long time national homosexual activist with zero experience in criminal law. Katine agreed to represent the criminal cases for no fee all the way the U.S. Supreme Court to challenge Texas' statute 21.06.

This defense version creates certain mental-visual impressions that stimulate thought to certain conclusions based thereon.

But what I discovered about the events of September 17, 1998, detailed in the chapters of this book, clashes in meaningful ways with the defense version—creating very different mental, visual, logical and commonsense interpretations consistent with a choreographed setup:

> My thesis is that a close examination of *Lawrence* reveals inconsistencies, trajectories of events, interlinked alliances, stonewalling, information gaps, evasions, effronteries to common sense, and circumstances too incredible to be coincidence.
> The meticulous planning and execution of the "facts" in *Lawrence* appear to have a knowledgeable masterfulness so brilliant, that—under other, less controversial circumstances—the planner(s) might be tempted to step forward to take a bow.

The first obvious aspect creating suspicion is the stone wall Katine erected, and still patrols, around Lawrence and Garner long after any attorney-client relationship has been dissolved and the U.S. Supreme Court has ruled.

Why wouldn't Katine allow the defendants to be interviewed separately in 2004, even *in* his presence? Why wouldn't Katine allow the defendants to be interviewed outside his presence? Outside his law office?

If there isn't a shred of evidence of a setup as Katine says, why couldn't I just meet Lawrence or Garner separately, without Katine, at a restaurant or anywhere for their freewheeling review of what transpired before, during, and after September 17, 1998—the way I did with the five deputies?

If Katine and the defendants have nothing to hide, why Katine's gatekeeper, clamped-down, double-locked, iron-lid posture—sealing their lips years after the events?

The answer suggests itself.

Katine's various explanations are that interviews were "not necessary or appropriate," describing the defendants as "private and shy"…"not comfortable talking about their lives."

In 2004 when Katine allowed me to submit written questions to the defendants, to which Katine would then provide defendants' answers, he said obtaining responses to my questions was: the first time, in the five-year pendency of the case, that he learned Lawrence, Garner and Eubanks were comrades spanning 23 years; the first time he knew what events transpired in Lawrence's apartment before deputies arrived; and the first time he knew any biographical material about his clients.

Most attorneys, or even lay people, would laugh out loud at that.

No even remotely competent attorney would be so ignorant about his clients in a case that went to the Supreme Court.

Katine's inability or unwillingness to provide a date on which he first told Lambda Legal about the arrests is a mismatch with Katine's ability to produce, from his meticulous records, every scrap of similar information. The phone call to New York to his longtime friend Ms. Goldberg, whenever that call was made, should have been one of *the* climactic moments in Katine's life as an attorney, certainly in his record keeping.

Was there no such call?

Or were there many such Lambda-Katine calls even before the arrests? Minutes after the arrests? Hours after the arrests?

Suzanne Goldberg is equally vague on this point, relating only what she terms a fortuity that Katine's call came at the exact moment she was heading into a full staff meeting of Lambda decision makers. Was Lambda perhaps *awaiting* such a call that day?

Katine often tells groups that for media purposes, he wishes the defendants had been attractive men with impressive work histories and without criminal records. However, common sense dictates the exact opposite would be true in staging an arrest scenario for Homosexual Conduct.

It is extremely unlikely that anyone with no prior arrests would agree to be arrested for a sexual offense. There would be a shortage of teachers, physicians, attorneys, CEOs, and other professionals waiting to apply for such notoriety. The negative career impact of that kind of an arrest, and the resultant publicity, would most likely dull the enthusiasm of anyone except volunteers who already *had* criminal records.

Ideally, at least one of the volunteers should be unemployed, with no career to be destroyed. Unemployment usually equates with financial need as well. Eubanks and Garner were chronically unemployed and, according to police reports, used cocaine—an expensive addiction. The employment status of the shadowy Velez is unknown. Only Lawrence had a steady work history at a nonprofessional job that, demonstrably unaffected by Lawrence's prior criminal arrests, was unlikely to be affected by another misdemeanor arrest. Eubanks was already a felon, possibly with AIDS, who had nothing to lose whatever he did.

And if an arrest sham was ever discovered? Diverting blame to blue-collar miscreants and a felon wouldn't be difficult.

The three were *nonpareil*.

Katine said he never knew about the existence of the fourth man, Velez, until April 2, 2004, when during my interview of Katine, I read from the police report to question him about Velez.

Katine asked me for a copy of the police report, which he said he had never seen in the nearly five years *Lawrence* crept up the appeal ladder. For five years Katine never asked the prosecution for a copy of the police report about his clients whose case went to the U.S. Supreme

Court? Wouldn't an attorney *start* with scrutinizing the police report and every other piece of paper connected with the arrests, seeking any and all information?

The district attorney's office has always had an open-files policy for attorneys representing clients. Attorney David Jones, Katine's co-counsel in representing the two men, is a grizzled, competent veteran of criminal defense in Harris County, Texas. If Katine didn't know that a criminal representation begins by asking to see police reports, Jones certainly did.

Further, for five years, according to Katine, his *clients* Lawrence and Garner never mentioned to Katine that there was a fourth man in Lawrence's apartment on September 17, 1998? Highly improbable.

After obtaining police reports, the second question defense counsel usually asks a client is: Who are the witnesses?

Katine's explanations of many salient points of the *Lawrence* events vary greatly from the explanations of others, and from the circumstances of the case. Some of Katine's most intriguing, inconsistent statements involve the October 2000 homicide of Robert Royce Eubanks—the boisterous felon who waited for police outside Lawrence's apartment the night of the September 17, 1998, arrests in order to literally lead the deputies to where the homosexual sex was in progress. (These provocative disconnects are detailed in subsequent chapters.)

On the surface, Katine was extremely helpful to me.

His impeccable manners vanished only when I pressed him for more specific biographical details about his partner Walter, and on the occasions Eubanks' name was mentioned.

Whenever Eubanks' name came up, Katine's persona seemed to descend—to some basement of his psyche, reserved only for Eubanks. Katine's facial expression became negative; his eyes appeared to disengage, and uncommunicated, dark, angry thoughts seemed to move through his brain. Even Katine's voice became harsh, cold, dispassionate.

Eubanks. No other topic we ever discussed—including Walter, precipitated this unsettling transformation.

Throughout my research, Katine and I played intellectual cat and mouse.

We sparred as two veteran lawyers. Usually I played cat.

But not always.

I often wondered why Katine was so helpful? Did he truly have nothing to hide? Did he think I was too inept to stumble toward the truth?

Or did Katine—unable or unwilling himself to be the vehicle for explosive post-_Lawrence_ revelations disclosing a setup—calculate that with my journalism-judicial background, I would be one of the few persons competent to correctly assemble all the pieces from the clues Katine provided to me? Then Katine, who admittedly craves limelight, could step from behind the curtains to effulge.

# Defendants John Geddes Lawrence, Tyrone Garner and Robert Royce Eubanks

At the time of his arrest on September 17, 1998, John Geddes Lawrence worked as a medical technician at Bayshore Medical Center, Pasadena, Texas. After graduating from high school in Koontz, Texas, Lawrence, one of four children, joined the U.S. Navy in 1961 where he served until honorably discharged in 1966. He used skills learned as a military hospital corpsman to earn his living for 40 years at various Texas medical facilities.

Born in Beaumont, Texas, but reared in Brazoria County, Texas, Lawrence, who has two sisters and one brother, has lived in Harris County since 1971, having moved from Halletsville, Texas. He took some college courses at Lamar University in Beaumont, Texas.

Police records list Lawrence as a white male, five foot ten and weighing 170 pounds, with brown hair and brown eyes, born on August 2, 1943.

Lawrence was no stranger to criminal courts in Harris County, Texas. On November 3, 1978, according to courthouse files, Lawrence pleaded no contest to a charge that on January 7, 1978, he drove while intoxicated. He received probation, which he successfully completed. On October 31, 1988, Lawrence was again charged with DWI. He pleaded no contest on December 21, 1988, and again received probation, which it appears he successfully completed. Harris County criminal records before 1976, if any, with regard to Lawrence and the other defendants, are unavailable through the clerk's office. Criminal records outside Harris County, if any, usually may be obtained only by law enforcement agencies for official purposes, and public distribution is highly restricted or totally prohibited.

Tyron Garner, an African American, born July 10, 1967, in Houston, became involved in the Harris County criminal court system at age 19. Police records describe Garner as a black male, five foot seven and weighing 140 pounds, with black hair and brown eyes. On April 3, 1986, he was charged with possession of marijuana under two ounces, a misdemeanor. The case was dismissed on August 28, 1986, according to courthouse records.

Garner did not graduate from Houston's Jack Yates High School.

Based on the usual trade-off of plea agreements in criminal cases, dismissal of the drug charges was most likely part of a plea agreement to his felony charge of Aggravated Assault of Peace (Police) Officer J. K. Schooler, filed April 3, 1986, the same day the marijuana charge was filed.

Garner's felony, striking Officer Schooler with his fist, was reduced to a misdemeanor assault—to which Garner pleaded guilty on August 28, 1986, and was assessed punishment of three days in jail and a $750 fine. It is probable Garner, having served three days in jail after being arrested, was given credit for his jail time already served, meaning he did not serve any additional jail time.

On July 24, 1990, Garner was back at the criminal courthouse pleading no contest to charges that on July 23, 1990, he drove while intoxicated. He was sentenced to 10 days in jail, and a $100 fine.

On February 14, 1995, Garner pleaded no contest to a January 28, 1995, misdemeanor assault with bodily injury and was sentenced to 35 days in jail, no fine.

While the September 17, 1998, Homosexual Conduct charge—to which Garner and Lawrence pleaded no contest on December 22, 1998, and were fined $200 each—was creaking slowly up the appeal court ladder, Garner then 33, was charged on May 2, 2000, with another misdemeanor assault with bodily injury—on Robert Royce Eubanks, as well as violation of a protective order that Eubanks had obtained seeking to protect himself from Garner.

Three days later, on May 5, 2000, the Violation of a Protective Order charge was dismissed, and Garner pleaded guilty to the assault, for which he received a 90-day jail sentence. The dismissal of the violation of a protective order was most likely a routine plea agreement where Garner pleaded guilty to one charge in exchange for the dismissal of another charge.

Were it not for the notoriety conferred on Garner by the publicity surrounding the Homosexual Conduct case, such routine court matters probably would have gone unreported.

However, a *Houston Chronicle* article about Garner assaulting Eubanks in May, notes: "According to the police report, Garner and Eubanks had been out drinking Sunday night and began arguing when they returned to their room at the Montague Hotel, 804 Fannin.

"Eubanks told police that during the disagreement, Garner swatted him with a belt. Eubanks waited for Garner to go to sleep, then left the room to call police," the *Chronicle* quotes police spokesman Fred King.

King added, according to the *Chronicle* article, that the police report indicated, "Garner and Eubanks had a history of filing false reports against each other."

Garner, the 10th of 10 children, lived all his life in Harris County. His father died in 2001, followed by his mother's death in 2002. After high school, Garner says—through Katine—that for nine months he studied word processing at Hargast, a vocational trade school on South Main Street in Houston. He then attended an eight-week truck driving school, later working briefly as a nurse's assistant. He has been unemployed longer than he has been employed.

Robert Royce Eubanks, five foot nine, 150 pounds—also known as Roger David Nance and Robert Lee Smith—was born July 22, 1958, in Muleshoe, Texas. He grew up in Texas, Pennsylvania, Arkansas, and Copenhagen, Denmark, according to his mother. He has one sister.

Eubanks pleaded no contest on September 21, 1998, to the misdemeanor of Filing a False Report to a Police Officer, involving the same September 17, 1998, occurrences surrounding the Lawrence-Garner cases. He apparently had no attorney representing him on the plea, four days after the offense date. He was sentenced to 30 days in jail, with four days credit for the time he previously served in jail after being arrested.

For Eubanks, like his longtime companions Lawrence and Garner, the 1998 False Report conviction wasn't his first time as a defendant in the Harris County, Texas, criminal courthouse.

Records for Harris County reflect that on September 7, 1978, Eubanks pleaded guilty to a May 16, 1978, felony arson, and received probation. He violated his probation, which was revoked on August 28, 1985, when he was then sentenced to four years in prison.

Months earlier, on February 15, 1985, Eubanks had been charged with felony theft, plus another felony arson, and sentenced on August 28, 1985, to four years in prison. It is probable from the record that the 1985 theft and *second* arson offense were the reasons for having his

1978 arson probation revoked. The two four-year prison sentences on new felonies, imposed on the same date, would run concurrent with the "old" felonies. No records were checked under Eubanks' alias names.

On a standard self-reporting form with the 1998 False Report case, Eubanks stated that his prior employment included working for five years as an auditor at the now-razed Shamrock Hilton Hotel in Houston, and employment for an unspecified time at a "medical center" in Houston. He indicated on the form that he was a high school graduate, with 18 years of education.

He listed defendant John Lawrence as a reference.

Katine asked that I come to his office February 17, 2004, to receive answers to my written questions to Garner and Lawrence, submitted to Katine earlier. Katine declined to provide the answers by e-mail or on the telephone. Katine read the two men's answers from his handwritten notes. Suzanne Testa, my research assistant, accompanied me.

Katine said he obtained the information from both Garner and Lawrence. The information from Katine is:

> Lawrence, Garner and Eubanks spent the day together Thursday, September 17, 1998. Lawrence was going to give Eubanks some furniture, which Eubanks was going to take the next day. "Garner and Eubanks were together." [Katine said he couldn't define "together" in that context.]
>
> Eubanks and Garner had lived together for eight months, Katine relayed.
>
> The three went out to dinner together. When they returned, Eubanks wanted Garner to leave, so Eubanks could spend the night with Lawrence. But Garner didn't want to leave, causing a conflict between Eubanks and Garner. [According to deputies, Eubanks said he had lived with Lawrence in Lawrence's apartment for quite awhile. Deputies said they found many of Eubanks' pos-

sessions in one bedroom. But if Eubanks planned to spend the night to move furniture the next morning, that could explain the presence of Eubanks' possessions as well.]

Eubanks said he wanted a Coca-Cola, so Lawrence gave Eubanks money to purchase a Coca-Cola. Eubanks left Lawrence's apartment, but instead of buying a Coca-Cola, Eubanks phoned police, according to the information Katine said he obtained from Lawrence and Garner.

Eubanks and Lawrence were friends since 1978. Katine implied, but did not state, that Eubanks and Lawrence also had a sexual relationship.

Eubanks introduced Garner to Lawrence in 1989, Katine said. According to police reports, Eubanks and Garner had a sexual relationship for many years. [On September 17, Lawrence was having sex with Garner.]

A couple of months after our meeting on February 17, 2004, Katine changed his stance—allowing me to interview Lawrence and Garner in person.

He said he acquiesced to a long-standing *Houston Chronicle* interview request. He invited me to interview the two men in person on April 23, 2004. We agreed that the *Chronicle* would have a 2-hour interview, immediately followed by my 1-hour interview. Katine was present at both interviews, which were conducted in his law office. He said those were the first interviews the men granted since their 1998 arrest.

The tepid *Chronicle* interview, printed shortly thereafter, contained little information that hadn't already appeared publicly. The *Chronicle* reporter, like everyone else, apparently made no attempt to elicit information from the five arresting deputies. (Certain information provided by Lawrence and Garner during the April 23, 2004, in-person interview is omitted below, and distributed within chapters matching that subject matter or time frame.)

Lawrence said his job as a medical technologist involved doing chemical analysis of blood and urine. He lived in the 794 Normandy, Colorado Club apartments for about 15 years prior to 1998. He said he lived alone at the time of the September 1998 arrest.

At the time of the interview, Garner had a job selling sandwiches.

Lawrence described himself as: "Outgoing and enjoy life."

"I'd say I'm a very nice person. Loveable," Garner responded about himself. He speaks very softly.

Neither remembers Emergency Medical Services responding, or offering them medical attention in response to their complaints to the deputies on the night of their arrest.

In the early morning hours of Friday, September 18, 1998, they were released together from the county jail in downtown Houston. Lawrence, who alleges deputies had refused to allow him to dress at his apartment the night before, was wearing a borrowed T-shirt and jeans given to him at the jail. Because Garner obeyed police orders to dress at the scene, he was wearing his own clothes.

Lawrence said they flagged down a taxi, which drove them back to Lawrence's apartment September 18.

"I had to go upstairs to get my billfold to pay the taxi driver, since I was taken out of my house only in my underwear. No keys, no billfold, no discussion," Lawrence remembered in bitter tones.

"I had only a couple of dollars and my identification," Garner said.

A magistrate, before whom they were arraigned in the jail's 24-hour court, authorized their release on personal recognizance. PR (personal recognizance) bond—granted to defendants who have community ties, who are not charged with a violent offense, and who have no recent criminal history of violence—does not require money to post a bond.

Lawrence's father was the first person he phoned after

arriving home. "My dad said, 'You *will* get a lawyer.'" Lawrence did not have to report to work until Tuesday.

"When I got out of jail I went to bed. I went to sleep. After I woke up, I got a phone call from [Lawrence]. He wanted to get a lawyer. I told him if he wanted to get a lawyer, then we will get a lawyer. Whatever you want to do. After that conversation with [Lawrence], I discussed it with my brother," Garner said.

He and his brother are closest. His brother didn't advise Garner to get an attorney. "But he thought it was a good idea that I do it."

Lawrence admitted the deputies were correct—that during the confrontation in his bedroom, Lawrence continually threatened to call his lawyer.

Who was Lawrence going to call?

"No one.'"

Was that just an idle threat then?

"Right."

Did Lawrence have an attorney on September 17, 1998?

"No," Lawrence said, smiling at his apparent deception.

Given the scenario that Eubanks' phone call summoned police to Lawrence's apartment, triggering Lawrence and Garner's arrest, why did Eubanks accompany Lawrence and Garner to the initial interview with Katine? Weren't they at least annoyed with Eubanks?

"Because we felt that since [Eubanks] was part of the case, that he should be there in case they needed any information from him," Lawrence explained.

"[Eubanks] wanted to come. So we said, why not?" Garner added.

"I was very upset with [Eubanks] but I felt since he was part of the case that he probably . . . I did not know if he should or should not be there," Lawrence continued.

Was Lawrence still angry with Eubanks?

"Yes. I was just aggravated at the fact that he caused such a situation."

On the day all three of them went to Katine's office, had Lawrence forgiven Eubanks?

"I have never forgiven him," Lawrence said coldly.

Does Lawrence still feel bitter toward Eubanks?

"I don't feel bitterness. I feel aggravated that someone [Eubanks] could be so stupid," Lawrence said angrily.

Was Garner still angry with Eubanks when they first went to Katine's law office?

"No. We had made up," Garner said.

They were friends then?

"Yeah. Forgive and forget. That's the way it was on my part," Garner remembered.

So Garner's attitude toward Eubanks was different than Lawrence's?

"I imagine," Garner said softly.

Garner's comments are a complete contradiction to how attorneys Jones and Katine characterized Garner's feelings toward Eubanks.

What were Eubanks, Lawrence and Garner doing in the hours immediately preceding their arrest?

"Eating. Came home and had a couple of drinks," Lawrence explained. "I was getting ready to watch the news and go to bed because I wanted to get that furniture out early the next day. I had gotten new furniture and taken all of my old living room furniture, and put it in the front bedroom. [Eubanks and Garner] were supposed to get a truck the next day and move it to an apartment that they were supposedly getting."

Did either Lawrence or Garner own a gun on September 17, 1998?

"No."

Did they ever own a gun?

"No."

Was there a gun in Lawrence's apartment on September 17?

"There has never been a gun in that apartment," Lawrence said.

Did they hear the deputies announce themselves and burst into the apartment?

"No. [The deputies] just walked in the door. I seen them walking in," Garner said.

Before Lawrence saw the deputies in his bedroom did Lawrence hear anything?

"No."

Was Lawrence surprised when the deputies walked in?

"I was asleep..." Lawrence began, apparently denying that he was engaged in the sexual act to which he twice pleaded no contest, which is the same as a guilty plea.

Katine cut Lawrence off before Lawrence could finish his sentence.

"We are, what the sexual information that the police gave, we are, due to their privacy, we are not going into that type of question," Katine cautioned, motioning to Lawrence and Garner not to continue their answer.

"I was surprised," Lawrence continued with Katine's permission.

"I thought [Eubanks] was going down to get a soda. That's what [Eubanks] said. He was going to go down to the Coke machine," Garner recalled.

With few exceptions during this interview, Garner parrots Lawrence's responses.

"Well before that they were having an argument," Katine interjected, answering the question *for* Lawrence and Garner. [Eubanks] wanted [Garner] to leave and Garner didn't want to leave."

"[Eubanks] wanted me to leave," Garner said. "I stayed. [Eubanks] and I came over to [Lawrence's] house together. It was like [midnight] and the buses had stopped running. I didn't have a way to get home anyway."

Why did Eubanks want Garner to leave?

"I don't know. I think he had a friend or something that he was talking to on the phone. He probably was inviting somebody or something. I don't really know. [Eubanks] wanted me to leave. I know that," Garner said.

After his arrest, did the deputies prevent Lawrence from dressing?

"They did not allow me to get dressed. They were sort of brutal to me. They threw me down on the couch and broke some porcelain birds. [Garner] was allowed to dress. They handcuffed us. I was sort of taken downstairs roughshod. I was not allowed to get my billfold or my keys. I was not allowed to lock my apartment," Lawrence complained.

Why did they allow the statute of limitations to expire without filing a civil suit against the deputies?

Lawrence looked questioningly at Katine.

"Not until today [April 23, 2004]. No it is not anything that we thought," Katine answered for them.

"I don't really think a civil suit would have accomplished what we have accomplished," Lawrence responded.

"No, I really didn't. They didn't do anything to me, not physically," Garner added.

On the same subject, why didn't they file a complaint about the deputies with the sheriff's Internal Affairs division?

"We didn't want anything to detract or distract from our case. We didn't want to criticize the deputies. We didn't want it to get political," Katine said.

The deputies contend that when they came into the bedroom Lawrence and Garner were engaged in a sexual act that they continued as the police stood there. Is that true or not?

"We are not going to get into that," Katine interjected, stopping Lawrence for the second time as Lawrence started to answer. Was Garner physically in the same bedroom that Lawrence was when police arrived?

"Let's not go there," Katine again cut Garner off as Garner started to answer. It appeared from his face that Garner, before Katine interrupted, was forming the word "No."

What, in their opinion, should the deputies have done?

"If they are coming for a gun, they should ask you, 'Is there a gun in the house?' They did not approach that question. They merely went through the front side of the house. They did not go into the second bedroom. They did not go into the bathroom. They frisked us down. Like someone in their underwear was going to put a gun in his whatever. It was just poor law enforcement as far as I am concerned," Lawrence complained.

"I think they should have left when they didn't find a gun." "They should have left and let us go," Garner added.

Did either of them resist the deputies?

"I probably did," Lawrence admitted.

To what degree?

"Well when you think how big those boys were, it wasn't very much," Lawrence added.

"I didn't resist," Garner said.

Who was the male in Lawrence's kitchen who identified himself as Ramon Pelayo Velez, date of birth July 2, 1962, whom the deputies described as Hispanic?

"I do not know anything about the guy," Lawrence said. "[Garner] says he thinks it was a friend of [Eubanks]. That [Eubanks] had been on the phone and was trying to get the guy to come over. But we don't know really anything."

"I don't know who the guy was in the kitchen," Garner echoed.

What did he look like?

"I think he was a tall Hispanic guy. He came about 15 minutes before the police got there," Garner said.

Did he walk in and just start using the phone?

"I went in the bathroom and when I came out, he was in the kitchen," Garner said.

Did Garner say to him: Who the heck are you?

"No, he was in the kitchen talking to [Eubanks]. So I just assumed he was [Eubanks'] friend," Garner said.

Have they seen that person since September 17, 1998?

"No."

Do they remember the deputies bringing all of them into the living room?

"I don't remember the Mexican being in the living room at all," Lawrence said, apparently referring to Ramon Pelayo Velez.

Does Garner remember while in the living room with

the deputies that Eubanks said to Garner, "How could you have done this to me?"

"No," Garner said.

Did Garner have a sexual relationship with Eubanks?

"Yes," Garner said.

Did Lawrence have a sexual relationship with Eubanks?

"No!" Lawrence said emphatically.

"We did say we thought that maybe [Eubanks] was jealous," Katine answered, again interjecting his theory of why Eubanks may have contacted law enforcement.

"I believe that he probably was. On his part," Garner echoed Katine's answer.

Why did they pursue an appeal of their case to the U.S. Supreme Court?

Lawrence focused his response on what he felt were the personal indignities of his arrest, rather than passion against 21.06, or intellectual identification with homosexual rights issues.

"Because I was an angry person," Lawrence said. "I was very, very angry at having had my rights violated. I am an American citizen. I am not some throw down. And when this happened, I said, 'No, this has gone too far. I am not going to let these people stomp me down.'"

But Lawrence allowed at least a week and a half to elapse after his arrest without trying to hire an attorney. Did his anger grow during that time?

"I was mad from day one. Because I was turned out of jail in a pair of pants that didn't fit, barefooted with no shoes, no money, no billfold, no car keys, and having to hitch a ride home in the middle of the night to get a billfold to pay the cab driver," Lawrence said.

Garner was more philosophical.

"I thought about it, and I think I thought it was just the right thing to do. To try to get some justice," Garner added.

Would they have preferred a trial?

"I thought we did have a trial!" Lawrence exclaimed, apparently shocked. He looked toward Katine questioningly.

"No, you pled guilty," Katine reminded him.

When did they first realize they are homosexual?

"I guess I have been gay all of my life," Lawrence said. "I've never even thought about it. I guess I was born gay. My mother always said I was her special son. In 99.9 percent of the cases, it's biological. It's not some inherent trained thing. You either are or you are not." Lawrence said he has a relative who is gay.

"I was born gay," Garner added. "One hundred percent. No one made me this way. My brothers or my sisters, none of my friends made me this way. It is just the way I am. I have always been this way. It is biological."

After interviewing Lawrence and Garner in Katine's office that April, Katine and Jones' description of Lawrence and Garner clashed sharply with my observations.

Although not eloquent, John Lawrence was articulate, adroit with words, knowledgeable of political subtleties, and had above-average intelligence—almost a quick study.

Lawrence easily and correctly used such words as "inherent," and "entity" and "merely." In a country where fewer than 50 percent of the population votes, Lawrence has a strong voting record.

Far from being the shy personality attorneys Katine and Jones described, Lawrence was feisty, almost steely at times, struggling to suppress an edgy argumentative demeanor.

Clearly Lawrence dominated Tyron Garner, who presented himself meekly. Garner's persona is somewhat reminiscent of Johnny Mathis, a singer popular in the 1950s and '60s. The passive demeanor Garner displayed sharply contrasts with his past convictions for violent assault, including assaulting a cop. But what may seem a contradiction—is not unusual based on my courtroom experience.

In my years practicing criminal law, I have noticed an

inverse relationship between the violence of the crime with which a defendant is charged, and the passive personality he or she presents in court. It is an odd juxtaposition, but not a phenomenon.

If an arrest report details some horrific violent or murderous behavior, often the defendant described in the report will appear before me in court as overly polite and mousy. Conversely, a defendant charged with some nonviolent offense will often be obstreperous and sassy in court, although it is more rare.

Although Garner is no Rhodes scholar, he seems to have at least average intelligence, is articulate, and street smart. Not at all the bashful person Katine and Jones described. Of course it could be argued that even though they have not spoken publicly, both men's personalities were altered from their "original" personas by being in the international spotlight for five years. But media attention does not confer innate perception nor expressive ability. Lawrence and Garner have both in above-average measure.

In 24 years as an attorney, and about 14 years as a journalist, I have never participated in an "interview" as controlled, implicitly and explicitly as the April 23, 2004, interview with Lawrence and Garner.

Katine held the reins shockingly tightly.

When we entered the conference room at his law firm, Katine directed us where to sit. We could not select our seat. He sat on my right at the head of the long conference table, with first Lawrence then Garner on his right. Katine sat sideways in his chair much of the time, facing the two men who almost never took their eyes off him.

The three were in constant, intense eye contact.

After each question, Lawrence and Garner would look at him before answering. It was as if Katine controlled their every word and move with invisible strings.

It is commonplace for witnesses to be woodshedded

before giving a deposition or other statement. Attorneys rehearse with them questions that might be asked, and discuss probable answers. Witnesses are told repeatedly to answer monosyllabically when possible, and never, never to *volunteer* information. Such preparation is routine. There is nothing improper about such rehearsals. But such careful, advance preparation usually is for situations involving potential legal liability or culpability.

This was supposed to be an interview for a book about a concluded case. Lawrence and Garner followed the answer pattern, usually dictated by attorneys, exactly: monosyllabic when possible, don't volunteer anything, look at the attorney for guidance if you are unsure of the answer.

They did as they had been told. They appeared to have been extensively rehearsed.

I could tell when a question I asked had not been covered in their rehearsal. They looked uncertainly at Katine before answering.

Very often during the April 2004 "interview" Katine rested his left elbow on the table, holding his left hand flat to cover as much of his face from my view as possible. Although I pretended not to be watching him, from my peripheral vision I could clearly see him behind his hand, silently mouthing responses to Lawrence and Garner. He also signaled them by slightly shaking his head "yes" or "no" as an answer to a question.

In my years as a criminal court judge, when a witness testified, I spent little time watching the witness. I kept my eyes glued on the defendant and his attorney, or even family members in the audience, to watch for signaling, which sometimes takes ingeniously subtle forms. Several times I have excused a jury to warn the parties that I have observed this conduct, and that if it is occurring, it is to cease immediately.

I did not reprimand Katine of course. There was a kind of horrified fascination, like watching a train wreck, in watching Katine in action—particularly since he didn't seem to realize that I had caught on, and was watching his choreography out of the corner of my right eye.

But why Katine's resolute obsession with keeping Lawrence and Garner from an unfettered, uncontrolled, freewheeling interview? The case is about as over as any case can be!

The Supreme Court of the United States has ruled.

Why was Katine feeding them answers?

What was Katine trying so desperately to conceal?

What information and why, was Katine guarding?

The thought occurred to me after, that maybe a reason Katine continues to allow the defendants to be interviewed only in his presence—under tight restrictions, and never interviewed separately—is not that Lawrence and Garner are poor communicators, but that they are excellent communicators!

A public image of the defendants as verbally adroit, intelligent, articulate, even feisty—would be at variance with Katine's structured spin, perhaps casting an entirely different light on the events of *Lawrence v. Texas.*

Because Lawrence, Garner, and Eubanks were friends with interlocking sexual relationships for more than two decades, the sudden sexual jealousy Katine publicly postulated as a motive for what the defense said was Eubanks' call to police, seemed unlikely, given human nature. Impetuous sexual jealousy between comrades of 23 years?

Lawrence's too-adamant denial of ever having a sexual relationship with Eubanks rang false. The Lawrence-Eubanks friendship predated the Lawrence-Garner friendship. It is unlikely that the glue of the two-decade Lawrence-Eubanks relationship was rarified intellectual discourse.

More as a trial judge than as an attorney, one learns to listen closely to every word a witness speaks. Even sentences or fragments that seem insignificant turn out to have crucial significance. With all the issues Lawrence said he was angry about as a patrol car whisked him from the scene, he listed with some prominence that police didn't allow him to lock the door of his apartment.

Locking his door was something Lawrence obviously cared very much about. Locking the door was so strong a concern or habit that Lawrence worried about it even under intensely emotional circumstances.

But on September 17, 1998, late at night—with Lawrence at home (Lawrence said he was getting ready to watch the news and go to bed or to sleep), and a man they said was a stranger in Lawrence's kitchen talking on the phone—both the outer door to Lawrence's apartment, and his bedroom door, were unlocked, allowing police convenient entry.

If impetuous sexual jealousy is discarded as Eubanks' motive for assisting the police in locating Lawrence and Garner, why would Eubanks rat out his friends of 23 years? He had to know his friends would quickly find out he fingered them. The suspect list would be short. As an ex-con who served prison time, Eubanks knew that in criminal subculture, snitches are universally despised.

Perhaps Eubanks had Lawrence and Garner's permission to rat them out. Maybe they were never really angry with Eubanks at all. Maybe the trio had been partners from the beginning.

Maybe that's why all three showed up at Katine's law office, conveniently after Eubanks finished serving his jail time for the False Report charge. Maybe Eubanks was showing up with his pals in expectation of something. Maybe forgiveness had nothing to do with it.

Perhaps it was business.

Lawrence's professed umbrage at his arrest is inconsistent with his discarding bagfuls of form solicitations from defense attorneys. If he was *that* furious, he'd be trying to get an attorney right away. His post-arrest inaction, for which he offers no explanation, is consistent with a defendant who knows he already *has* an attorney—a defendant who made arrangements for legal counsel well in advance of a planned arrest.

Maybe Lawrence *wasn't* lying when he told the deputies he already had an attorney.

CHAPTER
5

# JP Court and the
# Fax that Roared

The Class C misdemeanor Homosexual Conduct case, so longed for by the homosexual community to test Texas' sodomy law, was almost jettisoned at Justice of the Peace Court level the morning after the arrest, according to Sheryl Roppolo, chief clerk since 1995 to Precinct 3, Position 1, Justice of the Peace Mike Parrott.

Roppolo said as soon as she got the fax very early in the morning on September 18, 1998, outlining the Homosexual Conduct charges, she quickly walked through the clerk's office, down the long hallway through the adjacent constable's office, and out the back door at 14350 Wallisville Road.

A bit past 8 A.M. in Judge Parrott's parking spot behind the satellite courthouse, Roppolo stood smoking Virginia Slims menthol cigarettes, nervously glancing at her watch, and looking out toward the bordering fields of pine trees. A white Crown Victoria vehicle rounded the corner to her left. She stepped aside to allow Judge Parrot to pull his vehicle into his assigned space near the back door.

"'He said, 'What's going on?'" Roppolo explained. "I

said, 'Just stop! Before you go in there, we need to decide how we are going to handle some of these things because the media is fixing to converge on us big time!'

"'Why?' he asked.

"So I read the complaint to him.

"His initial response was 'Well, I'll just dismiss it.' Because the way it read you could tell—and this officer was somebody that was known to have problems anyway. And I said, 'Nooooo. You cannot dismiss it!'

"I mean it. It was just that close. That tells you what difference it makes by having somebody that knows. Because [Judge Parrott] is clueless. This is not an area that he knows anything about as far as homosexual issues. It's never been an issue that is dealt with in this JP Court. Prior to his taking over [as judge], he was a parks director for Precinct 3. So [homosexual issues] were just never anything he really knew about," Roppolo amplified.

"Homosexuality and the issues associated with that. Like same-sex benefits. Those things never crossed his mind as far as having to deal with it. I have never asked [Judge Parrott] but I doubt that he has many friends who are homosexual that would explain [issues to him]," she conjectured.

"We talked about it a little bit [standing outside by the back door], and Judge Parrott said, 'OK, fine.' He said, 'Just run the media through you. I'm not talking to anybody as long as the case is in the court,'" Roppolo recalled.

"I needed [Judge Parrott] to know. I knew it was going to get pretty wild around here. These are pretty quiet courts. I wanted him to understand that this was a really big deal. I wasn't sure he would understand because we've never had anything like that before. This is lazy East Harris County. You would be more likely to catch somebody in the act of bestiality than homosexuality. It is just a different kind of place. The last place in the world you would have thought this case would have originated," Roppolo observed.

"Once we came through the [back] door, I pulled the

rest of the staff together. 'You are going to be bombarded,' I said. Because everybody here answers the phone. We don't have just one operator.

"I told [the staff] 'You're fixing to be bombarded with calls and possibly people coming in the door. Refer them all to me.'"

"Within 2 hours the phone started ringing. People [media] started coming to the window," she remembered.

Roppolo's recollections of time frame are not supported by newspaper accounts or other witnesses. From September 17 to early November, members of the local news media, apparently unaware of the arrests, were silent. Publicity did not begin appearing until approximately November 17 on radio, and may have appeared slightly earlier on local television. The first *Houston Chronicle* article that researching could establish appeared November 21, 1998, almost two months after the arrest.

Confronted with the apparent discrepancy in time frames, Roppolo remained adamant that massive publicity began September 18, 1998, within hours after the JP Court opened.

"In fact, attorney David Jones [from Katine's law firm] was phoning me September 18, asking me for a copy of the arrest report within a couple of hours after I came into work," she remembered.

Roppolo and Jones are close friends.

Roppolo named several activist leaders of the Harris County homosexual community who she said, "...were calling and saying we are so glad that case is there at this court because they knew that: a) the guys would be treated fairly and treated with courtesy, and b) that Judge Parrott was going to be there on the whole thing."

Roppolo wasn't the first person to be waiting at the door of Precinct 3, Position 1, Justice of the Peace Court, on September 18, 1998. At about 7:30 A.M., her administrative assistant, Nathan Broussard, was waiting for Roppolo in the clerk's office doorway.

"Look at this!" Broussard exclaimed, handing Roppolo the fax of the deputies' report. Police officers who make night shift arrests fax their reports from the jail to the clerk's office. So a stack of arrest reports awaited Broussard when he arrived. As he thumbed through the reports, scanning each, Broussard first noticed the Homosexual Conduct charge, according to Roppolo.

"As soon as [Nathan and I] read the complaint, we knew this was the case," she said. "He [Nathan] is gay. I'm politically active. So both of us knew what it meant. Both of us knew this was the case that they [homosexuals] had been looking for—for 15 years or longer," she said.

Broussard, 38 in 1998, is a tall, sullen, muscular guy with a glistening, clean-shaved head, and a long, white-blond, droopy moustache. A dead ringer for wrestling personality Hulk Hogan. He gruffly refused all public comment. "I don't want to talk about [the cases]. I don't want to be involved in any way," Broussard snapped when Roppolo introduced me to him.

While I was in Roppolo's office, Broussard remained at his desk 15 feet away, hunched over with his head down as if he were trying to hide. He would not allow me to photograph him.

"He was like that when the media were here too. They tried to get him to talk and he wouldn't," Roppolo explained.

Broussard has the deep, permanent, leathery tan of someone who either has a side job outdoors, or a lifetime membership in a tanning studio. There isn't much sun exposure while daily staffing a desk in the clerk's office. He appeared to be a disciplined bodybuilder who has hefted weights at the gym for many years. Broussard obviously puts effort into his physical appearance.

His voice, high-pitched and childlike, is a jarring incongruity—a startling mismatch with his jock-like physicality.

Roppolo said that Broussard has not been politically active. "He's very private," she added.

❈

Broussard, listed in voter records as Nathan Paul Broussard, was born July 12, 1960, in Louisiana, according to Roppolo.

An Internet photograph depicts Broussard donating blood in a radio-station-sponsored blood drive in Morgan City, Louisiana, on an unspecified date.

"Nathan is a big boy. He is a very powerful presence. The long goatee. The shaved head. I know him very well," said his longtime friend Clovis Lane Lewis, the prominent local gay activist who was one of the major players in *Lawrence*, and who also is a longtime Katine confidant.

Is Nathan Broussard openly gay?

"Yes." Lewis said.

"[Broussard] has a gorgeous tat [tattoo] on his back. It is wings from shoulder to shoulder with a goat head, and a human below the belt. Or maybe it's eagle head on a human body with wings. Sort of like a very muscular leg and torso with arms stretched out with wings," Lewis said.

What does Broussard's tattoo mean?

"I have no idea. I'm not a tattoo guy," Lewis responded.

Lewis said he was friends with Broussard for about three years before September 17, 1998.

"[Broussard] is a clerk at Judge Parrott's. He is a gay guy who works in Justice of the Peace Court. I know [Broussard] very well," Lewis said again.

They met years ago in a Houston gay bar known as Club Pacific Street, owned by Jay Allen, where Broussard was a regular customer, according to Lewis.

"Nathan Broussard used to hang out at Pacific Street, which I was managing at the time [about 1995 on]. For a very short while [Broussard] was managing when I was bartending the same club several years before that. [Broussard] didn't manage it for very long. It was more like a part-time thing . . ." Lewis explained.

Is Broussard a bodybuilder?

"Yes. Obviously," Lewis said.

In June 2004, I showed the Internet photo of Nathan

Broussard to Lawrence and Garner who were attending a Lambda-sponsored breakfast in Houston to celebrate the one-year anniversary of the *Lawrence* ruling. The breakfast was attended mainly by attorneys.

Katine was there as a featured speaker. As in my April 2004 interview with the defendants, I discussed information about the case with them together at the breakfast, and in Katine's presence.

I asked if they knew or recognized the person in the photo.

Lawrence barely glanced at the photo—maybe a nanosecond—then quickly looked away.

"No," Lawrence said.

In the color Internet photo, Broussard is wearing a baseball-type cap. But his features are visible. It is the photo of him at the blood drive in Louisiana. I showed the photo to Garner.

Garner looked at the photo for 2-3 seconds, then looked at Katine. Then Garner laughed. "No," Garner said.

"Well, who is that?" Katine asked me.

A clerk in JP Parrott's office, I responded.

"Oh," Katine said. Then the trio left to join the Lambda breakfast.

Sheryl Roppolo is a graduate of Channelview High School, class of 1976—two years before Deputy Quinn graduated from the same school in Harris County. She speaks disparagingly about Deputy Quinn at every conversational opportunity.

Born in Pasadena, Texas, (the same home ground where Lane Lewis was born and grew up) a blue-collar southeast Houston suburb, Roppolo began political activism early, and continues, enthusiastically hopeful of a Democratic resurgence.

"Yes, definitely there was an idea [within the local homosexual community] that I was sympathetic to [homosexual] causes. I wasn't at one time. I grew up out here with all the Bubbas too," she said. Roppolo, blond and plumpish, has a daughter who is in Hollywood seeking a career as an actress/model.

"I wouldn't say I wanted a case [to test 21.06]," Roppolo said. "It was not anything that I had pondered on especially. But when it happened, I realized the significance of it."

Roppolo said that for Judge Parrott the sodomy cases were "a scary thing out here, running in the precinct that he has to run in. Homosexuality is a very unpopular issue."

In managing what she perceived as possible negative political fallout for Judge Parrott, Roppolo consulted local lesbian activist Sue Lovell on September 18 or the next day.

"We had a conjillion [sic] conversations about this case," Lovell said in a May 17, 2004, interview, describing the numerous phone calls between her and Roppolo.

Lovell, then 48, said she was the first and only openly gay person from Texas elected to the Democratic National Committee. She and Roppolo are friends of 20 years who habitually speak weekly or more by telephone. Lovell works as director of a private jobs training program in Houston.

"My role was to reassure Judge Parrott that this [case] would not cost him any votes," Lovell said. "Democrats for a long time have opposed the sodomy law. Gays, lesbians and good Democrats would be worried about prosecuting people on the sodomy law. If Judge Parrott doesn't prosecute them, we don't go to the Supreme Court."

"We didn't want Judge Parrott to dismiss it," Ms. Lovell explained because, "We were using it as a test case."

Although Judge Parrott confirms that Sheryl Roppolo was waiting for him at his parking space the morning of September 18, 1998, he emphatically denies that he ever discussed dismissing the Homosexual Conduct cases with Roppolo or anyone. He denies that he ever even thought of dismissing the sodomy cases, or any other case, because he knows he does not have that authority.

"Only the prosecution has that authority. That part of our conversation never happened," Judge Parrott responded. Further contradicting Roppolo, he remembered publicity about the cases beginning in November, and not in September immediately after the arrests.

There was only one truck from a Houston television station when Justice of the Peace Mike Parrott pulled into his parking space about 8:30 A.M. on November 20, 1998, the day Garner and Lawrence were scheduled to enter pleas.

"I saw that TV truck and I thought, '*Hey! We don't have those often at JP Court!* And within an hour, my staff was telling me the parking lot was full of TV trucks from several stations. Some of them had those big towers," Judge Parrott remembered, explaining how the media multiplied.

"Then not long after I arrived November 20, a guy from the district attorney's office came into my chambers," Judge Parrott remembered. "It wasn't no *ex parte*. But he had a file in his hand. He said, 'This is what's going to happen.' Usually they [prosecutors] do their own thing, and I do my own thing. I knew something was up, because he was one of the top prosecutors in the district attorney's office. He wasn't one of the normal [beginning] prosecutors I usually see out here. He didn't tell me how to rule or nothin'. He just briefed me. 'Here's what's coming before you in about an hour,' the prosecutor told me. 'It's going to be simple. They *want* to plead guilty. What you want to do is assess a fine,' the prosecutor explained to me."

Parrott is a native of Lufkin, Texas, and was 49 when the two Homosexual Conduct cases came before him as the first rung on the legal ladder. He is neither an attorney nor a college graduate.

Parrott is a tall, exceedingly affable man with a firm handshake, whose broad-shouldered V-shaped physique is an immediate clue to his past football career at the

University of Houston, where he attended, but did not graduate.

Texas law allows non-attorneys to serve as Justices of the Peace.

Parrott said, "The TV people kept asking me if they could film in my courtroom. I said, 'Absolutely no!' But I allowed them to film through the courtroom door, which is what they did.

"So in court here comes the first defendant. I think it was Lawrence, with an entourage of lawyers. Maybe there was even more lawyers than that. They said 'Judge, we want to plead guilty,' which the defendant did. So I assessed a $100 fine plus court costs, and they all paraded out the courtroom door."

Attorney Suzanne B. Goldberg of Lambda Legal's New York City office was with Katine and co-counsel David Jones on November 20, 1998. Broussard and Katine's friend, Lane Lewis, said he was present too.

"Then comes the second defendant, I think it was Garner," Parrott continued. "He also had an entourage of three-to-four attorneys, maybe more. I think they might have been different attorneys than the attorneys with the first defendant. But I'm not sure. He pled guilty. I assessed a $100 fine, and they all paraded out the courtroom door. I thought it was finished.

"Then in just a few minutes, my clerk whispered to me, 'Judge, they want a set-aside.' That means they want the plea and judgment just taken, set aside. So I went back to my chambers. All the big entourage came in. 'Judge, the fine has to be the full amount before we can appeal,' the defense attorneys told me.

"I looked at the prosecutor and he nodded 'Yes.' So I said OK. They wanted to redo the pleas back there in chambers. But I said, 'No, we'll do it outside in open court.' So we all went back into the courtroom," Judge Parrott explained.

"We granted the set-aside [voiding the prior pleas and fines] and they pled guilty again. This time I assessed a $150 fine, which allowed them to appeal, they said."

Roppolo described the grand entrance, grand exit, second grand entrance, and second grand exit part of the plea proceedings as "really kind of comical."

Judge Parrott recalled that he "...didn't hear much more about the cases until about two weeks later. I was driving past a convenience store near here. Deputies were processing a crime scene where a man was shot to death in a parking lot. I stopped to see what was going on. Deputy Joseph Quinn, the arresting officer in the sodomy cases, was helping process the fatal shooting. Deputy Quinn came over, shook my hand, and started apologizing to me [about the cases].

"I told him, 'Don't apologize to me! You didn't do anything wrong!'

"Deputy Quinn started telling me about the cases. Of course the cases were out of my court and up on appeal by then. He said his superiors are not reprimanding him, but they had criticized him for arresting the two men for Homosexual Conduct.

"His superiors said when Quinn witnessed the two defendants having sex, he should have just shut the bedroom door, said excuse me, and moved on. I told him, you guys are trained to do what you do.

"Deputy Quinn said when he witnessed the two men having anal sex they continued sexual activity for at least 10 seconds—which is an eternity, after the [armed] officers entered the bedroom.

"'They [the defendants] put on a show. The defendants rubbed our face in it. We rapped on the door with nightsticks, we announced our presence. There is no way the defendants didn't know we were there. That's why I wrote them up [arrested them].' Deputy Quinn told me," Judge Parrott recalled.

"He asked me, 'Judge, what would you [have done]? I had to do something," Judge Parrott remembered the later conversation with Deputy Quinn. In two interviews,

Judge Parrott volunteered many complimentary remarks about Deputy Quinn, praising his work as a deputy, and specifically his work in arresting Lawrence and Garner.

At the conclusion of the JP proceedings, Lawrence, Garner, and their defense team held a press conference in the large, gray-tiled lobby of the satellite courthouse.

When I first heard about these cases initially assigned to my county criminal court, I assumed the arrests took place in Houston's near-downtown Montrose area, described in a 1987 U.S. Supreme Court case as "an eclectic neighborhood which is the center of gay life and culture." (That case, involving Ray Hill, a prominent Houston homosexual activist, was handled by Katine's law partner Gerald Birnberg. The court ruled in Hill's favor).

I was astounded to discover when I began research that the arrest scene was not in the Montrose area, or anywhere else in the City of Houston. The arrests were in a blue-collar area of southeast Harris County, which Sheryl Roppolo calls "Bubbaland." "The last place in the world you would have thought this case would have originated," is how Roppolo had put it.

But *that* is precisely what attracted my attention. Why *there* and not Montrose?

Another trajectory of absolute genius.

Stunning brilliance if you puzzled it out.

If the arrests occurred in the City of Houston, the cases would be sent for random assignment by computer to any one of about 65 full- and part-time judges in the Houston Municipal Court system, all attorneys—not subject to pressures of election, and of widely disparate political leanings.

Potluck.

If the case went to Municipal Court, the chance of getting an unsympathetic judge would be real. And the judge, by virtue of being an attorney, would have some degree of legal training and sophistication in terms of closely scrutinizing the high-profile cases.

Since the municipal judges are appointed by Houston's mayor, any covert political pressure would be less successful.

However, a clever planner could pre-select a court and judge most favorable to the cases simply by prearranging the arrests in a specific geographical area of Harris County where the case would automatically go to a pre-chosen, specific Justice of the Peace with jurisdiction over that area. Ideally, it would be a JP or a JP's staff who already had longtime connections and sympathies with local homosexual activists.

If the JP was a non-lawyer, so much the better.

If the JP was not a college graduate, even better.

If the JP's head clerk and campaign manager had 20-year friendships with most of *Lawrence*'s major players—much, *much* better.

Bingo!

By what seemed coincidence to the undiscerning eye, the cases found a *perfect* home at Precinct 3, Position 1, before Justice of the Peace Mike Parrott.

Years before the September 17, 1998, arrests, *every* major player in *Lawrence*, which includes nearly every prominent homosexual activist in Harris County—many who were nationally known, had interlocking friendships, partisan political sympathies and overlapping activist ties to that JP Court.

In fact, they were the same activists who *shepherded* the case after the arrests, including Lane Lewis, the Katine protégé who said he learned of the case by happenstance.

So, contrary to Ms. Roppolo's observation that the rural southeast area was "the last place in the world you would have thought this case would have originated," discerning analysis reveals Precinct 3, Position 1, JP Court as the *first* place one would have thought this case to originate.

Lane Lewis' close friend is Nathan Broussard, Sheryl Roppolo's assistant.

Lewis and Katine have been close confidants over many years as activists.

Roppolo is close friends with Katine's co-counsel David Jones, Katine's friend Annise Parker, and everyone's friend Sue Lovell, who is friends with Lane Lewis.

Roppolo knows and admires Katine, but does not describe him as a close friend. She said she has "heard of" Lane Lewis, but does not recall whether she ever met him.

All have Democratic ties.

Some of them are gay.

In recounting the day-after events of September 18, 1998, Roppolo indicated that her early arrival at work before 8 A.M. in time to receive the fax from her assistant Broussard, and then early enough to intercept Judge Parrott before he took the bench, was her routine behavior.

Several times during the weeks after interviewing her, I phoned the court about 8 A.M. and asked for her. She was never in. Personnel who answered the phone said Ms. Roppolo usually doesn't come into the office until later in the morning.

Did Sheryl Roppolo come in very early the morning of September 18, 1998, because she *expected* to find something?

Speaking privately to a judge about a case pending before him or her is an ethical no-no. Even most laypeople know that. But it was my experience as a judge in Harris County that such ethical rules are sometimes circumvented by using intermediaries—often court employees, whose routine of accessing the judges can easily be converted into an *ex parte*, which is less likely to appear to be a violation of the rules.

As head clerk, and as his campaign manager, Sheryl Roppolo had Judge Parrott's ear, and a shot at controlling his actions.

If the longed-for arrests were made, but the planner(s) had no control over the cases through the trial stages, all the brilliance of the arrests might be for naught.

Sue Lovell described how Sheryl Roppolo was a conduit for Lovell's "reassurances" to Judge Parrott. She thinks conversation with Roppolo regarding *Lawrence* began perhaps two days after the arrests.

Lovell said she never spoke directly with Judge Parrott. "That would be unethical. I don't want any sort of innuendos that Judge Parrott was influenced in any way," she said in a gruff, direct manner.

# City Councilwoman
# Annise Parker

Mitchell Katine's traits of political ambition and persistence fueled then Houston City Councilwoman Annise Parker's recommendation that Katine should represent defendants Lawrence and Garner. Those same Katine qualities clashed early on with the equally ambitious and entrepreneurial Lane Lewis, *and* with the Ivy League advocates of Lambda Legal.

Lewis is a local, gay activist and Katine friend.

Annise Parker is the only openly gay elected official in Harris County, Texas.

She recalls how—from the beginning—Katine, Lewis, and Lambda Legal engaged in a figurative shoving match vying for local, state, national, and international center-stage prominence as *Lawrence* progressed to the U.S. Supreme Court.

Parker was 43, serving her first term as an at-large member of Houston's City Council, when Lewis phoned her at her city hall office seeking input "within a few days" after the defendants were arrested. After serving on City Council until 2003, she was elected Houston's City Controller, her current position.

77

Parker knew Katine, Lewis, and Lovell as gay activist colleagues over many years.

"[Lewis] called me and said, 'I got these two guys. They were arrested for violating 21.06. We have been looking for some opportunity to challenge it. I think maybe this is it. What do we do?'" Parker remembered, in a May 10, 2004 interview.

"It is serendipity that [Lewis] happened to be an activist plugged into the implications, and finding out about [the case]," she added. "[Lewis] was in the right place at the right time."

Parker said she and Lewis conferred on the phone for at least 30 minutes.

"We brainstormed about what the next steps should be.

"I said, 'Make sure [Lawrence and Garner] don't plead out. We have to find them an attorney who knows the import of this case.' We discussed various attorneys [including] Stonewall Lawyers, the local gay-lesbian attorney group, and individual criminal defense attorneys. I said, '[Katine] has been active publicly in organizing the attorneys.

"I said, 'I know [Katine] is ambitious. This is not his area of law. But I think [Katine] would jump all over this, and do what he needs to do to make sure we go through the right steps now, whether or not he carries through with it in the future,' Parker recalled telling Lewis. 'This is an attorney [Katine] who I know will be both politically motivated, but also a community activist who will be willing to put his time into it.'"

"We knew Katine would understand. We wouldn't have to explain the political implications. I think I may have expected [Katine] to hand the case off to someone else. Lane Lewis and I also discussed that Williams, Birnberg and Anderson [Katine's law firm] litigated [another local case] that went to the U.S. Supreme Court.

"[Katine] was so perfect. He understood. He was an activist. He was plugged in. He was ambitious, and he is persistent.

"I think [Katine] may have had an eye on the future.

He said, 'I'm going to document this [case], and someday I will be famous.' Which is why we picked him. It worked!" Parker said, smiling.

Is Katine going to run for political office?

"I think so. I think [Katine] wants a judgeship someday when the political tides turn,' Parker speculated. Katine is a Democrat. Republicans have dominated Harris County politics since 1994.

The local gay community wanted to keep the September 17, 1998, arrests *off* media radar for a few days, Parker revealed.

Gays kept the secret very well. As the homosexual community buzzed with news of the arrests, the heterosexual community remained unaware of the high-profile case about to burst onto an international stage.

"There were a number of reasons," Parker explained. "[Lewis], then I, then [Katine] and others immediately recognized the implications of [the arrests]. But these guys [Lawrence and Garner] were unknowns. Particularly recognizing that their legal histories were maybe a little spotty—they weren't activists—and maybe they would get spooked by the whole thing, and bolt. Maybe [the defendants] wouldn't want to cooperate. We needed to get as many of the players engaged as possible before anything got out of hand. We didn't want them to plead out. We didn't want the case to be dismissed. We wanted to be able to keep it going."

During those days immediately after the arrest, there was a lot of activity in the gay community, trying to get organized, she remembered.

Is Justice of the Peace Court Clerk Sheryl Roppolo mistaken that publicity commenced within a few hours of September 18?

"It may have felt that way to her, but it probably wasn't immediately after. It was a few days," Parker remembered.

❈

Clashes among homosexuals over control of the case began early.

"Lane Lewis befriended Lawrence and Garner," Parker said. "He shepherded them through the process. Kind of babysat them. Then maybe at some point he started kind of controlling them a little too much. I know Lewis and Katine began to clash fairly early on. This was while it was still ... because while the [gay] community needs to be grateful that [Lewis] stumbled on this, recognized it, and worked with the guys ... I think at some point, [Lewis] wanted to represent Lawrence and Garner and keep control."

"From a community standpoint, we had to do everything right legally," said Parker, who is not an attorney.

How could Lewis, who is not an attorney, represent the defendants?

"He wanted to be part of the process. He was really passionate about it. I think [Lewis] wanted to be compensated [for] representing them in terms of being a spokesperson for [the defendants]," Parker remembered.

Did Lewis want money?

"I think so," Parker said unhesitatingly.

"Not [money] from [the defendants] in the sense of exploiting them. But like: 'I am doing all of this for them. I am working with them. There wouldn't be a case if I hadn't recognized it. I need to continue to be part of the process. But I need to be able to support myself through this too,'" she quoted Lewis. "More like an agent. That's how Lewis viewed himself. I think that is how he tried to represent himself."

Was Lewis employed then?

"Yeah. He is usually a bartender."

Did Lewis ever ask anybody for money?

"I don't know."

But that was implied?

"We certainly had that conversation. [Lewis] said after [Katine] was involved and other folks began to get involved that we wouldn't have a case if he hadn't gotten involved, and he ought to be compensated for all the hours he was putting into it. And yes, these guys were his clients. That he was the one who was able to relate to them, and keep them engaged," Parker stated.

Lewis phoned Parker throughout the proceedings with updates; once a week in the beginning, then every other week or so while Lewis was involved. "Once it progressed, we didn't speak about any of it," she remembered.

On April 30, 1999, about six months after Lewis brought the three defendants to Katine's law office, Lewis purchased a house for $90,000. The property, for sale just over a month, was listed for $97,500.

The three-bedroom, two-bath, 1,571-square-foot home, built in 1950, is in an older, middle-class section of north Houston, far from Lewis' family in working-class Pasadena, Texas.

Lewis, who had worked as an on-again, off-again bartender, and at other low-paying jobs all his life, put $4,550 down, and qualified for an $85,450 30-year mortgage loan on the home in the Oak Forest subdivision.

Lewis moved out of his San Felipe Court Apartment on the fringes of Houston's upscale Galleria area known as Uptown.

What did Lambda think of Lane Lewis?

"They couldn't understand what [Lewis] was doing. He isn't a lawyer, so they didn't want to talk to him. He was interfering."

How did Parker know Lane Lewis?

"We have just known each other a long time. Working together on projects. We ended up spending a lot of time together. I was the police liaison for the gay and lesbian community. I taught at the police academy and served on the Civilian Review Committee of the Houston Police Department. I recommended him to replace me on the CRC and at the police academy."

The unpaid positions involve studying hundreds of police reports and becoming familiar with police procedures and personalities—an education in copthink.

Lewis is a masterful chameleon, skilled at altering his "look" at will—morphing in appearance to fit any situation he is navigating, then morphing again to suit the occasion, Parker explained with amazement, and some admiration for Lewis' persona-altering abilities.

"When I first met Lane Lewis, he was working for Intercare Hospital and he was Mr. Corporate. Suit and tie. Yes!

"Then he kind of dropped out. Didn't know what he wanted to do. He was running a program for gay street kids. I guess he was identifying with them.

"He went through a couple of transformations. For the past few years he has been a bartender. But Lewis definitely went through a phase where he colored his hair. He always wore double earrings. He was more the out activist.

"Lewis could transition from that to the more street activist. He knew how to present himself professionally, especially to teach police officers at the academy. He appeared for a while in the colored hair and earrings. But then he sort of morphed back. I think by the time [*Lawrence*] was happening, Lewis was more on the coming back toward the center a little bit," Parker explained.

Katine-Lambda discord developed early too, she said.

"Again, I didn't expect that Katine would end up working on [the case] all the way through. We fully expected that if we could do all the things that we were supposed to do, execute it at the local level, that some day the national organizations would weigh in. I attended national meetings with representatives of Lambda. They are a well-established organization.

"There were some discussions at the beginning. [Lambda] seemed to be trying to ease the locals out and take over," Parker said.

But Katine stuck like glue.

He wasn't going to be pushed out of the klieg lights by

anyone. Lambda Legal's New York lawyers had met their match in Mitchell Katine.

In our various 2004 interviews and conversations, Katine strongly implied that the post-*Lawrence* relationship between him and Lambda is distant, cool. But he stopped short of openly criticizing Lambda.

"I don't think Lambda was particularly happy about sharing things with [Katine] either. I got the distinct impression that they are Lambda. They are national. They know what is going on. They were ready to move Katine out of the way. Katine wouldn't move! [Lambda] realized they had to partner with him," Parker explained.

Katine e-mailed her regular case updates over the nearly five years the case pended, she said.

Annise Parker, born May 17, 1956, in Houston, graduated from Rice University in 1978 with a BA in sociology, anthropology and psychology. A photo of uniformed Houston Police Department officers is prominently displayed on her City Hall office wall. She said she knows some police officers who, in order to be hired, lie about being gay.

# Enter Stage Left
# Lane Lewis, Provocateur

Clovis Lane Lewis is an angry man. Nothing "gay" about him in the traditional definition of the word.

Life's an unceasing rant.

He's enraged at bumper stickers, police, the U.S. Constitution, airplane passengers who fart in his face, "churches and other nefarious organizations, people who dislike homosexuals," and lots more he'd be glad to tell anyone about.

Even at 36, sliding toward middle age in 2004, Lane Lewis has not mellowed.

An anger usually attributed to youth still boils hot in his soul, radiating from his being with such force, that his anger and his persona are inseparable. His face is angry, his fingers are angry, his voice is angry, his writing is angry.

In face-to-face meetings, Lewis' emotional energy seems siphoned toward quelling his anger to socially acceptable levels, a self-torture he endures uneasily. His anger control appears tenuous.

His humor on his elaborate Web site is mocking others, finding fault, scathing ridicule.

Lewis, like activist Sue Lovell, is a past president of the local Gay and Lesbian Political Caucus. Like Sheryl Roppolo, Lewis was born in Pasadena, Texas. The Shell Oil refinery takes up the major portion of nearby Deer Park, a blue-collar Houston suburb like Pasadena, and where Lewis graduated from Deer Park High School in 1986.

Seventeen years after graduating, and within a few days of the June 2003 *Lawrence* decision, Lewis received a bachelor's degree in interdisciplinary studies from the University of Houston, downtown. After receiving his degree, Lewis continued as a bartender or bar manager, jobs he held off and on during most of his adult life.

Lewis enthusiastically identifies with other angry males. In an October 2003 entry in his Web log, he reveals his fantasy soul mate—the singer Eminem whose defiant rapper lyrics Lewis admiringly reprints for pages and pages on his pleonastic Web site.

"...you're a Maltese. I'm a pitbull off his leash, all this peace talk can cease," Lewis admiringly quotes Eminem.

Lewis includes on his blog a photo of the surly rapper, his shoulders covered with tattoos, staring sullenly at the camera.

"okey dokey. i just bought my first Eminem CD and I have not stopped listening 2 it since i put it into the player (and that is saying alot considering I bought Annie Lennox's CD on the same day and i have liked here [*sic*] since the early eighties ... in fact i have not even listened to the CD yet).

"I have this habit of wanting to know more about anything that white america does not want me to know about (i.e. malcom X, hip hop, history, the law, Lacan, Zinn, people who speak out against the Bushitt administration, etc...) With that said, off i went to the store and bought The Eminem Show. 3 words ... Fab You Lous," Lewis writes for September 30, 2003.

"Granted [Eminem's] lyrics can at times put one off ... especially if you r female, gay, or against violence in general. However, the crux of [Eminem's] lyrics contains honesty. That raw emotion at the heart of angst," Lewis wrote.

Scanning Lewis' hundreds of pages of multi-target diatribes on his Web site is mind numbing.

A sample from a September 18, 2003, Lewis Web log: "I am not a Democrat so please don't attempt [*sic*] dismiss or delineate me by the dichotomize catagories of a failing duplicitous (but actually singularly incestuous) political system."

It is difficult to ascertain from Lewis' loquacious writings whether he is expressing original ideas, or has copied verbatim passages from arcane books.

In a March 5, 2004, blog entry, Lewis says of the U.S. Constitution: "The Constitution and its subsequent pages upon pages of laws is a magazine for the powerful to subscribe the masses to. An article the authors rarely read or subscribed to themselves. The Constitution then creates a false 'we' that can be forcefully exerted to the capitalistic intent of nationalism."

From reading Lewis' incoherent ramblings on his Web site, the clashes Annise Parker described—between Lewis and the *au courant*, East Coast intellectual, media-savvy Lambda Legal attorneys—were predictable. Lewis' in-your-face, up-yours *déclassé* approach must have appalled Lambda's NYC, aristocratic upper echelon.

It's easy to see how Katine, needing to placate both Lewis and Lambda to achieve his own agenda, got bounced around in the turbulent middle.

Lewis, then 35, wrote for his September 10, 2003 entry: "I do not consider myself to be white. In part because I recognize I have Creek blood in my veins and, most likely, other colors as well. Actually, anyone who calls himself white at this point knows nothing of history.

"Even if you don't believe we all came from Africa and the Middle East (which i hate that term because it forces interpolation to England as the center of the world. I must admit grandparents of the 18th century were doin a lot of fuckin).

"Furthermore, because I acknowledge openly the destruction of white colonization and greed, I chose to dis-associate myself with the lineage. I do however, acknowledge my basic appearance is white and therefore, have a responsibility to that facade. I say this as a preface to my conclusion in an attempt to say that I, as a white male, am also harmed by the mentality of my white brethern [sic]."

In apparent forgetfulness of his writing on racial identity a week earlier, Lewis wrote in a September 17, 2003, book review: "...this commin [sic] from a Pasadena Texas white boy."

Pasadena, near the same southeast part of the county in Deer Park where Lewis was born November 17, 1967, (at 7:01 P.M. he says), is a blue-collar community where Lewis' parents still live. His only sibling, a sister 10 years older, lives in a southeast, Ship Channel-area community.

The September 17, 2003, blog entry—five years to the day of the 1998 Lawrence-Garner-Eubanks arrest—features a color photo of Lewis in a strappy T-shirt, head slightly back, his mouth partly open, seductively positioning his tongue as invitation.

In person Lewis is tall, medium-to-thin build, dark curly hair, handsome face. His skin has a gray pallor.

For some weeks after I first contacted Mitchell Katine on January 15, 2004, he didn't mention Lewis' pivotal role in *Lawrence*, despite my increasingly probing questions as to how Katine, a real estate and employment law attorney with zero experience in criminal practice, had connected with two defendants in a criminal case?

Did Lawrence, Garner and Eubanks just turn a wrong corner one day, wandering unannounced into Katine's law office on U.S. Highway 59?

Did Katine just happen to be sitting at his desk that day?

I persisted.

On February 17, 2004, Katine revealed the name Lane Lewis as involved in brokering in what Katine said was an initial liaison between Katine, Lawrence, Garner and Eubanks. Although Katine was vague about details, Katine later provided contact information for Lewis.

Lewis responded to my March 2004 initial e-mail inquiry, replying that in 1998 he was "just an activist with his ear to ground looking for the case." Lewis explained that he was then tending bar in Houston at Pacific Street, which he described as "a gay bar."

A person identifying himself as Lane Lewis confirmed in a March 30, 2004, e-mail that he was the initial liaison between attorney Mitchell Katine, and defendants Lawrence, Garner, and Eubanks: "It came to me quite by coincidence (although there r no coincidences) by a friend within the TC judicial system. i never met them prior to first contacting them about the case—once i was confident that this was the case i had been looking for, I consulted several people and we all agreed that Mitchell (Katine) deserved the case and was best suited.

"i then consulted with the 3 men and they agreed to let me take the case to a lawyer (Mitchell) after meeting with them we agreed to move forward. There is of course much more to the story but difficult to write within the confines of an e mail."

In an e-mail, Lewis delineates his background, with punctuation: "i have a license to practice social work and a Bachelors degree in interdisciplinary studies. -i have worked as youth teaching specialist, counselor, marketing, I currently teach police cadets and voluntarily act as the Mayoral Appointee as the Co-ordinator of the Citizens Review Committee of the Internal Affairs Dept at Houston Police Dept."

In a March 5, 2004, entry on his Web site expostulating on same-sex marriages, Lewis preens over his participation in Lawrence: "As the individual that first brought the supreme court sodomy case together in Texas several years ago, I apply these same principles to that. I do not thank the Supreme Court for striking down 21.06. NO governing body had the right to take that act away from me in the first place. By thanking them I am subscribing to their terms."

Responding by e-mail, on April 1, 2004, Lewis declined an in-person interview about *Lawrence* unless he could know in advance the "intent . . . motivation . . . and message of the text."

Besides, Lewis said, he is in India.

Why was he in India?

"I am writing a new psycho-social theory as to the motivation and formation of the human mind—I believe Buddhism to be the vehicle of spiritual healing which will be necessary after the western mental paradigm shift occurs, illusions of textural authority shattered and emptiness revealed."

Lewis' September 17, 2003, entry on his Web site featured another photo of Lewis—tan, buff, grinning, and stripped to the waist with low-hung jeans.

After Lewis' return from India, Lewis proved elusive for a personal interview.

After my request to Katine for assistance in obtaining the interview, Katine talked privately to Lewis, who then met my husband and me at a local cafeteria for an April 29, 2004, interview. Fresh from exercising at the gym, which he said he does regularly, he carried an orange fabric bag that appeared similar to those carried by monks. He twirled prayer beads.

Add "neophyte Buddhist" to the list of Lewis' chameleon forms.

According to Lewis' March 29, 2004, blog—his flirtation with Buddhism began in 1998, coinciding with his "bringing together" *Lawrence.*

In 2002, Lewis began to have what he calls "odd dreams"—"visions" that he connects back to his 1998 introduction to Buddhism.

He explains in a March 29, 2004 Web site entry: "In

1998 a book *Awakening the Buddha Within* by Lama Surya Das found its way into my hands. As I read, it seemed not so much familiar but more like "not foreign." The text spoke to me as if I had read it before. It all simply clicked.

"...I have never been one to have many dreams while sleeping. I am sure I have them but I rarely remember having them or even remember the topics or details when I do. That changed in November of 2002, when I turned 35.

"I began having odd dreams that would wake me. Not so much dreams actually. More like visions (for lack of a better term). They occurred both while asleep and within those moments between slumber and wakefulness.

"Sometimes they come to me during the normal activities of the day although I have often tried to shrug these off as mere storytelling or mental chatter except for the fact they occur randomly and often inconveniently. It is not so much that these visions/dreams are plural but rather singular in that they all have the same theme and occurred frequently over many months. They ceased last summer.

"In October or November (a little before turning 36) of last year, they began again and have increased. Additionally, varying topics I randomly pick up seem to fall open to pages that point me. TV, movies, conversations, random interactions with strangers all have something to do with the increasing urgency of moving in this direction.

"To the point that Thursday (not sure of the date) I was watching TV late at night (sometime sleep scares me) and for 2 hours every show I watched kept pointing me (even the X files).

"...This must all sound crazy and sometimes I think it is but I have come to realize that this view (crazy) is probably a conditioned thought of a conditioned reality.

"The dreams/visions repeatedly have me in Dharamsala during March and April of this year [2004]. I have no idea what the significance of these months are or why they are singled out. I feel I am supposed to go to Dharamsala to prepare myself for whatever the next step is," Lewis concludes, just before his departure to India. He solicited funds for the trip using his Web site.

"Ultimately however, all language will need to be done away with. Only telepathy is true communication," Lewis adds a few paragraphs later in his blog.

India's major religion is Hinduism, not Buddhism.

In 1998, about the time sheriff's deputies discovered Lawrence and Garner having sex, Lewis' psyche was affected by another influence: a professor from the University of Houston where he was a student.

"I was in a constitutional law class [in September 1998] ironically when this thing [*Lawrence*] was going through," Lewis explained in an interview.

"I didn't arrange it that way. I am sitting in a constitutional law class and somehow Dr. Brigman who was my professor, got wind on [*Lawrence*]. And that was an interesting discussion because his specialty was constitutional law and sex law. He was quite a character. He had a student in his class that had a case going through the Supreme Court."

"We discussed [the *Lawrence* case] at great length. He still gave me a B," Lewis lamented, apparently expecting that his discussions with professor Brigman would result in a higher grade.

Brigman died in 2004 of a heart attack, Lewis said.

Lewis' academic study of constitutional law in 1998 supplemented his street knowledge of the daily interplay of constitutional law and police officers; knowledge he began accumulating years earlier.

From about 1991-96 Lewis taught a one-day, 2-to-4-hour course to police cadets, which addressed issues in the local homosexual community—a mayoral initiative aimed at increasing police officers' sensitivity in dealing with gays. Resuming in 2001, he continued occasionally teaching the course to groups of 60-80 cadets. In teaching the human-relations-type course, Lewis replaced Annise Parker who recommended him after she relinquished the unpaid job upon her election to City Council. Both confirmed they are very close friends.

Lewis knows copspeak and copthink.

Lewis understands cop culture. He knows what cops like, what makes them angry, and how cops view the world. He knows precisely how cops approach a crime scene, what they do on arrival, and what makes them take action.

The teaching job educated Annise Parker to the ways of police as well. Both she and Lewis, veteran homosexual activists, were apt pupils.

"Hanging around cops, working with them, spending time at the police department. Spending time at the clubs, talking to the cops that are working the bars. I'm not an expert, but I'm probably well above average," Lewis said.

Is Lewis familiar with cop culture?

"Yes, I would say that. Sure."

Lewis said he carries a police badge.

Lewis' practical knowledge of police practices and procedures, which was already extensive, increased in 1998 when then-Mayor Lee Brown appointed Lewis to the Citizens Review Committee (CRC), one of the layers of the Houston Police Department's Internal Affairs division. The committee reviews investigative reports on complaints made against officers, and has a role in deciding punishment, if any.

As a committee member, Lewis was privy to the most intimate non-public information about local police officers: detailed reports of which cops were accused of screwing up, or committing crimes and with what frequency; what situations invited the most difficulties for cops; investigations by fellow police officers of alleged personal and professional misconduct; what complaints were sustained and why; who got punished and who didn't. The committee membership served as Lewis' education in the law as well as in the nitty-gritty of police procedures.

Lewis now chairs the CRC.

Lewis' access to law enforcement culture extended to the topmost echelons of the Houston Police Department.

"I was gay and lesbian liaison to the police department, called PAC, the Police Advisory Committee," Lewis said. "Annise Parker and I served on that together. Once a month we would meet with the police Command Staff over lunch, and talk about concerns in our community."

Lewis has been an agent provocateur in the gay community for years. He has held office in several organizations, among them—ACT UP (AIDS Coalition to Unleash Power) where he was executive director of AIDS Equity Leave.

"I was head of the civil disobedience section of Stonewall 25. We had a planned arrest event on July 24, 1994, at the United Nations. I was coordinator. I did not want to take an arrest because I was head of the thing. We had people arrested there. We were doing it on purpose," Lewis said.

"My talent is more in the area of putting things together," Lewis said, describing his academic studies.

His self description was similar to the language of his March 5, 2004, blog—that he: "brought the Supreme Court sodomy case together."

What exactly was Lewis' role in *Lawrence v. Texas*?

Could Lewis detail his involvement with the sodomy cases that became *Lawrence v. Texas*?

"I didn't know them," Lewis volunteered instantly, answering an unasked question with a non sequitur.

I assumed he meant Lawrence, Garner, and Eubanks.

How did Clovis Lane Lewis become involved in the Homosexual Conduct cases?

"Somebody, who to this day wants to remain unnamed, faxed me an arrest report. They told me they were going to fax it. I bumped into them in a bar. They knew who I was, and what I did, and that I was looking for this case."

Man or woman?

"Man."

How long after Lewis bumped into him was the arrest report faxed to Lewis?

"The next day. Day after that."

Someone Lewis knew?

"Oh yeah. He knew I was looking for this case. Not this case in particular, but this case, and had been [looking] for a couple of years. I knew it was just a matter of time. He faxed it to me and I read it. Knew what I was looking at. First I contacted Lawrence. Couldn't get a hold of [Garner]," Lewis said, lapsing for the first time into shorthand speech, different than his ordinary previous spoken speech patterns, and the patterns from his Web site.

How long after Lawrence, Garner, and Eubanks' September 17 arrest did Lewis receive this fax?

"I tried to put that together. I have gone back and looked at my notes." Lewis did not answer my question.

Lewis kept notes on all this? (Katine told Annise Parker Katine kept notes too.)

"I've got all that. [Lawrence, Garner, and Eubanks] were already out [of jail]. It was like the very next week. They were scheduled to appear in court. Some time had passed by the time it got to me. I don't remember. I'd have to go back and look at the arrest report. It's kind of hard to see because it was a fax, and is so faded." Again, Lewis did not answer my question.

Their arrest was September 17, 1998.

"Released on the 18th," Lewis volunteered instantly. "I don't know what day of the week it was. This was probably a week or so after."

They were arrested on a Thursday.

Lewis knew in advance the subject matter of our interview. If he had detailed notes on all the matters he knew I would be asking him about, why didn't he bring those notes to our interview? Lewis was not an absentminded person. Either he had no such notes, or he chose not to bring them.

Why would a man in the bar have selected Lewis to tell

about the arrests? Because Lewis had a reputation in the homosexual community as a liaison-type person?

"Yeah."

How did the man tell Lewis? Did he sit at the end of the bar, beckoning Lewis over?

"I was standing in front of register number 1, near the front door. I was walking by him. I said hello. He grabbed my arm. He said, 'I've got something I want you to see.'

"What is it? 'These two guys were arrested and charged with sodomy.' I said, 'Oh really? Wow! OK.' And he goes, 'Well, how can I get it to you?' I said fax it to me. Here is my fax number at the house.'

"I had the exact same response that everybody else did. Alright fax it to me. I'll take a look at it, blah, blah, blah. I really did. I don't know if he faxed me that day or the day after because this was probably a Friday or Saturday night when he told me. They were arrested on a Thursday. I didn't see it Sunday. I think it was like a Monday.

"If I remember correctly on my notes, it was a Tuesday when I got ahold of Lawrence. So he probably faxed it to me on a Monday or so," Lewis concluded. That would have been four days after the arrests.

Does Lewis know the name of this man?

"Oh yes, I know him very well. I have known him a couple of years. Not intimately or anything like that. But I knew who he was. I knew where he worked. I knew what he did for a living when he told me. I knew that he would have access to this kind of information," Lewis revealed.

Does this man work in the Texas judicial system?

"Yes. I asked him a few months ago if he wanted me to release his name. He said, 'I want [Katine] to know.' So I told Mitchell [Katine]. This was six months ago," Lewis said in the April 29, 2004, interview.

Does Lewis know a man named Nathan Broussard?

"Yes. He is not the one that faxed it to me. But I know he works for Justice of the Peace Mike Parrott," Lewis volunteered.

In the early morning hours of September 18, 1998,

Broussard is the court clerk who first received a copy of Deputy Quinn's arrest report, faxed overnight from the jail to Judge Parrott's office.

Does Lewis know Broussard?

"Very well."

How does Lewis know Nathan Broussard?

"Nathan Broussard used to hang out at the bar that I was managing at the time. For a very short while, [Broussard] was managing when I was bartending the same club several years before that. He didn't manage it for very long. It was more like a part-time thing. That is how I knew Nathan."

When Nathan Broussard's name first came up mid-interview, Lewis maintained the confident, blasé demeanor he affected during almost the entire interview, twirling the Buddhist prayer beads on the index finger of his right hand. Lewis' question to me about Broussard was the first time *he* asked *me* anything, other than whether I had talked to the cops.

"Where did you meet Nathan? I'm just curious. How in the world did Nathan's name come up?" Lewis asked me near the very end of our 2-hour interview.

Lewis' demeanor changed drastically when he asked me that question. His arrogance, his chutzpah, fell aside. Lewis was the supplicant seeking information. Clearly he was worried.

Lewis looked frightened. Frightened of Broussard? Frightened that I had connected the dots? Perhaps frightened for other, more complex reasons that were coalescing in my mind.

Lewis became transformed in that instant, a completely different persona—again the chameleon Annise Parker had described.

I told Lewis I met Broussard when I went to the Justice of the Peace Courthouse to interview Chief Clerk Sheryl Roppolo and Judge Mike Parrott.

Wouldn't Lewis' friend Nathan Broussard be the most logical man-in-the-bar to have faxed Lewis the arrest report on the defendants?

"Yeah. Well, that's interesting. That's what I have been told," Lewis responded enigmatically. Another non sequitur. He did not answer my question because his mind was reeling at this confrontation for which he had not prepared a response.

"That was interesting because when I called they..." Lewis began stumbling over his words, dissembling, melting like the wicked witch in The Wizard of Oz. "I remembered that he [the man in the bar] was really impressed that I hadn't even told [Katine]," Lewis stammered, trying to regain mental footing.

The man in the bar who Lewis says faxed Lewis the arrest report—is he an activist?

"No."

With the arrest report in hand, Lewis said he began to take action.

"So I called John [Lawrence] and identified to him who I was."

Who did Lewis tell Lawrence he was?

"Said I was Lane Lewis. I was a human rights activist and that I had some concern over his arrest. I wanted to know what action if any he had taken. That I thought we might have a Supreme Court case. If he was willing, I would like to find him an attorney at no cost to him. I would find the attorney, and find the funding to take care of this, if he would agree not to plead on it.

"I said, 'I'm not going to bug you. If you want to hang up, feel free to do it. I'm not going to call you back,'" Lewis said.

Did Lewis phone Lawrence at home or at Lawrence's work?

"At home. I used the phone number right off the police report. [Lawrence] said OK, he was interested."

How long did Lewis converse with Lawrence?

"Ten to fifteen minutes at the most." Lewis said he told Lawrence he would get back with him.

Did Lewis phone Lawrence at night or day?

"I called him that day when I got that blotter. I stared at it for a couple of hours. What am I looking at? Does this make sense? I'm thinking in my head how police operate. That came into play some."

How so?

"How arrests are made. How search and seizures are made. How people enter apartments. I am looking at it from that mindset first to ascertain whether it was a good arrest. Because if it was a blatantly bad arrest, well we are not going anywhere with it. Because the county is going to drop it. It was a [Harris] County arrest, not a [Houston] police arrest. So I had some concern over that. I wanted to make sure at least on paper, that it was a good arrest."

Was it?

"On paper it was. They had probable cause to enter the apartment. Man with a gun, etc. Now I'm not commenting on whether it happened the way they said it happened. It was a good arrest. As long as the officers stuck to the story they wrote down. It was a good arrest."

Did Lewis consult with anyone else during that time?

Lewis said after he called Lawrence, he phoned several local gay activists, including Annise Parker. "I don't remember them really latching on because it was unbelievable. We all knew it was going to happen, but something as simple as an apple falling from the tree.

"Of course I had a very short list of attorneys, which I ran through with [local activists]. Mitchell Katine was the only attorney I really seriously considered. Not just because he is a good attorney, and had access to money because he was at a fairly substantial law firm. But also because of his participation, volunteerism and assistance with not only me and my projects, but with other projects. There was a sense of debt, of [Katine] paying his dues.

"This was very important because from the beginning I never saw it as my case. It was a community case. I did not feel like I owned it. I did not want to get myself into a situation where I had this case and I was going to decide how it went forward."

Lewis said all three local gay activists with whom he consulted agreed that the cases should go to Mitchell Katine.

"Also keep in mind that the Lesbian-Gay Rights Lobby would have wanted this case. The Texas Human Rights Lobby was looking for this case. The Gay-Lesbian Task Force was looking. Everybody wanted this case. They all had their eye out. Because we all knew it was a matter of time before something like this happened. I didn't want to put myself in a position where I was making decisions for something that belonged not to me, but to everyone," Lewis remembered.

Did Lewis specifically want a gay attorney to represent Lawrence and Garner?

"Yes I did. I believe in taking care of our own. I wanted someone I knew.

"I called Katine first. He didn't really believe me either. He said fax it over to him. Katine got calls like this all the time: Can you help my friend? Then come to find out they weren't arrested for sodomy, they were arrested because they threw a vase across the room. Stuff like this.

"Less than five minutes after I put that thing in my machine, Katine called me back. His first words were, 'Do you know what you have?' Yeah, I have a pretty good idea of what I'm looking at."

Was Katine excited?

"Katine was very excited. 'Do you know what you have in your hand? Do you know what this is? Who are these guys? Can I call these guys?'

"When I faxed Katine the original thing, I blotted out the [defendants] names and phone numbers," Lewis said.

Lewis' version of events conflicts with the statements of Sheryl Roppolo, chief clerk in the Justice of the Peace Court where the case was filed. Roppolo, who has known attorney David Jones for years, said Jones phoned her the day after the September 17 arrests, requesting a copy of the arrest report.

Jones, co-counsel in the case, is in Katine's law firm.

Jones' office was about 30 feet from Katine's office.

If Jones had the arrest report within 24 hours of the arrest, it is certain Katine had it.

Why did Lewis white out identifiers on the arrest report he says he faxed to Katine?

"Because I didn't feel like their information should be released to people that weren't necessarily going on the same ship yet. I didn't want to start faxing their names all over town. I felt like it was private to them. They had not agreed to [Katine] as their attorney.

"They had only agreed to me as their representative. If Katine said no. If they didn't like Katine. If they wanted to . . . whatever it was, I didn't want that information out there. I didn't feel like it was appropriate. So I blotted their stuff out," Lewis explained.

"Katine didn't even know until [about November 2003] how I got [the arrest report]. Through all this, Katine never asked. He never pressured me. Until [November 2003] the two guys didn't even give me permission to tell Katine who they were."

They? Lewis now seemed to be saying there were *two* guys in the bar.

"The guy in the bar. So anyway, Katine wanted on board. I set up a meeting with [Garner, Lawrence, and Eubanks].

How long after Lewis talked to Katine was the meeting? A day or something?

"Yeah. Of course I never spoke to [Garner or Eubanks] because they were floaters—all over the place with their own set of issues. All going through Lawrence."

Did Lewis speak to Garner before that?

"I don't think I did. I don't remember talking to [Garner]. If I did, he was very agreeable. I don't remember. Somehow or other they all three ended up in my car going to [Katine's] office. I really don't remember how."

"I drove to Galena Park or Channelview where [Lawrence] lived. I'm almost positive. Because I would not have trusted them to find Katine's office. Thinking about the way I think, I don't remember how we got [to Katine's office]. I don't think I would have trusted them to get there on their own. Knowing my personality, I would have wanted to pick them up and put them in the car and make sure they got where they were going," Lewis said. He said it was the first time he had been to Lawrence's apartment.

Lewis picked [Lawrence, Garner, and Eubanks] up at Lawrence's apartment?

"I'm almost positive."

When was this?

"Probably two weeks after their arrest. [Katine] may have a better timeline. I don't know if he took better notes than that," Lewis added, confirming that Lewis knew Katine, like Lewis, was documenting everything.

What did Lewis tell the three men as they drove?

"I'm going to introduce you to a lawyer. Hear what they have to say about your case. You do not have to make a decision then and there. If you don't like him or you don't like the team that he is putting together, let me know and I will get another one. Don't go in thinking this is who you have to use. This is my first choice. I didn't tell them that. I'm sure they figured it out. So we went in."

In my April 23, 2004, interview with Lawrence and Garner, Lawrence described how *he* says he and Lane Lewis met. His account differs considerably from Lewis' version.

Lawrence said, "As usual, after you get out of jail you get all these flyers, flyers, flyers [from criminal defense attorneys soliciting business].

"I got a phone call one night about a week and a half later. This person told me that he was not a lawyer, but that he was an activist. He felt he knew someone we should be able to talk to and should be able to get to handle this case. He referred us to Mitchell Katine."

Who was that person?

"Lane Lewis."

In the week and a half between the time Lawrence phoned his father, and Garner consulted with Garner's brother, what did Lawrence do? Did Lawrence talk to other attorneys?

"No. I did not speak to anyone."

Criminal defense attorneys always stress to clients: Don't talk to anybody about your case. Lawrence's post-arrest silence and disinterest in hiring an attorney would be consistent with someone who already *has* legal representation arranged in advance of arrest.

So Lawrence's life just went on as usual after his September 17 arrest?

"Well I had made up my mind after I had spoken with my dad that I would find someone. It was just like he was telling me to wait. So I didn't hurry anything.

"I took the flyers and threw them in the garbage. I put them in black bags and drug them down to the trash so no one would know what I was getting in the mail," Lawrence said.

Did Lawrence know Lewis prior to this?

"No," Lawrence said.

Did Garner know Lewis prior to this?

"No," Garner said.

"We didn't know Lewis at all," Lawrence added.

How did Lawrence meet Lewis in person?

"About two nights later, Lane met me at the hospital [where Lawrence works]. We talked and he came to our house and we talked some more. A couple of days later, we came to Mitchell Katine's office. We made an appointment."

How did Garner meet Lewis?

Garner repeated, "We made an appointment, John and I, we met in [Katine's] office."

"He [Garner] didn't meet Lane," Lawrence interjected.

Did Lawrence tell Garner about Lewis' call?

"Right. I said I had been approached by someone who said he would like for us to meet with someone. [Katine's] office called us. They set an appointment up and we met on a Monday afternoon," Lawrence recalled.

Was Lewis at the meeting?

"I think Lane was there. He waited outside," Lawrence said, looking at Katine.

"Did Lane wait outside?" Katine asked Lawrence. Attorneys sometimes use information, imparted as a question, to telegraph to a witness the desired answer.

"Yes!" Lawrence and Garner then chorused simultaneously, the only time they spoke in exact unison during the interview.

Was anyone else other than Lewis involved in getting them an attorney?

"No," Lawrence said.

"(Eubanks) was drunk as a skunk when we were in Katine's office. Lit like a candle. I don't think I ever saw Eubanks sober," Lewis said.

"I remember they sat in the order: Lawrence, Eubanks, and Garner. Then two seats down was me. Across from me was Katine. I think Jones and Birnberg were on the end. So Katine and his [legal] team stepped out. I gave a little speech to the three boys," Lewis remembered.

"I talked about gay history, the Mattachine Society. I talked about how whenever we would dance we would always have to dance near a lesbian couple so we could switch partners if the police walked in. Talked to them about the importance of the case.

"I was very upfront with them about the amount of publicity they would receive in the media. That it would affect their work to some degree. I think Lawrence was the only one working at the time. I didn't want them going into this under any pretense of nirvana. They needed to understand what we were talking about doing and I wanted to have this discussion with them outside the ear of the lawyers. I wanted absolutely no pressure on them for that," Lewis explained.

"I said that if at any point they wanted to stop this process, to tell me and I would pull the plug. But they needed to understand that there would come a point in the case where I would not have that control. Up to a point if it gets overwhelming, I can put a stop to everything and you all can go back to your lives. But that at a point, we were going to cross that threshold, and they were not going to be able to turn back. They agreed to move forward.

"I believe I even quoted the JFK thing: 'Ask not what your country can do for you, but [ask] what you can do for your country.' Very sappy. Very emotional. It was an emotional thing because I wanted it to happen, but I didn't want it to happen under the pretense of them not really understanding. I have been in the paper. I know what that does," Lewis said.

Lewis said he spoke for 10 minutes. Then Katine re-entered the conference room.

I believe Lewis did make such a battle cry speech to Lawrence, Garner, and Eubanks. But long before they appeared together in Katine's law office.

"I remember Mitchell was very excited when they came back in, and I said that they were going forward. Big smile. Said great. Let's move forward. We have a court appearance."

What did attorneys Jones and Birnberg say?

"I don't remember. They didn't have any emotional tie to it because they are straight," Lewis said.

Lewis remembered the meeting continued another 20 minutes.

What was discussed?

"What the law was. What the legal thing was. Until they agreed to move forward, I don't think Mitchell and them really even knew the story of what really happened that night," Lewis said.

Didn't they have a general idea from the arrest report Lewis faxed Katine?

"They didn't even know that information at the front end of that meeting. Their job was simply to convince my clients that they knew the law. That they knew how to proceed. These are the resources that they had. That sort of thing."

Although Lewis is not an attorney, he several times referred to Lawrence, Garner, and Eubanks as his "clients."

"When [the attorneys] got back, they [the defendants] had to say what happened. They had to talk about the particulars in what actually happened. Then we left."

Was Lewis concerned that Katine was a real estate attorney with zero criminal law experience?

"...No because I knew Katine was not going to be trying that case. I knew that Lambda Legal or somebody like that was going to be trying this case. Mitchell was simply going to be a point man. Someone helping them fill out all the paperwork locally, and give a local face to the attorneys. To field questions. That kind of thing."

"There was no discussion of who would be told what and when. I would have waited until November 20 after we got through the no contest plea in the first court (JP Court)."

Why?

"My sole purpose in addition to the case, was the clients. I wanted to keep it under wraps. I wanted to keep it as quiet as possible for as long as is necessary, for several reasons. To protect the anonymity of the clients. To keep them as private, as secret as long as possible.

"Secondly, we live in a Republican state. If the religious right knew what we had, they could very easily influence the case being dismissed. It would only take the DA saying we are not going to prosecute and it's over. It's done," Lewis theorized.

Lewis is a gay person who wants gays prosecuted?

"Yeah! We all did! It had to happen! I knew the religious right was on their toes, they saw what it was and where it was going to go. I'm sure in hindsight, they wish they had. Nobody knew. There was nothing in the paper [immediately after the arrest]," Lewis said.

"Mitchell Katine called everybody that day, after the [October 12] meeting. I did not know he was going to do it. I was a little upset. I called him back. What are you doing? I wasn't angry. I was a little disappointed.

"It had gotten out of control very quickly. There was wrangling with other [homosexual] organizations, sending out e-mails and letters that they had the case. The Texas Human Rights Foundation sent out something that *they* had this sodomy case. Suddenly everybody had this case!" Lewis recalled.

So the Katine-generated publicity (after October 12, 1998) caught the three defendants off guard?

"All four of us," Lewis corrected.

"[The defendants] did not need to know that their lawyer [Katine] and I were not on the same page in that [publicity] regard. I couldn't be upset. I had to constantly assure them that it was OK. *It is all part of the plan.* I didn't want [the defendants] losing faith in [Katine]. Not that they would have. But they didn't know [Katine] at that point. They just knew me, barely," Lewis added.

If Lawrence and Garner were physically mistreated by sheriff's deputies, why didn't they file a civil suit against the police, and/or file a complaint with the sheriff's Internal Affairs unit? Because of Lewis" work, Lewis was very familiar with such complaints.

"I did not advise them on that. I had thought about it.

"I don't know if [Katine] ever talked about it with them or not. Mitchell and I never talked about it because it wasn't even something I wanted to put into anybody's head. Then what the story becomes—you're just trying to get money. It's a very touchy issue.

"There are so many ways that this *story* could have been spun that would have cost us the opportunity to do what eventually happened," Lewis explained.

Did Lewis feel a civil suit or internal affairs complaint might cost them the criminal case?

"I do and I did at the time. *I needed this story to be credible on its face.* I don't know if Mitchell thought of all this. I don't know what Lambda thought. We never talked about it," Lewis said.

Lewis' repeated choice of the word "story" caught my attention. Webster defines story as a fictitious literary composition.

Did Lewis know any of the three (Lawrence, Garner, Eubanks) before?

"Never heard of them."

If Lewis was a complete stranger. Why did they trust him?

"You will have to ask them. Because I was always honest with them. Probably when I called and told [Lawrence] that if he wanted to hang up, I wouldn't call back. And I wouldn't have. There wouldn't have been no *story.* It would be over," Lewis said.

Did Lewis or Katine patch up [their disagreements]?

"Mostly me. The other concern was that we didn't have boy scouts as clients. That was the other reason I wanted to keep it out of the press as long as possible. I knew these guys. I knew it was going to be difficult to keep them behaving so to speak.

"So that became difficult. Of course it fell into me whenever [the defendants] got into trouble or the press was getting too close, or whatever, to maintain the integrity of the proceedings," Lewis said, adopting a martyr-like tone.

Did Lewis have to babysit the defendants?

"Sometimes. Not so much with Lawrence, but especially Eubanks. He was a handful. He is dead now, so I don't mind saying that.

"Riding herd. Exactly what my job was. Keeping them out of trouble. They went to jail. I got them out as fast as I could. Because the media is trying to figure out who these three guys are. Who are these people (Lawrence, Garner, and Eubanks)? Trying to put a face on the case.

"We are trying to keep the face off the case," Lewis said.

"I was trying to keep the *story* on task—two people dragged out of their place. Papers will write about what you tell them to write about. [U.S. Senator] Phil Gramm [R-Texas] knows that better than anybody," Lewis continued.

"The *story* was not race. The *story* was not age. The *story* was not even sex. The *story* was privacy. The *story* was Fascism. The *story* wasn't what the paper would have made it out to be, had they been given a chance. So that was one of the reasons why were trying to keep them [Lawrence, Garner, and Eubanks] away from the papers," Lewis explained the strategy.

Was Lewis at the Justice of the Peace Court on November 20, 1998, when the defendants pled no contest there?

"Yeah. I have a picture in my kitchen," Lewis said. "I think we are all standing together right after. We won. We lost. Because we wanted to lose."

Did Eubanks ever tell Lewis what happened September 17? Did Lawrence and Garner ever tell Lewis what really happened?

"We have had several conversations about what went on that night."

What did Eubanks say happened September 17?

"[Eubanks] used a pay phone, I remember that. But I remember that being a big concern of mine. Because of my experience with the police department is, he [Eubanks] didn't have possession of the property. He didn't own that apartment. He didn't live there. Why didn't the cops ask that question? Because if they had asked that question, they could not have gone into the house unless there was eminent danger to the property owner. Which they couldn't ascertain without going onto the property," Lewis theorized.

Where did Eubanks use the pay phone?

"I'm thinking there was one down like in the parking

lot of the complex. They usually have one by the pool or by the mailboxes or something like that. It was outside the apartment, I'm almost positive," said Lewis. Lewis said earlier that October 12, 1998 when he picked the three men up at Lawrence's apartment, to take them to Katine's, was the first time he had been there.

Did Lewis discuss the September 17, 1998, events with Eubanks and Garner and Lawrence at various times?

"I've tried."

Did Eubanks say he went to use the pay phone because he was jealous?

"I think that is what they [sic] told me."

What did Eubanks say?

"I don't remember. He was so out of his mind drunk most of the time. Bless his heart. I don't think he was in a state of mind or education to exactly identify why he did what he did," said Lewis, joining Katine and David Jones in volunteering derogatory remarks about Eubanks' credibility.

Did Eubanks ever give a motivation for summoning the police?

"No, not really that I can remember."

When Lewis brought the three to Katine's office October 12, had Lawrence and Garner forgiven Eubanks?

"Oh yeah! They had been friends for years, was my impression. And they stayed friends afterwards," Lewis confirmed, contradicting Lawrence's statements that the 24-year friendship ended a few months after September 17.

"As far as I know, they were friends right up until he died. I didn't even know when he died. They told me. I didn't even know he was dead until the case was almost over."

How did Lewis find out Eubanks is dead?

"[Lawrence] told me. I think he told me [June 26, 2003] the day the Supreme Court decided. It was a Thursday, right? I always call that 'Lane's Day' because it was the day I took my last final. I knew I made an A on it. So I knew I was going to graduate. So I got my degree that day, technically." Lewis graduated from high school 17 years earlier.

"We had won the Supreme Court case that day, and (U.S. Senator) Strom Thurmond (R-South Carolina) had passed away. I know that is really horrible," Lewis said.

Wasn't Lewis in charge of watching Eubanks?

Did there come a time when Eubanks disappeared? (Eubanks was murdered in October 2000 while the case was pending a crucial re-hearing ruling in an intermediate appeal court in Houston.)

"Oh no. I disappeared. It had reached a point where I was so far out on the fringes. Publicity doesn't mean anything. I've been there. I've done it. So there's a point where I was stepping further back. I was being pushed further back. Whatever," Lewis explained, indirectly confirming Annise Parker's statement that Lambda wanted Lewis off the stage.

"I think [the defendants] slipped a little bit away, particularly with Eubanks. Lawrence was fairly stable. But Garner and Eubanks were nomads. They were living with brothers to sisters to friends to jail to whatever they were doing. Garner is very docile. Very quiet, tender, kind," Lewis said. "Eubanks was very loud and boisterous."

"Lawrence and Garner are sweet men. Very congenial. They weren't choirboys by any stretch. They enjoyed their bourbon," Lewis said.

"So I really didn't talk to those guys very often," Lewis said. "About once a year or so Mitchell [Katine] would call and say this is going on. The boys want you here or there. Then I would go."

Annise Parker said Katine, an enthusiastic e-mailer, sent her frequent updates throughout the years *Lawrence* pended. Parker and Lewis are in frequent contact. All three activists are very close friends.

❈

When is the last time Clovis Lane Lewis saw Robert Royce Eubanks?

"I do not remember. Whenever the last time Garner was arrested [May 2, 2000, for assaulting Eubanks]. That was probably the last time I saw Eubanks. They were staying at the Montague Hotel in downtown Houston. A charming facility. That is where they were staying more or less. So whenever I visited them, that's where I would go," Lewis said.

Is Lewis aware of a May 2, 2000, criminal case where Garner was accused of assaulting Eubanks?

"Oh yeah. That was ongoing. Usually it was Eubanks kicking Garner's butt. And Garner had just had enough."

Was Lewis still involved with Lawrence, Garner, and Eubanks then?

"Yes. In fact because I have a police badge, because of my work in the police department, that is how I got in to the jail see Garner," Lewis revealed.

Lewis visited Garner in jail, using a police badge?

"Yeah. I have a police I.D."

What is that?

"I have an office at 1200 Travis [police headquarters]. So [the I.D.] enables me to get in and out of the parking lot, in and out of police headquarters, etc.," Lewis explained.

Does Lewis go to that office periodically?

"Periodically. It's not my office. It's the Civilian Review Committee coordinator's office. I just happen to be that person," said Lewis, smiling faintly for the first time.

Does Lewis think that May 2, 2000, might have been the last time he saw Eubanks?

"Probably. It was right around that time period. Because they would call me in the middle of the night. They would be in a fight. I would need to go over there and calm things down or whatever.

"Because if they got in too big of a fight, the police were called. Now we have got police records which are going to be accessible to the *Houston Chronicle*. Now we have a whole different *story*.

"Now we have criminals that *deserve* to be carried out of their house regardless of what they may or may not have been doing," Lewis projected.

Did the defendants ever tell Lewis that they weren't engaged in a sexual act on September 17 when the deputies burst in? Or has Lewis heard that rumor?

"Who told you that?"

It's a rumor.

"I've heard that," Lewis responded.

Is it true?

"I've heard that," Lewis repeated.

Is it true?

"I wasn't there."

Did the defendants tell Lewis they weren't having sex?

"I don't really know what happened in that apartment," Lewis parried.

"I will say this. Neither side's story matches up. The police story definitely doesn't match. Not in time frame. Not in what I know about police procedures. Not what common sense tells me," Lewis offered.

The defendants (twice in JP Court and once in county court) pled no contest, which is the same as a guilty plea, admitting that they were having sex as the State alleged in the charging document. Why would they say they were having sex if they weren't?

"You don't have much of a case if they weren't having sex, do they?"

Is Lewis saying the defendants agreed publicly and in court, that they were having sex, just to have this case?

Lewis does not answer the question.

"They were arrested for having sex, period. That is what they were charged with. The *story* isn't whether or not they were having sex. The *story* was: Does the State have a right to arrest and charge for particular acts? That is the story.

"Now whether or not they were actually doing it, to me was not the *story*. And not only that, I don't have to prove what they were doing. The State has already said what they were doing. All I have to do is respond," Lewis explained, confident in his knowledge of the law.

Were they or weren't the defendants having sex

September 17? Did they tell Lewis they were? Lewis said he talked to them about it.

"You'll have to ask Mitchell [Katine]," Lewis lateraled.

The police report says a man who identified himself as Ramon Pelayo Velez, date of birth July 2, 1962, whom police identified as Hispanic, was in Lawrence's kitchen on the phone during the events of the September 17, 1998, arrest.

Who was that man?

Lewis doesn't answer.

He tests the wind first.

"What did [Lawrence] tell you? What did [Katine] tell you?" Lewis responded.

I would rather hear what you have to say, I countered.

"I don't know who that was. I will say that I have never been able to ascertain who that was. I will also tell you that Lawrence and Garner have flip-flopped back and forth as to whether or not they even know who the man was," Lewis said.

Sometimes Lawrence and Garner said they *did* know who the man is?

"Sometimes they kind of remember someone being in the house. They kind of don't.

"The best that I have gotten the story is that Eubanks had invited someone over that they didn't really know. But that didn't really make sense to me because according to the police report, he was on the phone in the kitchen. So then I am saying: 'I'm at someone's house that I don't even know?'"

So sometimes Lawrence and Garner said they were aware that (Ramon Pelayo Velez) was in Lawrence's apartment, and sometimes they said that Velez wasn't there?

"They never really admitted that they were aware. At first they said they didn't know who the hell they were talking about. Then I kept calling them back on it, because it just wasn't making any sense to me," Lewis continued.

So that stuck in Lewis' mind?

"Yeah. Then again I didn't really start pressuring on all

this until after the case, six months before I heard from you," Lewis said. (I first contacted Lewis by e-mail on or about March 29, 2004.)

"Because these were questions I didn't want anybody else asking. That doesn't mean that [Katine, that doesn't mean Lambda, it doesn't mean the district attorney, because I mean these people didn't think about... [*sic*]

"But I didn't want them thinking about it if they weren't. So I didn't even mess with it until less than a year ago," Lewis added, implying that Lewis knew about Velez's name in the police report near the time of the 1998 arrests.

Did Mitchell Katine ever ask Lewis who Ramon Pelayo Velez was?

"Not that I know of. [Katine] never asked me."

Because if Lewis read the police report, obviously, Velez' name is there.

"Yeah, it's there."

Wouldn't any intelligent person say, 'Well, who was Ramon Pelayo Velez?'

"But the cops couldn't tell you who he was either, huh? Because they don't know. I can't find him," Lewis said.

The deputies released the man at the scene who said his name was Velez, because there was nothing with which he could be charged, according to on-scene supervisor Sergeant Adams.

"Yeah, they let him go. Which is—no information, no phone number, no address. And here is a witness to someone you are arresting. Probably the only credible witness to what you are arresting, because you know the other three are drunk. I don't know if this guy [Velez] was drunk or not. I don't know if it is someone they invented," Lewis speculated.

"They" meaning?

"The cops. To give themselves more credibility. They entered an apartment. And they're saying, 'County Deputies, Sheriff's Office,' whatever it was they were claiming to be saying. And there is one guy in the kitchen staring you in the face. And you're going to continue searching a house before you pat him down? No. Because let me tell you, if that was the way they did work, he would have been dead a long time ago."

(All the deputies agree that two deputies subdued Velez as soon as they saw him, and before deputies Quinn and Lilly continued their search of the rest of Lawrence's apartment.)

How did Lewis try to locate Ramon Pelayo Velez?

"Police blotters. Internet. Information. Everything short of hiring a private investigator."

How long did Lewis spend looking for Velez, months, weeks, a couple of days?

"Very little time, Lewis said. "Because everything was a dead end.

"There was nothing on the Internet. There was nothing. There wasn't even a name close. Then when I called Lawrence. He said, 'I don't have any idea who you are talking about.'

"Alright. Where do I go? I'm not going to call the cops!"

# "It Was Brilliant!"

In researching *Lawrence v. Texas*, I never anticipated finding a definitive smoking gun—a flat-out admission that every aspect of the arrests was carefully preplanned. I thought spontaneous confessions ("Yes! I did it! And I'm glad!") occurred only on television's Perry Mason reruns.

In real-life courtrooms where I spent my life almost every weekday for 24 years, I never witnessed one.

Never say never.

In a moment of hubris during our April 2004 interview, Clovis Lane Lewis came breathtakingly close to confession, implying that he put together the incidents comprising *Lawrence*. His implications of his role fit my projected profile of the planner(s) exactly: someone who knew and understood street cops; someone who was connected to the blue-collar world—the bar world—to find recruits for the arrests; and someone intelligent, daring and furious enough to put it all together.

Hearing Lewis' unguarded, detailed remarks was one of those once-in-a-lifetime, fall-off-your-chair moments.

"This guy admits he did it!" exclaimed Nanette Primeaux, looking at me in astonishment when she handed me the Lewis interview tape after transcribing it.

I had said nothing in advance to Primeaux, my transcriber, about the tape's contents.

A confession standing alone is insufficient proof. By law, in most states, a confession has to be supported by some other evidence consistent with the confession. This is because confessions are subject to fabrication or coercion.

On April 29, 2004, I was nearing the end of about a 2-hour interview with Lewis, whose cocky, self-assured demeanor began to waver only when I suggested the involvement in the case of his friend JP clerk Nathan Broussard, who Lewis seemed to actually fear.

Was the case a setup?

"No," Lewis said

Why wasn't it a setup?

"Why wasn't a case ever set up? Or why wasn't this case particularly?" Lewis clarified.

If the homosexual community wanted a case, why didn't you just set up a case? Phone the police and say, 'So-and-so and I are getting ready to have homosexual sex! Come on over!' I asked Lewis.

"I don't know. I remember when I was in my more radical days, I used to always tease that we should all go have sex on the steps of Congress."

That would be public. That's different.

"It makes it difficult because they have to have probable cause to go in. I would have had to of called and said, 'My house is being robbed! I'm trapped in the bedroom!' They could have come in and then you get in trouble for a police report. Then, 'Why did you make the police report? Because it was a setup.'

"Being Buddhist, everything always happens the way it is supposed to happen," Lewis said of his recently adopted religion.

In the 1960s lunch counter sit-ins, everyone knew it was a setup. They were supposed to be arrested. It is age-old civil disobedience.

"Yeah, we could have done that. I don't know. I wouldn't begin to know how the process would have happened, without it being public. Because then the story isn't that; it's vulgarity. It's—'See, all you people just want to . . . whatever.'

"So I can't really answer from a general point of view. But from my own point of view, the reason I never thought it would work was for that very reason. How do you find the *story*? As an activist, that was one of my strong suits. And a setup, or in public, or trying to get someone in there. I mean the *story* would have been very different if Lawrence had said there is a black man with a gun. But because this third party did it, it becomes even more bizarre. It's all really a bizarre *story* if you think about it. But it was only a matter of time," Lewis added.

Why wasn't *this* case a setup?

"You met [Lawrence and Garner]. I don't think they have the experience, the knowledge nor the motivation to have made up something like this. Certainly not Eubanks. These are guys that have never had any political aspirations. As far as I know, they have never even been a member of any political party. It's just so far outside the realm of their world.

"Which, in my opinion, made it even better. These were not people anybody knew," Lewis added in counterpoint to his own prior argument.

From observing Lewis sitting across from me in the interview, and from having read his Web site, his predominant characteristic seemed to be egotism. Lewis thinks very, very highly of himself. Sensing that I had temporarily edged Lewis somewhat off-message by my conclusions about Broussard, and realizing my window of opportunity with Lewis was rapidly evolving to an end, I decided to try two of the oldest cross-examining gambits: flattery, and asking for the witness' advice.

If Lewis was going to put this case together, how would you put it together differently than it actually existed? Or was it a good case the way it existed? How would you have improved on it?

"Legally?"

Any way. Both legally, and any other way.

"Other than I would have gone slower at the beginning, publicly."

What about the facts and circumstances of the case itself?

"Oh. Of course it would have made it easier if they [Lawrence and Garner] were big buffed gym bunnies. Would have made it easier if they were both white males. It would have made it easier if they had been sober. If it had a different face on it," Lewis said.

More reputable-type people?

"That would have made it easier. It's not how I would have changed it," Lewis said, shifting in his seat in the cafeteria booth. He seemed to warm to my question, leaning forward across the table, discarding his nonchalance and the Buddhist prayer beads. Lewis was fully engaged.

I had focused on Lewis' favorite topic: himself.

"*I wouldn't have changed it at all!*" he exclaimed, consumed with enthusiasm.

"I think it is brilliant that they were different races!

"I think it is brilliant that they were of different ages!

"When I was working at a project in New York one time, an African American gentleman worked for GLAD, the Gay and Lesbian Anti-Defamation League. He said, 'A movement's credibility or success can directly be related to the way in which they perceive the most disenfranchised members.'"

Now that was a comment, I responded.

"Yeah. I was 22 at the time. I had never heard that before. Now at 36, I can see why that is so important," Lewis said.

Lewis was drifting toward polemic. I tried again.

Why was it brilliant that (Lawrence and Garner) were of different races and different ages?

"Most disenfranchised members. Ageism, sexism, racism, weightism. They weren't bodybuilders. They were just average guys with bellies. Diseasism. Closet, what the closet does," Lewis expounded.

Were Lawrence and Garner in the closet? (Not publicly acknowledging their homosexuality).

"Well, [Lawrence] pretty much was at work. Not any more. Because I remember Lawrence called me when he was going through that process. And it wasn't as bad as I think he thought it was going to be. I'm not going to sit here and say it was easy. But he didn't lose his job. He didn't find used condoms in his sandwiches at lunch. And I know people that do.

"I wouldn't have changed anything other than I would have kept [the arrests] a little more private until it got out of a couple JP Courts," Lewis added.

*Lawrence* was brilliant in that it did combine a lot of things, I mirrored.

"*It was wonderful!*" Lewis responded, almost lifting himself up from the booth seat in excitement.

Lewis had dropped all pretense. He was riding a mental roller coaster right to the top of his ego. His whole body language was exuberant, joyful in the way athletes describe hitting the home run that won the game, students acing the exam, or players winning the lottery.

Lewis spoke as a creator. Lewis seemed to be talking about the case as his personal achievement, just as our transcriber heard on the tape.

Age and race . . .

"Weightism, because weightism is a big thing in the gay community. They want to be big and buff and cut and whatever."

(Lawrence and Garner) were people who already had some contact with the criminal justice system, I observed.

"Exactly! Because if they both had been lawyers . . ."

It was brilliant because they were people for whom being arrested wouldn't damage their career irreparably, like a dentist or an accountant?

"Yeah, I thought it was brilliant!" Lewis exclaimed.

Lewis' demeanor during this exchange was one of those you-just-had-to-be-there moments. That's what Nanette Primeaux, the transcriber, recognized in Lewis' proud tone on the tape. It seemed apparent—the brilliance of which Lewis spoke was his.

Lewis revealed unhealed psychological wounds for which the arrests and the successful ruling in the U.S. Supreme Court were apparently sweet balm.

"And it also . . . the organizations, Log Cabin Republicans [a gay Republican group], etc., they are a little bit exclusive. Now they owe a debt to the type of person that they wouldn't walk in the parade next to: feminine black man, drunken blue-collar worker. If one of them [Lawrence and Garner] had been a drag queen, all the better. So that sort of pushes their envelope too. Because now they are somewhat beholden to these two incredibly brave men that allowed themselves to be put out front," Lewis said.

Although Lewis attended a 2003 rally on the steps of Houston City Hall to celebrate the Supreme Court ruling, he balked at giving thanks to the court "for doing something they should have never have not done [sic]."

"If there was anything I could say as far as my part in this," Lewis said, "it was never my intention to simply change the law. Because the law on its face didn't matter. What mattered was the increased awareness to the plight that the law was affecting."

The masterful, politically correct make up of arrestees Lawrence and Garner attracted my notice the first time I saw a large color photo of them on the front page of the *Houston Chronicle*.

Although Lewis phrased it differently, it was as if someone had selected arrestees who would be representative of every permutation in the gay community—or the heterosexual community for that matter.

Lawrence is Caucasian, not openly gay at that time—having sex with Garner, who is black, and openly homosexual.

At 55, Lawrence was 26 years older than Garner when

both were arrested. A blue-collar worker, Lawrence had some college. Garner, chronically unemployed, never graduated from high school.

The *exact* politically correct composition seemed too, too perfect—as if someone had cast a theatrical production to placate every faction of a target audience.

Lewis said he did not know the three men before September 17. Yet their employment backgrounds share an interesting commonality.

Lewis worked several years in a hospital, Intercare.

On court forms, Eubanks reported working in "a medical center."

Garner's sporadic self-reported employment also included working as "a nurse's aide."

Lawrence's entire work experience has been as a medical technician.

All four frequented gay bars. Lewis is a veteran bartender who has managed several gay bars. In his interview, Lawrence referred to his lifestyle frequenting bars. Garner, a drinker like Lawrence, has been convicted of DWI. Eubanks, by all descriptions, drank to excess.

Gays who frequent the local, gay bar scene usually know other gays of like interests. Particularly since their gay barhopping lifestyle spanned 23 years. Both Lawrence and Lewis lived at least 15 years in the same southeast Harris County area where the arrests occurred.

Lewis said he only spoke to Lawrence once on the phone and had never been to Lawrence's apartment except for picking him up to drive him to Katine's office.

However, Lawrence said Lewis came to Lawrence's apartment for a long visit and even met with Lawrence at night in the parking lot of the medical facility where Lawrence worked.

Lawrence admitted that after his arrest, although he was "angry," he not only made no effort to hire an attorney, but discarded bags of solicitation letters from attorneys. In that do-nothing context, when Lawrence received a phone call from a non-attorney who he said was a stranger, it seems inconsistent that Lawrence would go with him.

Lewis' story that he learned of the arrests via a fax from a guy in a bar is completely lacking in credibility. Lewis and Sue Lovell are close friends. Lovell is best friends with JP head clerk Sheryl Roppolo who communicated the arrests immediately to her many friends in the homosexual community.

Katine's confirmation of his protégé Lewis' story about the fax is equally suspect. Roppolo said Katine's co-counsel David Jones was asking her for a fax of the arrest report the day after the arrest!

Katine and Lewis were clearly trying to distance themselves from having immediate knowledge of the arrests. *How* immediate was their knowledge?

Lewis said the last time he saw Robert Eubanks was in May 2000 when Garner was arrested and charged with assaulting Eubanks. About six months after that assault charge, Garner and Garner's brother were subpoenaed to a Grand Jury investigating Eubanks' homicide. Eubanks was murdered in October 2000 when the *Lawrence* case was pending a crucial rehearing from a mid-level Texas appeal court. Lewis' babysitting duties were not over because the case was not yet even out of Texas' courts.

Lewis said he did not even know Eubanks was dead until "the case was almost over" in the summer of 2003.

Lewis' claims of lack of knowledge are not believable.

Lewis didn't notice when Eubanks, whom Lewis described as the most difficult of the trio to babysit, was no longer around?

From 2000 to 2003, Lewis never asked anyone: Hey! Where's Eubanks?

Lewis, who did maintain contact with Lawrence and Garner, didn't know that Garner had been subpoenaed regarding Eubanks' murder?

Didn't wonder at the absence of Eubanks and Garner's fights after October 2000?

Didn't wonder why his babysitting duties became less burdensome after October 2000?

Further, Eubanks' death was being investigated by the homicide division of the Houston Police Department— where Lane Lewis has an office.

# "You Got the Sodomy Cases"

In early November 1998 I was elected Judge of Harris County Criminal Court Number 5, defeating an incumbent who was the last Democrat judge in the county. But under Texas law, newly elected judges would not be sworn in until January 1, 1999.

There is a transitional eight-week lag time of being "judge-elect": You *are* the judge; you just haven't taken office yet.

It is a time to prepare by completing paperwork, hiring staff, and visiting with courthouse staff as to customs and procedures. Backed by Harris County's efficient Republican machine, I defeated the incumbent.

With religious right and conservatives as THE political base necessary to be elected to any office countywide; *no* judges, new or incumbent, wanted the sodomy cases assigned to their court, fearing political retribution however they handled it. The cases were a hot potato grandissimo.

As thousands of cases poured in to the 15 county, criminal misdemeanor courts in 1998, a clerk turned the crank on an old-fashioned wire cage with 15 numbered balls representing the 15 county criminal courts. As the bingo cage spit out a ball, the clerk assigned the next in-coming case in the stack to the court number on the ball. She then put that ball aside, rolling the cage again until 15 balls spit out, assigning courts to the next 14 incoming cases. She then began again.

The alleged randomness of the process was the subject of long-time snickering. Misdemeanor court administrator Bob Wessels acknowledged that the felony courts abandoned the bingo-ball system long ago in favor of random assignment by computer. Wessels explained the misdemeanor courts had been working toward making case assignments by computer for several years, but just hadn't been able to accomplish it yet! The two courts shared the same computer system.

"You got the sodomy cases," the staff attorney told me on December 2, 1998. "I was there when they ran the bingo balls."

But had I really drawn the proverbial black bean—the assignment to preside over the Homosexual Conduct cases *nobody* wanted? Or, if the widespread rumors were true, that the events of the sodomy arrests were a pre-arranged setup designed to test Texas' statute, had I, by being elected, stepped between some pre-agreed-upon, teammate-to-teammate handoff involving my predecessor? Was I now perceived as an inconvenience blocking opportunity for someone's winning basket?

Almost immediately after the defendants' September 17 arrest, persistent rumors circulated throughout the courthouse that the Lawrence and Garner sodomy cases were a setup.

Technically, Hannah Chow, the incumbent Democrat judge I defeated, was still judge in Court Number 5 when the sodomy cases were assigned to her court—the next step up in the appeal process from Judge Mike Parrott's, Precinct 3, Position 1 Justice of the Peace Court.

What a further *amazing* coincidence that the sodomy arrests, which occurred in the jurisdiction of one of a few Democratic JPs, were next assigned to the court of the only Democrat county criminal court judge remaining!

Judge Chow, who had never served as a prosecutor, was a well-known liberal, and thus the daily bane of prosecutors' existence. "She would never put anybody in jail," grumped Chuck Noll, the assistant district attorney who headed all 15 misdemeanor divisions.

If the arrests were instigated, then, I predicted, the sodomy cases would be moved out of my court before January 1, 1999, when I took office. I wondered how that would be accomplished? I had to wait only a few days for my answer.

On a Friday, December 18, 1998, when the criminal courthouse is usually in well-known power-down mode, the pressroom is empty, and it is joked that after 10 A.M. you could be trampled by exiting judges and staff—an order was filed with the clerk, transferring the sodomy cases out of my Court Number 5, into Court Number 10 of Judge Sherman Ross.

Judges Chow and Ross, longtime close friends, both signed the transfer order.

It was 13 days before I was to be sworn in.

Once assigned to a court, a defendant's case usually stays in that court until it is resolved by a plea, trial, or dismissal.

Transfer orders are used only when a defendant's case, which should have been kept in a court because the case was in that court previously, has mistakenly or inadvertently been assigned to another judge. Or, if the lower-numbered case with several codefendants, is mistakenly sequenced to a court other than the court to which the case was originally sent. None of those situations were involved with the sodomy cases.

The Chow-Ross chess-like move, using a transfer order, was unusual, although perhaps not unprecedented; attracting raised eyebrows and comment from many attorneys, but going unnoticed by the media, who frequently have little background in the subject matter of their reporting.

The only other way criminal cases are reassigned to another court is when the assigned judge recuses, or is asked or required to recuse. Recusals are usually based on the judge's unspoken admission that he or she cannot rule fairly in the case because of some personal relationship or philosophical bias. Reasons are not usually written on a recusal.

Upon a *recusal*, a case is treated as a new incoming case, and is supposed to be reassigned randomly, using the bingo-ball system. This random assignment is to avoid what attorneys call forum shopping, that is, seeking deliberately to have a case assigned to a judge who a party or the parties feel will rule most favorably to them.

"I don't recall ever speaking to [Judge Chow] because that would be improper," Katine said in a 2004 interview. He opened a thick, indexed file, intently reading a page.

"This is a memo regarding county court strategy. You know you are, you were considered before you took the bench to be a conservative Republican judge," Katine began, looking nervously at me.

That's fair, I responded.

Katine pulled the memo from a file of carefully tabbed, meticulously arranged, neat folders chronicling the Lawrence and Garner cases. No sloppy record keeping here. Every date, every conversation, every nuance of the cases was in Katine's files.

"I think it was just . . . it was my understanding that this was a preferred transfer by Judge Chow. I'm not sure," Katine concluded, closing his file, and our discussion.

CHAPTER
10

# County Criminal Court:
# As You Like It

Judge Sherman Ross is diplomatic, circumspect as to why Judge Hannah Chow transferred the sodomy cases from her court into his court 13 days before she left judicial office.

When I asked Judge Ross that question, seated on a white sofa in front of the fireplace in his elegant, black-and-white decorated home in Houston's old-money museum area, my former judicial colleague momentarily broke eye contact with me, and did not answer immediately.

Judge Ross was thinking before speaking.

"Because Judge Chow didn't want to hear it before she left office," he finally responded.

But *why* didn't Judge Chow want to hear the sodomy cases?"

"She felt it more appropriate to be heard by someone [Ross] who would be there. She phoned me and asked if the cases could be transferred to me."

But *I* would be there [in that court].

Judge Ross ignored my observation.

"Judge Chow didn't say this, but she chose me I think

because we are friends. She figured that I could have ruled [as well as she]," Judge Ross said.

"Maybe it was her concern about possible political fall-out for her. Because Judge Chow didn't know what she would be doing January 1, 1999," he speculated. He said he meant that Judge Chow might be accepting some other employment after January 1, and her rulings on the controversial sodomy cases might affect that future employment.

Describing Lawrence and Garner's December 22, 1998, appearance in his court on case numbers 9848530 and 9848531, amid a blitz of television cameras and national and local press, Judge Ross remembers: "A lot of people came up to the bench for the [no contest] plea. When I saw everyone marching in, I knew the ultimate decision would have far-reaching effect, no matter what it was," Judge Ross said.

Each judge varies in how he or she handles pleas, or pleas that are known in advance to be on an appeal track. It would be common in Harris County, in a high-profile case, for the judge, prosecution, and defense to converse in open court as to how the plea would be conducted—a sort of advance "you-say-this, I'll say that" scripting.

However, a knowledgeable examination of the official transcript of the December 22, 1998, proceedings reveals some deviations from the norm.

Most often, the prosecution offers the probable cause affidavits into evidence as a factual basis for the plea. It is extremely rare to hear such a request from the defense. I remember only one such request from the defense in my 24 years practicing criminal law. When an attorney offers an exhibit for that purpose, the attorney implicitly vouches that she believes the exhibit to be true and correct.

The prosecutor, Angela Beavers, told Judge Ross she had no objection to the *prosecution* exhibits being admitted into evidence by the *defense*.

Not offered into evidence by either side was the standard two-page, single-spaced plea form that both defendants had signed under oath. The fifth paragraph of the form contains this sentence: "I confess that I committed the offense as alleged in the State's information and that each element of the State's pleading is true. In open court I freely and voluntarily enter my plea of *nolo contendere* to the offense charged in the Information and request the Court to make immediate disposition of this case based upon my plea."

On a case that the judge and both parties know is headed up the appeal ladder, it would be usual for either the prosecution or the defense to offer the standard plea agreement form into evidence because it contains the defendants' written confession to the charges. Once in evidence, the documents travel with the case up the appeal ladder.

This was not done.

So the plea agreements, the only documents sworn to by the defendants, would not travel with the case up the appeal ladder as part of the official record.

Equally unusual was the absence of oral argument on the defense motion to quash. A motion to quash asks a court to throw out the State's charging instrument. Both the State and the defense stood silent after asking Judge Ross to rule on the defense motion to quash.

Usually a prosecutor would argue against a defense motion to quash.

"All right. The court has reviewed the motions and considered same, and respectfully denies them," Judge Ross responded in ruling for the State.

Prosecutor Beavers read aloud the sworn probable cause affidavit from Deputy Quinn, adding to its 69 words by verbally stumbling once, telling Judge Ross the defendants engaged in "oral sex," then correcting her words to "anal sex."

"...officers observed the defendants engaged in deviate sexual conduct, namely, oral sex. I'm sorry. Anal sex," Beavers told Judge Ross.

Interestingly, in a 2004 interview, Deputy Lilly said the defendants were engaged in oral sex when he first saw them. Although the courtroom verbal exchanges imply that the defense and prosecution stipulated [agreed] to those written facts—that is, pre-agreed that the facts Beavers read from the probable cause affidavit were correct—no one formally recited the word "stipulation," as is usually done.

Therefore, neither side stipulated that what Beavers read aloud is what happened on September 17, 1998. Reviewed in the context of implications by the defendants and their attorneys (in our 2004 interviews) that the defendants were not having sex, the lack of stipulation is even more curious.

Were the defendants implying even in 1998 that they weren't copulating when arrested?

Those brief courtroom moments would constitute the only time in the case's history that any facts were revealed "officially" and publicly. From December 22, 1998, forward, all appeal courts premised their decisions on those 69 words in Deputy Quinn's report. On appeal, motions and argument are confined to legal issues. No "new" facts are permitted.

In the courtroom, Lawrence and Garner then pled *nolo contendere* (no contest), and were assessed a $200 fine each for the Class C misdemeanor, which is not punishable by jail.

Attorney Gary Polland, then chair of the Republican Party in Harris County, stood near the front of the courtroom when the pleas were taken. Polland, a criminal defense attorney, said he just happened to be there on client matters.

At any time, the district attorney's office could have

handed the judge a *nolle prosse* form, requesting that the case be dismissed, ending the case forever, dashing Katine and Lambda's hopes to ride the cases as far up the appeal ladder as they could go.

I asked Katine why curmudgeon DA Johnny Holmes didn't just pull the plug on the cases right there, ending their journey on December 22, 1998?

"I believe [the State] couldn't do that due to the political election of the district attorney and the Republican Party and how strongly they felt about it. They [the prosecutors] had to be seen as doing their job," Katine speculated.

Defense attorney David Jones, Katine's co-counsel for the cases, emphasized how solicitous prosecutor Angela Beavers was throughout all proceedings in Judge Ross's court. "She could not have been more friendly. I think I know why she was [friendly]."

Asked why, Jones responded, "I think it was in her own personal interest that this be taken up. I don't know for a fact, but I . . . let's just say she was very sympathetic with the aspirations of homosexuals. It would be unfair to say that I think Ms. Beavers is gay. I'm just saying she couldn't have been more sympathetic. She even expressed some encouragement about moving forward beyond [county court]," Jones remembered.

"I felt pretty lucky that Angela Beavers was the chief prosecutor of that court at that time because she knew how important, she just knew. She had just an instinct it seems for how important the case was," Jones added.

Since she was chief prosecutor in my court on December 22, 1998, what was she doing in Judge Sherman Ross' court shepherding Lawrence and Garner's no-contest plea there? Why wasn't Judge Ross's chief prosecutor handling the case, as would be custom? When cases are moved between courts, prosecutors in the receiving court usually take over the case.

"I knew the case was probably going to be high publicity," Beavers explained. "I just followed the case and handled it in Judge Ross's court. That is the only case that I handled in his court. Because it [was transferred] from my court, I dealt with [Katine] and the attorney from Lambda Legal, so I just went ahead. I thought it would probably be more expeditious that way."

Did anyone ask her to follow the case, or did Beavers do that on her own?

"I think I did it on my own. I felt like I knew the people involved. I felt pretty strongly about the issue as well," Beavers said.

Following a case in that manner was extremely rare. It was my experience as a judge that whenever cases were transferred from one court to another, Harris County prosecutors had to obtain permission from the chief of the misdemeanor divisions to follow a case.

Another rarity was the fact that the defendants' only sworn statements, contained in their written pleas, were not entered into evidence and so did not become part of the case record on appeal. The only sworn testimony to travel with the cases would be Deputy Quinn's two identical probable cause affidavits. Although the affidavits were entered into evidence—meaning that they would accompany the official record of the cases up the appeal ladder—neither side "stipulated" to them (a formal legal agreement that the affidavits are true). The prosecution and defense joined in shifting the legal focus away from the only sworn paperwork from the defendants—their pleas—and toward the deputy's affidavits, which neither side officially agreed to.

Thus, through brilliant, subtle, legal "nuancing" discernable only to the most practiced eye, each side avoided formally, legally committing to any set of facts as to what happened on September 17, 1998.

When Lawrence and Garner pled on December 22, why wasn't there a customary stipulation (formal agreement) of the facts Beavers read from Deputy Quinn's 69-word probable cause affidavit? Was that an oversight?

"I would think that since [the PC affidavit] was not objected to [by the defense], I guess we just both agreed to the facts. If that was a probable cause affidavit, then the State surely agreed," Beavers said.

In county court, why did the *defense* enter the two exhibits of the probable cause affidavits, rather than the State? Doesn't the *State* usually enter prosecution exhibits into evidence?

"Yes," Beavers said. "But I felt like [the defense] probably needed that somewhere in the appeal. I think we had maybe discussed that, and [the defense] had mentioned they might need that. I didn't see any harm in doing that. It was our document wasn't it? It was probable cause."

Why wasn't there any oral argument from the prosecution to Judge Ross on the defendants' motion to quash the complaint? Wouldn't the State customarily argue against such a defense motion? Was there pre-agreement that the State wouldn't make argument?

"Yes. It just seems like that was one of the things that [the defense] needed to do to be able to appeal. I don't think Lambda really needed to do as much as they did," Beavers added.

"I do have my own personal opinions about the case," Beavers stated. "But my job is to uphold the law, no matter how I feel about the law. I had definite feelings that the law [21.06] was wrong. But my function was not to give any kind of favoritism or anything like that."

"I want to make a really strong point here that all my dealings with Mitchell [Katine], David [Jones], and [Suzanne] Goldberg at that time were on a purely professional level. My personal feelings about the case or the sodomy law was totally irrelevant at that time. We have seen each other socially and everything. But as far as my handling of the case in court, I feel like I didn't handle it any differently than I would any other case.

What did Beavers mean that she and the defense team saw each other socially?

"Well, like David and Mitchell, outside of the workplace. And of course my opinions there are different from my professional opinions as far as upholding the law."

Katine said he never met Ms. Beavers before the case, and did not join her on any social occasion.

What are Beavers' personal feelings on 21.06?

"The law is wrong. But there might be a lot of laws I think are wrong," Beavers said. "My position here at the office is to uphold the laws that are there on the books."

CHAPTER
11

# Unwelcome Victory?
# 14th Court of Appeals

On November 3, 1999, when Yale Law School graduate Ruth E. Harlow, then 39, stood on behalf of defendants John Lawrence and Tyron Garner to argue their sodomy cases before a three-judge panel of the 14th Court of Appeals, her lawyerly brilliance dazzled the packed courtroom.

Harlow was employed by Lambda Legal Defense and Education Fund, Inc. headquartered in New York City.

The three, white male justices—who formed a review panel selected by a complicated system among the nine justices within the all-Republican, Houston-based 14th Court of Appeals—were Chief Justice Paul Murphy, Justice John Sharp Anderson, and Justice Harvey Hudson.

Assistant District Attorney William J. Delmore III, then 46, rose on behalf of the State of Texas to argue for the constitutionality of Texas' sodomy law. A 13-year veteran of the district attorney's appellate section, he enjoyed a reputation among admiring colleagues as a loyal advocate for the prosecution.

"I thought I was kind of off that day actually. I was a

little thrown off by I think all the press attention and the crowd at the courthouse and so forth. So I didn't think it was one of my better efforts. But I appreciate the compliment [of those who thought I did well]," Delmore said in a May 13, 2004, interview.

Delmore, born August 18, 1954, in Cleveland, Ohio, holds an undergraduate degree from University of Texas and is a 1982 graduate of the University of Houston Law Center. He earned no academic honors in either school. "I worked my way through school. I was an intern in the DA's office. That was always my focus," Delmore said. He became an assistant district attorney in 1982.

Although experienced attorneys agree that cases at any level of court are rarely won or lost on the basis of oral argument—the traditional public demonstration matching wit, intelligence, and style of competing attorneys, compels timeless fascination. It's a legal High Noon at the OK Corral.

On Monday, June 5, 2000, when the three-judge appeals court panel made public its 11-page written opinion, the panel's 2-1 decision to reverse Lawrence and Garner's convictions triggered a local political firestorm equivalent to lobbing a grenade into an ammunition factory. As the two-judge majority in favor of striking down Texas' sodomy law, Justices Anderson, 54, and Murphy, 64, had yanked the pin on the grenade.

The same religious right, and conservative Republican voter bases that elected Justices Anderson, Murphy, and nearly every other judge in Harris County since 1994, were not amused.

For the religious right, there was only one law, immutable, absolute.

It predated puny, upstart Texas' 21.06 by 2,000 years of Judeo-Christian thought.

It thundered triumphant, out of the Old Testament, from the Lord to Moses: "Do not lie with a man as one lies with a woman. That is detestable." (Leviticus 18:22)

And for the religious right, that law—God's law—transcends all other law.

Judicial heads would roll.

Political blood would spill.

It would not be pretty.

Because of the way court authority is constructed, the three-judge panel's decision would affect only the 14 counties around Houston that comprised the jurisdiction of the 14th Court of Appeals.

In the rest of Texas, 21.06 of the penal code was unaffected—still valid, enforceable law. As the lone dissenter, in favor of upholding Texas' law against consensual same sex-sodomy and the Lawrence and Garner convictions, Justice J. Harvey Hudson, 51, could merely sit back and watch the mushroom cloud forming over colleagues Justices Murphy and Anderson—followed by the reviling nuclear wind.

But before the radioactive dust settled, adversaries from both sides would be scurrying to basement cover.

Chief Justice Paul Murphy joined Justice John Sharp Anderson in concluding that 21.06 constituted gender discrimination under a 1972 Texas Equal Rights Amendment (ERA) to the Texas Constitution. They did not address federal constitutional issues.

For at least one legal strategist on the Lawrence-Garner defense team, the panel's ruling was an unwelcome victory.

David Jones, the experienced, criminal-defense attorney in Katine's firm, and who was co-counsel on the cases, termed the three-judge panel decision as "scary" for the defense. A "thanks, but no thanks" morsel.

Although it may seem to non-lawyers like another lawyers' game, strategically, Jones actually *wanted to lose* in the three-judge panel decision. Winning June 8, 2000, at the State appellate level could block the defense's intended journey up the appeal ladder to the United States Supreme Court, leaving the defense stuck with a legally ineffectual "victory" that applied to only

14 counties around Houston. It didn't even apply in Dallas!

In a 2004 interview, Katine unveiled a separate issue rising out of the three-judge panel decision of June 8, 2000.

If the decision of the three-judge panel had not been overturned later by the entire 14th court, Katine said he intended to use the rationale of the three-judge panel decision as the basis for filing a lawsuit in 2000, against the State of Texas and Harris County, for denying gay and lesbian people the right to marry. He would have based his lawsuit on the same Texas ERA rationale as the Murphy-Anderson opinion.

"But the fact that the three-judge panel decision was overturned, I can't use it," Katine lamented.

Justice John Sharp Anderson is a collateral descendent of Monroe Dunaway Anderson, an unmarried banker who amassed a great fortune, staggering by any standard—even Texas'.

M.D. Anderson, lived from 1873 to 1939, and was treasurer, then president, of Anderson Clayton & Company, the world's largest cotton merchandiser.

Justice John Sharp Anderson, a short, slight, balding man with almost translucent white skin and long slender fingers, moves in rarified political circles statewide.

Born August 2, 1946, Justice Anderson graduated from one of Houston's blue-blooded, private prep schools.

Running for judicial office successfully in 1995, he appeared uncomfortable on the campaign trail—distant, reluctant to join the required, public hand shaking, speeches and social chitchat.

Anderson received his BA degree in 1968 from aristocratic, 250-year-old Washington and Lee University in Lexington, Virginia. He received his law degree from the University of Texas in 1971.

Through a terse message from his attorney Jim Evans, a loquacious former host of local radio talk shows and a self-published author, Justice Anderson declined to comment on the Lawrence and Garner cases.

Although ethical rules prohibit judges from public comment on *pending* cases, there is no prohibition on judicial public comment once cases are closed, as are the Lawrence and Garner cases.

However, Houston attorney Frank Harmon—one of the triumvirate forming the political machine that elects judges in Harris County—was eager to talk. The machine, called Conservative Republicans of Harris County, also includes founder Dr. Steven Hotze, a physician, and political consultant Allen Blakemore.

Harmon defended Justice Anderson vociferously, blaming Justice Paul Murphy for everything. Justice Anderson is up for reelection in 2006. Murphy retired after the 1999 furor.

According to Harmon, Justice Anderson, to coin a phrase, "fell in with evil companions"—namely: his fellow justice, Paul Murphy.

"[Chief Justice] Paul Murphy talked John into that [June 8, 2000] decision! John Anderson wouldn't have issued that opinion if Paul Murphy hadn't influenced him to rule that way," charges Harmon, a close, longtime friend of Justice Anderson.

But according to one of Justice Anderson's judicial colleagues, it was the defense, not Murphy whose argument Justice Anderson found compelling. Justice Anderson privately has expressed admiration for Mitchell Katine, the defendants' Houston attorney, Anderson's colleague revealed.

"He says he likes Katine, and admires Katine's legal work," the colleague quoted Justice Anderson.

Chief Justice Paul C. Murphy III is a Houston native who earned both his undergraduate (1958) and law degrees (1962) from University of Houston. Justice Murphy, a burly, muscular man with florid Irish complexion, and thick salt-and-pepper gray hair, could easily be cast to play the role of a longshoreman.

He served as a U.S. Army captain from 1962-64, and was honorably discharged.

Justice Murphy served on the 14th Court of Appeals from 1981 to 2001, and as Chief Justice from 1995 to 2001.

His résumé includes pages of honors and awards, in years of Republican Party, community and professional work. He is married, and has three children.

Justice Murphy, who retired from the court on March 1, 2001, was a featured panelist speaking at a February 14, 2004, seminar on the Lawrence and Garner cases. Justice John Anderson, who was invited to the same retrospective event, sponsored by and held at the South Texas College of Law in Houston, declined to attend, sponsors said.

Having traveled out of Texas when the June 8, 2000, opinion was released, Justice Murphy revealed to the 2004 law-school-seminar audience how "hurt" he was on his return, by the stinging public attacks from his own political party—where he had served in various, volunteer grassroots posts for many years. His deep voice seemed to quaver a bit when describing his feelings during those weeks of nearly nonstop, negative publicity.

If he had to make the decision again, it would be exactly the same decision, Chief Justice Murphy said. He has no regrets.

He said the announcement of his retirement two years before his six-year term of office would have ended in 2002, was motivated by his age and the attractive retirement options available at that time. His early departure from the bench had nothing to do with the massive local publicity surrounding the sodomy law opinion.

Despite Justice Murphy's statements, attorney Gary Polland theorizes that the political furor and Justice Murphy's subsequent retirement announcement were related.

"Murphy took a lot of abuse. He quit," Polland said.

Gary Polland, the attorney who in 1999 served as chair of the Republican Party in Harris County, an elected post, was not shy about quickly, publicly expressing his anger and displeasure over the Justice Anderson-Justice Murphy ruling. Polland, skilled at 30-second sound bites and pithy observations, was quoted in television and print interviews attacking Justices Anderson and Murphy, and their ruling.

Gary Polland read Leviticus in the Old Testament too.

He shared his outrage at Justices Anderson and Murphy with his large, politically powerful, conservative Christian following that was equally outraged at what it considered an assault on family values.

Ever the consummate political activist, Polland decided to do something beyond talking.

CHAPTER
**12**

# The Letter Unsent,
# Gary Polland

Like Australia's duck-billed platypus, a furry mammal with a duckbill and webbed feet that lays eggs, Gary Polland is an amalgam of politically correct-politically incorrect, contrasting, and seemingly incompatible philosophies, characteristics and stereotypes.

A political platypus.

At first impression, Gary Polland and Mitchell Katine could be brothers.

Both are about the same age, short with dark hair, politically active, cause-oriented, self-confident, smooth public speakers, extremely intense, and so peripatetic it is as if they have a several motors whirring inside—attorneys, limelight seekers, smiling, friendly, intelligent, outgoing, articulate, Jewish.

"But *I'm* a conservative Jew!" Polland exclaims, only half joking, contrasting himself with Katine.

Each of their respective law offices is crammed with various awards and plaques from their constituencies, but Katine's office is neat and organized, while Polland's office is a shambles.

But the two men couldn't be more of a contrast politically: Katine, a homosexual liberal, whose law partner Gerald Birnberg was chair of the Harris County Democratic Party; and Polland, a fire-breathing, scorched-earth, right-wing conservative chair of the Harris County Republican Party, who relishes attacking liberals at the slightest opportunity.

Polland continually and publicly espouses far-right Christian principles. He enjoys an ultra-right Christian following that applauds almost his every pronouncement.

Polland's main legal work to earn a living is criminal defense. Many of the ultra-right intensely dislike criminal defense attorneys. Polland gives anti-crime speeches, then drives to the courthouse to earn a living defending accused child molesters, drug dealers, and murderers who the religious right regularly denounce.

The religious right and conservative vote is largely controlled by the Hotze-Harmon-Blakemore triumvirate that politically competes with, and dislikes Polland. The far right love Polland, but vote for the triumvirate slate, which does not include Polland.

Although the triumvirate never endorses Polland for anything, neither does it actively oppose him, perhaps fearing alienating its own religious-right vote on which it depends for its success. An uneasy symbiosis born of political practicalities.

Polland is vehemently pro-life, railing against abortion at every opportunity, public and private. Pro-lifers detest Planned Parenthood, and similar organizations they consider pro-choice.

Polland's wife served on the board of directors of Planned Parenthood in Houston.

Only in America.

Maybe only in Harris County, Texas.

Gary Michael Polland was born September 10, 1950, in Chicago. He graduated cum laude from William A. Wirt High School in Gary, Indiana. He graduated cum laude from the University of Texas in 1972, and from the University of Texas law school in 1975. He was president of the Texas Student Union. He and his wife Esther have two sons.

Unlike Katine, Polland considers himself a practicing Jew, for whom his religious faith plays a vital role in everyday life. He has served in major posts for many local and national Jewish political and charitable organizations.

He served as county chair of the Republican Party in Harris County from 1996-2002.

On June 21, 2000, at Chicen Itza in Mexico's arid Yucatan peninsula, thousands of spectators gasped in awe when the Sun Serpent, appearing as a shadow-cast light, crept slowly up the side of El Castillo pyramid. The summer solstice.

The entire Earth tilted on its rotation axis with respect to the orbital plane. The longest day of the year; maximum offset of 23° degrees, 27'.

According to superstition, it is one of four days a year when it is possible to stand an egg upright on its end.

A day of mystery and omens.

A thousand miles away, at a Houston hotel on that same evening, a glittering fund-raising gala for then Texas governor George W. Bush's presidential campaign was in progress. Governor Bush had been quoted as supporting Texas' sodomy law as a "symbol of traditional values." He said he would veto any attempt to overturn the sodomy law legislatively, according to a June 8, 2000, news release from the National Stonewall Democratic Federation.

As party chair of vote-rich Harris County, Gary Polland was at a prestigious table with other influential party activists. Harris County traditionally provided about 17 percent of the vote in any statewide balloting.

Paul Simpson, attorney, accountant, party treasurer, party counsel, and conservative, sat next to Polland, his close friend. Simpson, stocky with dark, thick hair, fancied running countywide to replace Polland as party chair if Polland decided to try for a new U.S. Congressional seat, which redistricting from the 2000 census might create. A local judge, whose name Simpson says he cannot remember, sat at the same table.

Golden opportunity beckoned.

Thirteen days had passed since the three-judge panel, by a 2-1 vote, issued its June 8, 2000, opinion striking down Texas' sodomy law.

Four days previously, 10,000-plus Republican delegates from across Texas held their June 15-17, 2000, annual party convention at Houston's cavernous George R. Brown Convention Center, a red and white confection that looks like a giant oceangoing steamship run aground at the edge of the downtown business district.

One plank of the state party platform addressed the June 8 Lawrence decision from the Houston-based 14th Court of Appeals:

> "Judicial Activism—The Party stands strongly against activist judges, who use their power to usurp the clear will of the people. We publicly rebuke judges Chief Justice Murphy and John Anderson, who ruled that the 100-year-old Texas sodomy law is unconstitutional, and ask that all members of the Republican Party of Texas oppose their reelection, and activist judges like them, and support non-activist judges as their opponents."

Another section of the 2000 party platform addressed the specific issue of homosexuality:

> "Homosexuality—The Party believes that the practice of sodomy tears at the fabric of society, contributes to the breakdown of the family unit, and leads to the spread of dangerous, communicable diseases. Homosexual behavior is contrary to the fundamental, unchanging truths that have been ordained by God, recognized by our country's founders, and shared by the majority of Texans.
>
> "Homosexuality must not be presented as an acceptable 'alternative' lifestyle in our public education and policy, nor should 'family' be redefined to include homosexual 'couples.' We are opposed to any granting of special legal entitlements, recognition, or privileges includ-

ing, but not limited to, marriage between persons of the same sex, custody of children by homosexuals, homosexual partner insurance or retirement benefits. We oppose any criminal or civil penalties against those who oppose homosexuality out of faith, conviction or belief in traditional values," the section continued.

Polland thought with that kind of state party support, he wouldn't be going out on a limb alone if he took even bolder steps.

And, in case Justices Murphy and Anderson and other judges didn't get the message from the June 15-17 state party convention, Polland wanted to up the ante.

Spell it out.

Smack down.

Polland wanted the *en banc* (in full court) rehearing, and he wanted to up the public pressure on the nine appeal court justices who would be reconsidering the decision of their judicial colleagues on the three-judge panel.

Polland had been thinking.

It wasn't difficult at the June 21 Bush fund-raiser to steer the table conversation to Justices Murphy and Anderson.

Both Simpson and Polland agree that the idea to send a letter to Justices Murphy and Anderson was born and agreed upon June 21 at the Bush gala dinner, but the two activists differ on whose idea it was initially, and on details of what transpired after that.

Both profess complete memory lapses as to who else at the gala table expressed support for their gambit.

The draft letter, which was never mailed to Judge Anderson, was dated June, 2000 and stated:

"Re: *Lawrence v. State of Texas* and the Texas Anti-Sodomy Statute
Dear Justice Anderson:
We the undersigned Republican County Chairs within your jurisdiction, are disappointed and appalled at your recent ruling that legalizes all sodomy in the State of Texas. Your June 8 opinion in Lawrence v. State of

Texas is wrong, constitutes the worse kind of judicial activism in overruling the will of the people, and violates the principles of the Republican Party. We urge you to retract your opinion or to resign immediately as a Republican candidate for the 14th Court of Appeals.

Texas has outlawed sodomy for over 100 years. It is your opinion that the Texas anti-sodomy statute violates the 1972 Texas Equal Rights Amendment. There is no basis for your conclusion. Texas citizens adopted that Amendment to eliminate certain types of discrimination, so the law would treat men and women equally. But—contrary to your holding—the people of Texas did **not** legalize homosexual conduct by adopting that Amendment. Ominously, the logical next step after your opinion would be the legalization of homosexual marriage.

The Texas Republican Party has long opposed decriminalizing sodomy and supported traditional marriage. As the Texas Republican Platform states, homosexual behavior tears at the fabric of society, contributes to the breakdown of the family, and is a hazard to public health. The Republican Party also opposes legalizing homosexual marriage and seeks to preserve the traditional institution of marriage as being solely between a man and a woman. Your opinion blatantly defies the Republican Party Platform and creates potential for further damage to our society.

Therefore we call on you [*sic*] reverse your vote and affirm the constitutionality of the Texas anti-sodomy statute. If you refuse to do so, we urge you to withdraw immediately from the race for reelection to the Fourteenth Court of Appeals, to allow all the 14 Republican County Chairs in the court's jurisdiction, time to nominate a Republican candidate who believes in and supports the principles of the Republican Party and the State of Texas."

No letter was drafted for Justice Murphy because Murphy was not up for reelection in 2000. Although Justice Anderson was up for reelection, he was already on the ballot with no opponent, assuring his automatic reelection.

But before Polland and Simpson could send their letter to Justice Anderson, someone faxed the draft of the letter to Justice Anderson's office.

Justice Anderson was not amused. Justice Anderson did what all attorneys would do. He contacted his attorney.

Simpson said, "I got a call that night [June 26, 2000] at home from [attorney] Jim Evans who said he represents Justice Anderson. Evans told me someone faxed the draft letter to Justice Anderson. Evans raised the issue of the legal propriety of sending the letter. We discussed it.

"After my conversation with Evans, I thought, [Evans] *is right*. Politically it is not a wise thing to do. The letter was really ineffective. We [the letter] couldn't *do* anything. The letter wasn't a threat. It wasn't change your opinion or step down. Why have a letter?"

"Since I was in New York, I asked [Polland] to send a letter to the county chairs canceling the letter to Justice Anderson," Simpson continued. "But when I hung up the phone, I thought, [Polland] is *never going to* [*not send the letter*]. So I called my secretary from New York, and [dictated] a letter canceling the draft letter to Justice Anderson."

But the controversy was just beginning. Someone contacted Harris County media about the draft to Justice Anderson—the letter never sent.

"It snowballed from there," Simpson remembered with a fatigued sigh.

"It just kept going in the press." The *Chronicle* printed an editorial denouncing Polland, and the letter, as an attempt to intimidate judges.

"The *Chronicle* had a nasty cartoon. They had an editorial that I should be indicted for trying to influence what the judges do. And my response was, 'Do you believe in democracy? Do you believe in freedom of speech? Hello? You guys [members of the *Houston Chronicle* editorial board] criticize judicial opinions all the time! Why can't I?' Then the manager of Channel 2 [the local NBC affiliate] had a television editorial against me! Intolerant!" Polland fumed.

❄

On June 28, 2000, the Harris County District Attorney's Office filed a motion in the 14th Court of Appeals seeking a rehearing and request for an *en banc* review.

In layman terms, the DA was asking all nine justices on the 14th Court of Appeals to publicly reevaluate the June 8, 2000, decision of three of their colleagues on the same court.

Public comment from both sides escalated the ideological battle until July 28, 2000, in Austin, Texas, when the judiciary committee of the Texas legislature voted 6-1 in favor of issuing subpoenas for a hearing in Houston to investigate the letter to Justice John Sharp Anderson.

At the September 27, 2000, hearing in Houston the judiciary committee members grilled Simpson early on, publicly turning him slowly on the spit over the fire, then hearing a parade of citizens speak their opinions.

After several hours, Polland was called last.

Committee chair, Democrat Senfronia Thompson, like Polland, a Houston criminal defense attorney, asked Polland if he would like to give an opening statement.

"I said yes!" Polland remembered with pride. "I ripped them to shreds in 10 minutes. After my opening statement they are apologizing that they are not against the Constitution and they do believe in freedom of speech. They were on the defensive the whole time. My philosophy always was you never go on the defense. You are always on the attack.

"Jamie Capelo [a Democrat judiciary committee member] starts giving me a hard time after I give my opening statement. I just hand him his head back. Like I'm on trial there. I know what I'm doing. I give people a hard time.

"I told them that the problem was not criticizing judicial opinions. The problem was out-of-control courts that are usurping legislative function. [You ought] to be having a hearing on these courts that are doing your [legislative] job for you. I said, 'You don't like sodomy? Vote to get rid of it. Don't leave it to the courts. We don't elect courts to be legislatures.'"

Polland is known for hyperbole when describing his abilities as an attorney. But, having watched a videotape of the hearing, I can attest that Polland wasn't exaggerating at all. Polland really did hand Capelo his head. That afternoon Polland was a *force majeure*.

Mitchell Katine sat in the audience watching.

CHAPTER
13

# Beaten to Death:
# Homicide

On October 11, 2000, while Lawrence and Garner's sodomy cases were pending a crucial rehearing ruling from the entire *en banc* nine-judge membership of the 14th Court of Appeals in Houston, and 14 days after the Judiciary Committee hearing in Houston—Robert Royce Eubanks, the talkative witness who literally led deputies to the scene of the September 17, 1998, sodomy—was murdered.

The medical examiner's autopsy report listed manner of death as "homicide."

Cause of death was listed as "blunt force head injuries."

Eubanks, then 42, had, in layman's terminology, been beaten to death.

Officer Randle Wayne Smith, who had been with the Houston Police Department since 1983, was field training probationary Officer Derrick R. Stone October 11, 2000, when they both drove to 3942 Faulkner after a 3:39 A.M. phone call about Eubanks. Officer Smith does not recall the source of the phone notification. Their complete written police report is not officially available as public information.

The neighborhood, colloquially known as Yellowstone, is one of the toughest in Houston.

"If I remember, it was a small one-story, wood frame house with a carport. Paramedics were already there. I saw [Eubanks] on the gurney, outside the house," Officer Smith said. Paramedics told him that Eubanks was in extremely critical condition.

A black male on the scene, whose description could fit Tyron Garner, and who identified the comatose Eubanks, told Officer Smith that Eubanks had left 3942 Faulkner earlier, returning in the beaten condition. "He told me Eubanks got beat up elsewhere. So I didn't think I had probable cause to be searching that house," Officer Smith rationalized.

Paramedics told Officer Smith it was doubtful Eubanks would live much longer.

An ambulance transported Eubanks to Houston's Hermann Hospital. "I don't know why Eubanks went to Hermann. Most cases like that go to Ben Taub hospital," Smith noted.

Almost immediately when Officer Smith and trainee Officer Stone arrived at Hermann Hospital, "...the nurses there told us they recognized Garner and Eubanks from prior violent incidents. They said Garner had physically assaulted Eubanks on prior occasions," Smith related.

Eubanks' autopsy report reflects that hospital staff were so concerned about the situation that on their own initiative, they put a false name on Eubanks' medical records.

"According to decedent's medical records, the decedent's name is Robert Royce Eubanks. The decedent was the victim of an assault and in trying to protect the decedent, the hospital staff put the alias name of *Russell Edison* on some of decedent's records," the official report notes.

Having received this further information from reliable sources about a history of violence between Garner and Eubanks, and being advised that Eubanks was near death, and only about an hour having passed since he was at the scene with the person he then knew had a violent history with Eubanks, Officer Smith did not seek to obtain a warrant to search 3942 Faulkner, nor did he return to the house to ask more questions or expand his investigation.

"On the way home, I told myself I needed to go in there [go into the house at 3942 Faulkner]," Officer Smith said in a June 2004 interview.

He never did.

Did either officer look near the house for a weapon?

"You mean in the driveway? We didn't see a rock or a board or anything," Officer Smith said.

Nationally recognized forensic pathologist Dr. Ronald Wright, who later analyzed the autopsy report on Eubanks, said the nature of Eubanks' injuries would indicate there were copious amounts of blood, as well as blood spattering, at the location where Eubanks was beaten to death.

After being transported to Hermann at 4:15 A.M. on October 11, 2000, Robert Eubanks lingered for almost four days, never regaining consciousness. Never able to tell authorities who inflicted his fatal injuries.

He was pronounced dead at 9:33 A.M. on October 14, 2000, at the hospital.

"By the time they found him, he was virtually already gone," said his mother, who was with Eubanks at the hospital when he died. She provided official identification of Eubanks' body, according to the medical examiner's report.

Hospital staff found a card in the unconscious Eubanks' pocket naming John Lawrence as the person to contact in case of emergency.

"I got a call from the hospital," Lawrence said. "They said he had been injured severely and that he was carrying a card in his pocket that said that I should be notified in case something happened to him.

"It [the card] had probably been in there [Eubanks' pocket] for probably 10 years," Lawrence speculated. Lawrence had known Eubanks since 1975, but denies they had a sexual relationship.

Knowing Eubanks lay dying in the hospital, did Lawrence visit his friend of 25 years?

"No."

Did Garner know what happened to Eubanks as far as the hospital goes? Did Garner visit his friend of 11 years?

"No. I didn't go see him," Garner responded.

After Lawrence and Garner came to Katine's office with Eubanks in 1998, when was Lawrence's next contact with Eubanks? Did Lawrence continue his longtime friendship with Eubanks?

"No. I would just speak to him on the phone. He became more irrational against me. So I just avoided confrontation," said Lawrence, who refers to Eubanks by his middle name, Royce.

Was Eubanks angry with Lawrence?

"[Eubanks] was an epileptic that was on a lot of medications that sometimes would, sometimes would not, sometimes would overdo. So I felt it best just to stay far," Lawrence said.

Did Lawrence sever the friendship after that?

"Yeah."

Does Lawrence remember the last time he saw Eubanks?

"I don't remember."

How long after the 1998 meeting in Katine's office did Lawrence sever the friendship with Eubanks?

"Probably six to seven months," Lawrence estimated.

Because Garner and Garner's brother Michael Garner were subpoenaed to a Grand Jury regarding Eubanks' death, I did not ask Tyron Garner when Garner last saw Robert Eubanks. Garner had previously invoked his Fifth Amendment privilege to not give evidence against himself about the Eubanks homicide.

According to police, Tyron Garner was the initial suspect in Eubanks' murder, said homicide Sergeant Ken Williamson of the Houston Police Department. Wiliamson, a supervisor in the homicide division, said that Garner's attorney, Katine's law partner David A. Jones, told prosecutors that if Garner was called to testify about Eubanks' death, Garner would invoke his Fifth Amendment right not to provide incriminating testimony against himself.

"And there was another witness who said that Eubanks was an epileptic who would injure himself all the time," Sergeant Williamson added.

"Clearly, the police dropped the ball on this case. But there is no Statute of Limitations on murder," said Kenny Rodgers, now retired, who served for 30 years as chief investigator with the Harris County District Attorney's Office.

HPD Homicide Detective L.D. Garrettson confirmed that although Eubanks' murder is still an open case, it is in the "cold" case file. He said he cannot provide further information because the murder remains unsolved. He did not respond to my several subsequent voice messages left for him, advising him that his supervisor Sergeant Williamson did not object if Detective Garrettson wished to discuss Eubanks' homicide.

Katine said he was not the attorney who advised Tyron Garner regarding Garner's invocation of Fifth Amendment rights before the Grand Jury investigating Eubanks' death, nor does Katine know who did represent Eubanks then.

It was co-counsel David Jones of Katine's law firm according to Sergeant Williamson. Jones' office was just a few feet from Katine's office.

When I asked Garner in the interview whether he visited Eubanks in the hospital, Katine interjected, "He [Garner] knows what happened."

Because Katine was not Garner's attorney with regard to the Eubanks murder, and Garner was therefore unrepresented regarding questions I might ask him on a crime that could trigger the death penalty—and because Katine is inexperienced in criminal law, and Garner had previously taken the Fifth—I told Katine I felt legally uncomfortable pursuing the information Katine volunteered suggesting Garner's knowledge of Eubanks' homicide.

However, during the April 23, 2004, interview with Lawrence and Garner, I told Katine if he wished to ask Garner any questions about Eubanks' murder, to go ahead.

"I won't go there," Katine said, backing off.

A police report, written by medical examiner and investigator J. Brite, states, quoting HPD Detective L.D. Garretson:

> "The decedent [Eubanks] has been in a violent homosexual relationship which often resulted in fights. [Eubanks] was reportedly struck on the head, approximately three blows, with a broom handle by his boyfriend Tyron Garner during an altercation on October 3, 2000, and he appeared to be OK since that time.
>
> "[Eubanks] and Garner had been using various pills and crack cocaine for approximately one week prior to October 10, 2000, and had argued and possibly fought on October 10, 2000. Tyron Garner had reportedly told Detective Garretson that the decedent and he had been staying for a while at Garner's mother's home at 3942 Faulkner.
>
> "On October 10, 2000, in the evening, [Eubanks] had gone out for a while and when he returned it appeared he had been beaten up while away from the house. [Eubanks] had gone to sleep and when Tyrone tried to wake him, he was unable to do so. An ambulance was called.
>
> "Detective Garrettson stated that Dr. Steven Koch had told him that the decedent, Eubanks, had a brain stem injury and the brain was off mid line," J. Brite concludes his report.

Dr. Morna L. Gonsoulin MD, the assistant medical examiner who performed the autopsy on Eubanks, listed the cause of death as "Blunt force head injuries." She itemizes Eubanks' injuries and scarring, including three broken ribs, in 1½ single-spaced pages. The relevant portions of Dr. Gonsoulin's autopsy report, written in dry, repetitive style, state:

"IDENTIFYING MARKS AND SCARS: There is a 6 inch area on the ventral left forearm with at least 20 horizontally-oriented, parallel, linear scars of apparently similar age, each ranging from 1 to 2 inches in length. There is a 2 inch, obliquely-oriented, linear scar of the right forearm . . . a 3 inch, vaguely triangular scar of the left knee. There are numerous (at least 25) linear scars scattered over all areas of the scalp, ranging from ½ to 1¼ inches. No tattoos are identified.

EXTERNAL EVIDENCE OF INJURY: There is a 1 inch contusion of the midline forehead. There are periorbital contusions of the left lower lid and the right lateral eye. There are three healing lacerations at the vertex of the scalp: a 2 inch linear laceration of the left parietal scalp, a 1¾ inch forked laceration at the vertex, and a ¼ inch laceration of the right parietal scalp.

There is a 1¼ inch laceration surrounded by contusion on the right parietooccipital scalp . . . a ¾ inch, curvilinear laceration of the left parietal scalp. There is a cluster of six red-purple contusions of the midline occipital scalp located in an approximately circular arrangement, ranging from ¾ to 1 inch. A ¾ inch curvilinear laceration is within the previously described cluster.

There is a 1 inch circumscribed red contusion of the sternal chest . . . a ½ inch crusted abrasion of the left upper quadrant of the abdomen.

There is a 2½ inch area of patchy red contusion of the upper right arm adjacent to two linear abrasions, measuring ¾ inch. There is a 2 inch laceration adjacent to a 1½ inch red contusion of the left wrist . . . ½ inch lacerations on each palm . . . three blue contusions of the proximal right forearm and antecubital fossa, ranging from ¼ to 1 inch.

The dorsal surface of each hand is covered in faint blue contusions. There is a 3 inch purple contusion of the posterior left thigh. There are two 1½ inch blue green contusions of the lateral right thigh . . . a ½ inch red contusion of the right knee . . . a 1 inch scabbed abrasion of the left knee.

INTERNAL EVIDENCE OF INJURY:
There is a 6 by 6 inch polygonal defict of the right

parietal skull corresponding to an area of softening in the scalp ... a 6 by 6 inch confluent hemorrhage concentrated in the right frontoparietal region.

There are two distinctly separate areas of parietooccipital subscalpular hemorrhage, measuring 1.5 and 1 inch respectively. There is a 20 milliliter epidural clot adherent to the dura in the previously described defect. The right subdural space contains approximately 90 milliliters of clotted blood.

There is marked subarachnoid hemorrhage of the right hemisphere of the cerebrum. A 4 by 3 by 2.5 centimeter area of necrosis and hemorrhage is present in the medial right temporal lobe ... marked cerebral edema with shifting to the left of the midline and cerebellar tonsillar herniation.

There is secondary (Duret) hemorrhage of the midbrain and the pons. There are scattered contusions of the inferior surface of the right occipital lobe.

The left sixth through eighth ribs are fractured," the autopsy report states in pertinent part.

The autopsy report contains a section on blood tests for drugs. Although the report says the samples were tested October 16, the day after Eubanks was pronounced dead, it does not state when the blood samples were extracted from Eubanks.

If the blood samples were extracted from Eubanks October 11, the day he was brought to the hospital, presumably any drugs he had taken including alcohol and cocaine, would still be in his system. However, if Eubanks' blood samples for testing were taken after his four days in the hospital, there is a greater likelihood that evidence of any drugs he had used would have dissipated.

The length of time drugs stay in the human system varies with the type of drug, some remaining in the system for as long as 30 days.

The medical examiner's report says no drugs were detected.

This included ethanol, methanol, acetone, isopropanol, marijuana metabolite, cocaine metabolite, phencyclidine, amphetamine, methamphetamine, opiate, and the standard basic drug screen.

Medical examiner and investigator J. Brite's report said that Eubanks and Garner had been using "various pills and crack cocaine for approximately one week prior to October 10, 2000."

How did Lawrence meet Eubanks 25 years ago?

"We were neighbors in a Houston apartment complex."

Did Eubanks live with Lawrence September 17, 1998? Deputies said they found some of Eubanks personal effects in Lawrence's other bedroom.

"No."

Did Eubanks have his own place?

"Yes."

On September 17 was Eubanks employed?

"I don't think so," Lawrence said.

How did Eubanks support himself?

"He was on Social Security Disability for epilepsy."

How long had Garner known Eubanks on September 17?

"Ten or eleven years. Since around 1990," Garner said.

How did Garner first meet Eubanks?

"He stayed behind me on the next street. I had seen him walking one day and we just started talking," Garner recalled.

How did Lawrence meet Garner?

"Through [Eubanks]," Lawrence explained.

In what way did Eubanks introduce Garner to Lawrence?

"I think we were down in the bar," Lawrence remembered.

Both Tyron Garner and his brother Michael Garner were subpoenaed to appear October 26, 2000, before a Grand Jury of the 339th District Court in Houston, which was investigating the beating death of Eubanks, police said. Assistant District Attorney Kelly Siegler was prosecuting the case.

A day before October 25, attorney David Jones, who offices two doors from Katine in the same law firm, phoned Ms. Siegler.

"Jones told her that if called before the Grand Jury, Tyron Garner would invoke his Fifth Amendment right [not to be forced to give self-incriminating testimony]," explained Sergeant Ken Williamson of the Houston Police Department's Homicide division. Jones represented himself to Siegler as Tyron Garner's attorney with regard to the Eubank's homicide, Sergeant Williamson said.

In a March 18, 2004, interview, attorney David Jones denied that he ever represented Garner in any case other than the September 17, 1998, Homosexual Conduct case(s).

After the case which became *Lawrence v. Texas*, the sodomy case, did you ever represent Garner, Lawrence or Eubanks in regard to anything?"

"No," Jones said.

In a June 25, 2004, follow-up interview with Garner, again in Lawrence and Katine's presence, I revisited this point, asking Garner if attorney David Jones acted in Garner's behalf with regard to the Eubanks homicide investigation?

"Yes," Garner said.

Ron Wright, MD, an attorney, is one of the most respected and well-known forensic pathologists in the United States. Dr. Wright served as Broward County Chief Medical Examiner in Fort Lauderdale, Florida for 14 years. He is author of numerous scholarly articles and frequently testifies as expert witness in civil and criminal cases.

He reviewed the autopsy report and other relevant material with regard to Eubanks' homicide.

"Mr. Eubanks was beaten to death with a baseball bat or similar. I doubt it was a broom," Dr. Wright concluded.

As to time frame, Eubanks was beaten not long before he came to the emergency room in the early morning hours of October 11, 2000. "There is a lot of blood [at whatever location] he was beaten. He was kicked too. That is what broke his ribs," Dr. Wright explained. "Eubanks was not so intoxicated that he could not fight back. He has defensive wounds to his hands and arms. But the lack of fracture to the hands and forearms indicates that the beating weapon was not a tire iron or similar weapon. It was not terribly heavy and hard."

Dr. Wright speculates that a baseball bat was the most probable weapon. "But a 2-by-4 or 2-by-6 will do also," he said. "There would be a huge amount of blood at the scene. That is from the head injuries alone. They would bleed. Also a lot of [blood] splatter."

Dr. Wright discounts any possibility that Eubanks was run over by a vehicle. "His injuries are a beating. Whoever did it was really enraged."

The killer was, or killer(s) apparently were so enraged that he/they continued administering blows after Eubanks was defenseless. "The worst blows are about six or more after he was down, and apparently no longer fighting back," Dr. Wright explained.

His assailant(s) apparently wanted to make sure Eubanks was dead.

As to purported testimony before the Grand Jury in Houston that Eubanks sometimes injured himself falling from epileptic seizures, Dr. Wright scoffs.

"There is no way Mr. Eubanks' injuries are from a fall from seizures. [His] injuries look like an altercation taken to the extreme," Dr. Wright concluded.

There is no indication that Eubanks was tortured.

"The pathologist did not describe dissecting the testes. The absence of description can be taken to mean no injury. Hardly any male is tortured without getting bonked on the nuts. So I think that torture is really not indicated, unless it is someone really good, which eliminates anyone working for the USA," Dr. Wright observed.

Was there more than one assailant?

"Of course that is possible," Dr. Wright said.

Based on Eubanks' injuries, can Dr. Wright postulate anything about the assailant(s)?

"Not very small children or infirm adults. Other than that, you have the universe of people. We do not know his level of intoxication. If Eubanks was very drunk (which is likely), then anyone. If he was sober (unlikely) then someone young and strong," Dr. Wright speculated.

Dr. Wright noticed that Eubanks, who was right-handed, had previously attempted suicide by slitting his wrists. "The suicide attempt was approximately six months before his death. Those wounds were completely healed," Dr. Wright concluded.

"He [Eubanks] appears to be a druggie," Dr. Wright added.

After Eubanks' beating, which Wright said occurred not long before Eubanks was admitted to Hermann Hospital on October 11, could Eubanks, given his physical impairments from the beating, have walked anywhere? Was Eubanks physically capable of self-locomotion?

"Yes. He could have walked perhaps for 10 minutes," Dr. Wright said.

# Backstage:
# David Allan Jones

Within 24 hours of the defendants' September 17, 1998, arrest—attorney Mitchell Katine stood at David Allan Jones' office door down the hall from Katine's office, Jones said.

"[Katine] gave me a general heads-up. That this [sodomy cases] was something that might be interesting to me, and would I help, because Katine didn't have any experience in criminal law," Jones remembers. In 1998, Jones, then 51, had practiced criminal law about 23 years.

Jones said he talked to Lawrence and Garner "certainly within a day or two of their arraignment," which date would have been set shortly after their arrest. Defendants must be brought before a magistrate within 24 hours of their arrest. Lawrence and Garner said they did go before a magistrate in the downtown main jail's basement courtroom shortly after their arrest.

Sheryl Roppolo confirmed Jones recollection. She said Jones was phoning her at the JP Court requesting copies of the probable cause affidavit less than 24 hours after the defendants' arrest.

"When Lambda Legal made their interest known to [Katine], I don't know. I do know that [Katine] and I talked about it as if it were a Supreme Court case from the first day," Jones revealed.

Jones, born in the nearby rural community of Wharton, Texas, graduated from El Campo High School there. He earned a BA degree in 1971, and a law degree in 1975 from the University of Houston, working as an assistant district attorney from 1976-78, then as an assistant attorney general of Texas from 1978-80. He is divorced, and childless.

A self-described, left-wing liberal Democrat, Jones never morphed into a conservative after he left college. "I never changed. Been a liberal since 1968," Jones said.

"I like to raise hell," Jones explained.

Lambda Legal of New York, who had taken a lead before the November 3, 2000, oral argument to the three-justice panel of the 14th Court of Appeals, took complete control after that, according to Jones. "I had pretty much since the 14th Court of Appeals time been leaving it to Lambda and not wanting to be feeling ... the handwriting on the wall that they [Lambda] were very much interested in this being done right, and they [Lambda] do it. I sensed that," Jones explained, regarding the shifting of control from Houston to New York City, from local to international.

"They [Lambda Legal] were very, very controlling in terms of who said what, and what was said. Not in any negative way. They were just on top of that. They knew of course that I was as likely to be [contacted] as anyone else at certain times, given the fact that my name was on the pleading[s]. So I recall visiting with them [lawyers at Lambda Legal] about how various things were characterized," Jones recalled.

Jones, like Katine, Lewis, and the defendants themselves, implies the defendants were never engaged in a sexual act on September 17, 1998. "These people [Lawrence and Garner] were so hesitant about talking about this. It was almost as if ... on many occasions I thought that from the way they were handling themselves, that nothing really happened. That something happened, but it wasn't necessarily anal intercourse."

Although Jones plays down his role, his law colleague Gerald Birnberg privately offers a starkly contrasting perspective of Jones' backstage activity.

"David [Jones] devoted his life to those cases. He handled everything. Katine was the front man but relied on David [Jones] because David is experienced in criminal law, and Mitchell [Katine] was not," Birnberg reveals, shaking his head in awe of Jones' unwavering, years-long, behind-the-scenes support.

Jones estimates he spent a mere 30 hours on both cases.

Although Jones is an out-front personality who, like Katine and Polland, loves center stage, Jones has another side.

Jones' reputation in the courthouse is for well-connected stealth, moving so skillfully to achieve his political goals that he rarely leaves fingerprints. Jones has the nondescript physical appearance intelligence agencies love: tall, thin, with graying hair, and smushed-in lower face—someone who fades unnoticed into the woodwork, and attracts no one's notice.

Despite Jones' aw-shucks averring that his role in *Lawrence* was minimal, common sense and Birnberg's statements about Jones indicate otherwise. Lambda, like all organizations litigating outside their jurisdiction, needed a local attorney knowledgeable in criminal law to direct the case. Katine knew zilch about criminal law. No matter what Jones says, Jones was probably in charge. Katine was the subordinate attorney.

Jones, like Lane Lewis and Annise Parker, has accumulated a sophisticated understanding of cop culture, copthink and police procedures from his years on both the prosecution and defense side.

Jones' statements that Katine appeared in Jones' office doorway almost immediately after the arrests to discuss appealing the cases to the U.S. Supreme Court, are in obvious direct conflict with Katine and Lewis' portrayal of themselves as clueless about the arrests until faxing each other more than a week later based on information from a guy who approached Lewis in a bar.

Given Katine and Lewis' local prominence, and history of activism in the homosexual community, their version of being clueless immediately after the arrests rings hollow.

Jones' joining Katine and Lewis in gratuitous attacks on Eubanks' credibility seems, anticipatory. They all particularly went out of their way to characterize Eubanks as a liar, not worthy of belief—laying the groundwork so that if Eubanks ever did make any statements, Eubanks would be discredited in advance.

What were they worried the talkative drunk Eubanks might say?

Jones' failure to mention that he represented Garner in Eubanks' October 2000 homicide is significant. Even with a lot of clients, forgetting representing a client who might be charged with homicide is unlikely. Particularly if the same client was also the defendant in an internationally famous sodomy case!

In fact, Jones went further. Jones said he never represented Garner on anything other than sodomy. Even Garner agrees that Jones represented him when Garner invoked the Fifth Amendment regarding Eubanks' murder. Homicide Sergeant Williamson also says Jones represented Garner.

Not only did Katine initially profess uncertainty as to whether Eubanks was dead, but also uncertainty as to who represented Garner, Katine's client, in the homicide!

It was Katine's co-counsel Jones, whose office was 30 feet from Katine's office.

Lewis, assigned to babysit Eubanks while the sodomy case languished in Texas' courts, seemed to say he didn't notice Eubanks wasn't around anymore! Garner, whom Lewis was also babysitting, was a suspect in Eubanks' murder, investigated by the Houston Police Department where Lewis maintains an office!

The topic of Eubanks' homicide seems to rapidly clear the room of people who normally never need encouragement to speak.

# 14th Court *En Banc*,
# Convictions Reinstated

Twenty days after the June 8, 2000, opinion of the three-judge panel, the Harris County District Attorney's Office filed a request for rehearing before the entire nine-justice 14th Court of Appeals, *en banc*.

*En Banc* court is a legal term meaning the entire nine justices. The terms *"en banc"* and "entire" are interchangeable.

To astute observers, the court's vote of *whether* to grant a rehearing of the June 8, 2000, ruling was a portend of what its later decision on the issues would be, since the court was unlikely to vote to rehear a decision with which it *agreed*.

Therefore, the legal battleground shifted to the motion for rehearing, since—if they granted the rehearing—it was almost a foregone conclusion that they would then vote to reinstate the Lawrence-Garner convictions, reversing what their two judicial colleagues had ruled on June 8, 2000.

What political chits were called in, what attractive carrots were dangled, and what sticks were brandished subtly or unsubtly, whatever political machinations may have transpired privately in the days between Assistant DA Delmore's rehearing request on June 23, and the justices granting the State's request on September 14, 2000, would be mind-boggling even to cynical, veteran political operatives.

In Texas, the observation that "politics is a blood sport" absolutely includes judicial politics. Big time.

Houston attorney Frank Harmon's wife is a federal judge. Harmon's brother is a felony State Court judge. His sister and his other brother are prominent local attorneys.

Harmon, acknowledged as a political genius even by his detractors, is one of three men who decide by their support, who will be a judge in Harris County, or who will win any countywide political office. The politically successful Republican trio's organization, Conservative Republicans of Harris County (described earlier), includes founder Steven Hotze, MD, and political consultant Allen Blakemore.

Harmon is so well-known, not only locally, but statewide as the triumvirate's up-front operative member, that he—like Cher, Elton, or Madonna—is known only by his first name: Frank. If you say Frank, no politico responds, "Frank who?"

Harmon is always self-effacing, describing himself as just an ordinary guy. "People always think I have all this power. I don't," he often says, prompting eye rolls or silence from insiders.

Although Harmon is a conservative, he is not a religious conservative, nor a disciple of the religious right. But he detests liberals, and criminal defense attorneys, railing against them at the least opportunity.

"It was the oddest thing," *Lawrence* attorney David Jones remembers, in what may rank as one of the greatest understatements of all time in Harris County, Texas politics.

Sometime between June 23 and September 14, 2000,

Jones said Harmon phoned Jones to offer advice on political strategies to aid Lawrence and Garner's defense.

It was the Texas equivalent of Israeli leaders phoning Palestinian leaders to advise the Palestinians how they could annihilate Israel, or vice versa.

Harmon transmitted a secret that was even more astounding than the phone call to Jones itself.

According to Jones, Harmon knew in advance what is supposed to be top secret in all courts at any level: how the justices of the 14th Court of Appeals were going to vote on the State's motion for rehearing.

That Harmon would know such closely guarded, inner-sanctum secrets was hardly a surprise. His Conservative Republicans of Harris County had put nearly all the justices in office.

A leak of this highly confidential information to Harmon, presumably could only have come from one of the justices, a relative or spouse of one of the justices, or someone who knows the justices extremely well. For a justice to disclose the vote on an upcoming case would be considered a shocking breach of judicial ethics—perhaps unethical enough to get a justice removed from the bench.

But knowing the information is not as shocking as Harmon's sharing the information.

To transmit this closely guarded secret vote to one of the parties in that pending case, as Jones said Harmon did, is an act so bold it is almost beyond comprehension.

As Harmon told Jones, Harmon did not like what he knew in advance about how the court would rule on whether to rehear the Anderson-Murphy opinion. According to Jones, Harmon did not want the entire court [*en banc*] to review the three-judge panel's decision, particularly because that would conform to what Polland wanted. Harmon detested Polland.

Although Harmon did not say it, if Polland appeared powerful enough to influence an appeal court to *Polland's* agenda, the triumvirate's authority over judges could appear weaker than Polland's. The triumvirate, who in some sense competed with Polland for voter blocs, could lose its political grip.

Given Harmon's position as one of the conservative, ruling Republican triumvirate, his action of phoning Jones—a Democrat and a defense attorney, to offer helpful advice about sodomy cases—was *nes plus*, ultra high risk politically. If Harmon's call became public, Harmon's clout with conservatives could be severely damaged.

Harmon, or a close friend of Harmon's, must have been wall-clawing desperate.

Maybe Harmon was Dr. Hotze's messenger with the blessing of the machine.

Maybe Harmon was Justice Anderson's messenger, bidden or unbidden.

Maybe none of the above.

Maybe Harmon had another personal unspoken agenda.

Even more unfathomable, Harmon, who had worked as a Harris County Assistant District Attorney, always publicly and privately championed the State, pledging his eternal reverence for DA Holmes. Now, Harmon was privately advising Jones how to foil what DA Holmes and the State were requesting from the appeal court.

Jones remembered, "[Harmon] all of a sudden phoned me and said, 'It's a vote one way or the other [on the 14th court].' He had wind that there was one vote that would make all the difference in the world about the motion for rehearing [*en banc*] being granted. He was dead set against Gary Polland and that crowd at the Republican convention—whoever else, I don't know—be successful in getting that motion for rehearing granted.

"[The vote for rehearing] was close enough to where he did not want to see that succeed. He wanted to try and turn the tide in some way. [Harmon] felt it was a political victory for the bad guys. Or else he just didn't like the idea of a court being turned around on such an important issue. What all his motivations were, I don't know."

"Either [Harmon] didn't know or he didn't want to say that he knew which way [the vote] was going," Jones said at first, changing that later in our interview.

"[Harmon] wanted the 2-1 opinion [of the three-justice panel] to prevail. Whether he had other interests, I don't know. He just did not want to see that result [the June 8, 2000, opinion] changed in the manner in which the effort was being made to change it. It being a political power play by certain party stalwarts," Jones continued, describing his 15-to-20 minute phone conversation with Harmon.

Did Harmon like the 2-1 decision of the three-justice panel striking down the sodomy law?

"I don't know whether he liked it. For all I know, he just wanted it to stand. He was offended by the political tactics of the political crowd that was opposed to it. They had set the stage for the DA to get [the State's] motion granted by politicking and the like.

"[Harmon] starts giving me the low down and the inside from the [14th] Court of Appeals."

What *was* Harmon's advice to the defense?

"He thought it [the prosecution's motion for rehearing *en banc*] was one vote from being granted. He thought there was something that might *embarrass* [the 14th Court of Appeals] as I recall. It was a pleading ... I just can't remember," Jones said.

"I'm thinking, 'Wow! That's interesting, Frank! I'll let them [Katine and Lambda Legal] know that that is your concern, that that is what you think they should do,'" Jones said.

Did Harmon say how he obtained this inside information about the court's vote or the information that might *embarrass* the justices?

"No. He just has so many of those [judges] that he knows. I knew it was any one of three or four people I'm sure [were] talking to him.

"I recall a specific piece of advice. I just don't remember the contents of it—all that should be done that would maybe turn the tide, shift the vote. My best recollection, it was a pleading, a responsive pleading *that would have in-jected new material into the debate, that if made public,* would have been, might have gotten, back them [the judges] off of what they were trying to do. Whatever members of the court were heading in the direction of granting the rehearing," Jones added.

Did Jones' Lambda Legal team act on Harmon's advice?

"I do believe it was ignored. I don't believe anybody did anything. I know nothing was done," Jones remembered.

Katine said he does not remember ever discussing this topic with his co-counsel Jones.

"Who is Frank Harmon?" Katine asked me.

"[Harmon's phone call] was such a . . . this was really off the wall for me to get the call like that," Jones explained. "At the time I'm getting this information, I get from the way [Harmon] is describing it [the information that *could be embarrassing* to the 14th court] that it is rather sensitive material. That [Harmon] doesn't want to be identified with this information. He doesn't want to be used. He just wants me to carry this message and relay this strategy [to Katine and Lambda Legal].

"I don't think Harmon gave me his consent to (use Harmon's name). If he didn't, I disregarded [Harmon's request not to use his name], because I wasn't about to go say anything to [Katine and Lambda] and not have some credible information. If it was *Frank Harmon*, it was credible information."

Why did Harmon phone Jones instead of phoning Katine directly?

"[Harmon] and I worked in the DA's office together in the mid-1970s. He is always in the Book Stop, as I am. So we are always at the magazine section talking about what to read," Jones explained.

"We are opposites except for great appreciation for the process, respect for institutional integrity and the integrity of courts. That to me is beyond politics. We have a great deal in common that we both like the grassroots part of it rather than the fund raising, and stay in touch with who is doing what at the battle level," Jones added.

But isn't Jones friends with Gary Polland too? They both practice criminal defense law every day at the criminal courthouse. Did Harmon's phone call put Jones in an awkward position vis-à-vis Jones' friendship with Polland?

"No. I was yelling at [Polland] at the time anyway, about all that he was up to."

Did Jones tell Polland about Harmon's phone call?

"I don't think I did. It didn't go anywhere that I knew of. I don't believe anybody acted on it," Jones concluded.

Shortly after what Jones said was a June 23-September 14, 2000, time frame, Eubanks was beaten to death.

So not only was Jones fielding surprise calls from a Republican political superstar who proffered helpful suggestions to Lawrence and Garner, Jones was phoning the assistant district attorney in charge of the Grand Jury investigating Eubanks' homicide, telling her that if subpoenaed, his client Tyron Garner would invoke his Fifth Amendment privilege.

On March 15, 2001, the *en banc* court voted 7-2 to reinstate Lawrence and Garner's convictions. They said the prohibition of homosexual sodomy is permissible if rationally related to a legitimate State interest such as the protection of morality. They said, based on *Bowers*, there is no right to privacy for homosexual conduct. (The 1986 U.S. Supreme Court ruling in *Bowers v. Hardwick* upheld the constitutionality of Georgia's law criminalizing consensual homosexual *and* heterosexual sodomy.) Justices Harvey Hudson, Leslie Yates, Richard Edelman, Wanda Fowler, Don Wittig, Kem Frost and Maurice Amidei formed the majority. Justices Paul Murphy and John Sharp Anderson dissented.

In a concurring opinion, Justice Leslie Yates defended the decision, writing:

> "There is simply no place for suggesting that the members of this Court are pandering to certain political groups or deciding a case as a means to achieve a politically desired end. And to do so only adds unnecessarily to the already politically-charged climate created by the people amicus curiae purports to condemn," she wrote.
>
> "We have done so [made our decision]—not because of political pressures, as amicus curiae has suggested, but despite them," she concluded.

(Justice Yates' above comments refer to a particular *amicus* brief that was submitted by a local college professor. *Amicus curiae* means "friend of the court.") But political opposites Polland and Katine remain unimpressed with Justice Yates' rhetoric. They agree that the March 15, 2001, decision *was* political, not judicial.

"I think there was a connection between the public outcry among the party faithful and the [March 15, 2001, *en banc*] decision," Polland said. "Just shows you the judges do respond. Because after we started agitation when the case went amok, they [the *en banc* judges] just flushed it [the case] big time."

Katine agreed. "There are commentators who felt it was embarrassing enough for them [the *en banc* court] to have done what they did with [Justice Yates'] concurring opinion, saying, 'Well there is no political influence here.' When, even by acknowledging that, they acknowledged there is [political influence]," Katine said.

Was the *en banc* decision the result of political pressure?

"I think so," Katine said.

Like spectators following a ball at a tennis match, eyes now turned to the next rung on the legal appeal ladder: the Texas Court of Criminal Appeals.

In most states, the highest state court hears both criminal and civil matters. Texas is one of five states where there is a division of legal labor. Criminal appeals go to the Court of Criminal Appeals, dubbed by attorneys as the "Crim Apps," which hears only criminal cases. The Texas Supreme Court hears only appeals of civil cases.

The Texas Court of Criminal Appeals is the forum where the Texas Supreme Court, in *Morales* seven years earlier, told the homosexuals they must go.

On May 16, 2001, on request of Lambda Legal, the sodomy case went up to the Austin, Texas, Crim Apps, which—like the 14th Court of Appeals—was all Republican. The burden to convince the Crim Apps was on the defendants.

After keeping the case for almost a year, on April 19, 2002, the Crim Apps, without explanation, refused to hear the case.

Cynical observers saw the Crim Apps as dodging a known political danger, containing the potential to separate them from their judicial careers. Having witnessed the public, bloody political battles in Harris County, and resultant judicial casualties—well-honed survival instincts told the Crim Apps justices to avoid the fray.

Lambda Legal's New York City-based lawyers and the Harris County, Texas, District Attorney's office cast their eyes eastward to One First Street NE, Washington, D.C. 20543.

Lambda Legal filed a Writ of Certiorari asking the Supreme Court of the United States if they would hear the sodomy case.

On December 2, 2002, "the Supremes"—as they are known to lawyers—said, "Yes." They granted Lambda Legal's Writ of Certiorari. In lay terms, the Supreme Court asked Texas' lower courts to send up the case records for review.

Usually such records include truckloads of paper, including authenticated trial transcripts or depositions (sworn statements). Here, the only facts for the high court to study were Deputy Quinn's 69-word, handwritten, probable cause affidavits—written within hours of the arrests.

Supreme Court watchers think it may be the first time in history that the Court ruled with virtually no factual underpinnings.

Lawrence and Garner, who pled no contest at every stage of the legal proceedings, left no factual trail on an official record, not even a stipulation to those probable cause affidavits.

It was brilliant.

# Inside the 14th Court:
# Some Regrets

Looking back on his service as a justice on the 14th Court of Appeals when *Lawrence* traveled through, Justice Don Wittig, who voted with the majority to reinstate the Lawrence-Garner convictions, regrets not seizing the opportunity to publicly sound the alarm about a setup, by writing his thoughts as part of the court's March 15, 2001, opinion.

"I regretted not writing a concurrence on the setup issue," revealed Justice Wittig in a May 25, 2004, interview. Justice Wittig served on the 14th Court from 1999-2001. A concurrence is a separate written opinion, agreeing with the majority opinion, but based on different reasoning or legal theory.

The 14th is comprised of 14 south central Texas counties, which include Houston, the fourth-largest city in the United States. The 14th court is one level below Texas' highest criminal appeal court.

"I started to write a concurrence that pointed out that this [*Lawrence*] was a setup deal. There was no expectation of privacy," Justice Wittig said, speaking out publicly for the first time.

"As I recall, Lawrence and Company actually had the police come and catch them. In other words, they knew the police were coming. They set it up so the police *would* come. So there was no expectation of privacy," said Justice Wittig, a Vietnam veteran who served 11 years as a Harris County, Texas, civil trial court judge, before moving up to the appeal court.

"I started to write a short concurrence to say that, but I just didn't see how. If I had known then what I know now, I would have," revealed Justice Wittig.

"I'm pretty sure that the call to police was somehow directed by Lawrence and Company," he said, adopting a derisive *sobriquet* for *Lawrence* figures.

What gave Justice Wittig that impression?

"If you follow the record back to: 'How were the police called? Who called the police?' Assume hypothetically that you were engaged in illegal activity in your home. When you let the police in, wouldn't that illegal activity stop? If you were smoking a joint or snorting cocaine, wouldn't you flush it down the toilet before you let police in the door?

"So the police come in the door and catch them *en para delicto* (in the act). Even that points to the fact that it was a setup deal. It was a test case from the beginning. That part you probably picked up, didn't you?" Justice Wittig inquired.

"I don't remember whether it was in the briefs," the jurist continued. "I don't remember whether it was innuendo. But the fact that you were doing something illegal and the police came to your door, you would not continue the illegal activity. That is strong circumstantial evidence sufficient to say that *Lawrence* was a setup test case from the beginning.

"And look at the history of [the case]. They could have had a $100 fine and they don't do it. They fight it all the way. And that is pretty unusual too. So that is another circumstance that indicates [that it was a setup case].

"I think it was a setup case," Justice Wittig added.

If *Lawrence* was a case manufactured for litigation purposes, would that change the U.S. Supreme Court opinion favoring *Lawrence*?

"Yeah it would! Because there would be no expectation of privacy. So that ground goes out. Now we are back to equal protection [grounds]. They [the U.S. Supreme Court] obviously didn't have a majority [for equal protection grounds]," he observed.

Were the five deputies who responded to Lawrence's apartment on September 17, 1998, used?

"In a sense they were, yeah. The police are used with false accusations, false reports. They were doing their duty. They got a call and they followed up on the call. I'm not finding any fault with the police. The police did what they were supposed to do. Were the police used if it was a setup? Yes they were!

"Was the United States Supreme Court used? Yes they were! There is not a privacy issue because the first question about privacy is, 'Was there an *expectation* of privacy?' If you call the cops into your home and have them come in, there is no expectation of privacy!" Justice Wittig exclaimed.

The veteran jurist explained that ultimately he decided not to write a concurring opinion because "[*Lawrence*] was already too complicated, and taking too much of the court's time and everybody else's time."

"You don't see many constitutional cases in your legal career," Justice Wittig mused. He thinks *Lawrence v. Texas* may be the only case in the history of Texas' 14th Court of Appeals that went to the Supreme Court of the United States.

Why did he think the decision of the three-judge panel should be reviewed?

"I agreed more with the minority, and I didn't think Texas' Equal Rights Amendment even came into play," Justice Wittig remembered.

He revealed that while his friend Justice John Sharp Anderson was still drafting his June 5, 2000, opinion for the three-judge panel to overturn Lawrence and Garner's convictions, Justice Wittig tried unsuccessfully to persuade his colleague Justice Anderson out of basing his legal reasoning on Texas' Equal Rights Amendment.

"I was not happy with Anderson going ERA. I talked to him about going Equal Protection. I said that is a better way to go. [Supreme Court Justice] Sandra Day O'Connor is the only one who went equal protection [in the U.S. Supreme Court opinion]" Justice Wittig added.

"[In talking with Anderson] I thought Equal Protection was a more cogent argument. I didn't think the Equal Rights Amendment was ever intended to apply to a situation like [Lawrence]," Justice Wittig said. He said he never discussed the legal issues with Justice Murphy.

Does Justice Wittig have any idea where Justice Anderson came up with ERA as applicable?

"No, other than ERA was argued by Lawrence," Justice Wittig said.

Justice Wittig, 63, was born in San Antonio, Texas where he earned both an undergraduate and law degree from St. Mary's University. He served in Vietnam from 1967-68 where he "investigated and tried a case just like the [infamous] Mai Lai massacre."

He is now in private practice doing mediations and arbitrations. His law partner, Larry Thompson, is the brother of the late Tommy Thompson who wrote the nonfiction, mega best seller *Blood and Money*, based on two sensational Houston homicide cases.

No one could legitimately accuse former Justice, Murry B. Cohen, of being a conservative. Justice Cohen served 19 years on the Houston-based 1st Court of Appeals beginning in 1982. He announced late in his judicial career that he was switching from Democrat to Republican, as had several Democrat judges who saw local political tides turning against Democrats. But Justice Cohen remained a quintessential liberal, despite any political affiliations changed on paper.

His wife, Meryl, and Gary Polland's wife, Esther, were both involved with Planned Parenthood, an organization despised by the religious right.

Justice Cohen did not serve on the 14th Court of Appeals, which handled the *Lawrence* case. But the two appeal courts share the same, small downtown building and friendships with appellate court colleagues.

He has left the court and is now in private practice.

"I hope you're going to write about the setup in the *Lawrence* case," Justice Cohen told me when we met at a November 2004 social function. It was his initial comment to me immediately after I told him about my book.

Was Lawrence a manufactured case?

"Yes, of course it was! I have no proof. But it was a setup. It just was! There were too many coincidences," Justice Cohen exclaimed.

He is no novice at parsing the nuances of arrests.

Justice Cohen has been board certified in criminal law since 1977. In 1983, he served as an examiner for criminal law certification on the Texas Board of Legal Specialization.

Born in 1945, Justice Cohen, a 1979 graduate of the University of Texas School of Law, served as a Harris County Assistant District Attorney from 1973-75. A Houston native, he graduated from George Washington University and has served as an adjunct professor of law at the University of Houston and South Texas College of Law in Houston.

# Who Is Lambda Legal?

Lambda Legal's mission statement describes it as:

"A national organization committed to achieving full recognition of the civil rights of lesbians, gay men, bisexuals, the transgendered, and people with HIV or AIDS through impact litigation, education, and public policy work.

"Lambda Legal carries out its legal work principally through test cases selected for the likelihood of their success in establishing positive legal precedents ... From our offices in New York, Los Angeles, Chicago, Atlanta and Dallas, Lambda Legal's staff of attorneys works on a wide range of cases, with our docket averaging over 50 cases at any given time.

"Lambda Legal also maintains a national network of volunteer Cooperating Attorneys, which widens the scope of our legal work and allows attorneys, legal workers, and law students to become involved in our program by working with our legal staff.

"Lambda Legal pursues litigation in all parts of the country, in every area of the law that affects communities we represent, such as discrimination in employment, housing, public accommodations and the military ... parenting and relationship issues; equal marriage rights; equal employment and domestic partner benefits, "sodomy" law challenges; immigration issues, anti-gay initiatives, and free speech and equal protection rights"

Several articles refer to Lambda as "the country's oldest and most prestigious gay legal advocacy organization."

A Lambda attorney said the origin of the organization's name is unclear. She said the most commonly offered explanation is that in the era when homosexuals feared being identified, the name "Lambda" was selected to camouflage from outsiders the group's true nature, and purpose. "Lambda" made it sound like a college sorority or fraternity.

For Internal Revenue Service purposes, Lambda is a 501(c) (3) charity.

Lambda's 2002 budget was $7 million, raised from private donations, and grants from foundations including the Ford Foundation. But IRS regulations do not require 501 (c) (3) organizations to list publicly which foundations are contributors. Eric Ferrero, Lambda's communications director, declined to respond to several requests to list foundation donors, and other information.

Lambda Legal maintains an extensive Web site.

Katine said that in a public speech, Lambda official Ken Lott of the Dallas regional office told his audience that Lambda spent $750,000 litigating *Lawrence v. Texas.*

Lambda headquarters occupy half a floor of ultra-upscale office space in some of New York City's most expensive real estate at 120 Wall Street, an art deco building on the corner of South Avenue, just down the street from the New York Stock Exchange.

Through a small reception area are warrens of perhaps 30-to-40 office cubicles. The decor is light beige, unfussy, plain. Clearly, the Lambda organization has no financial problems.

When Lambda Legal's New York City-based attorneys

said goodbye to cowboy boots and conservatives—yanking their briefcases after three years of litigating in Texas where they were outsiders—they headed for Washington, D.C., where Texas' clout wielders Hotze, Harmon and Polland wouldn't have as much sway.

In the nation's capital, Lambda's Ivy League educational degrees and professional attainments matched those of the justices before whom they would appear, and from whom they were seeking relief.

The Harris County, Texas, DA's office then would be the outsider in 2003 as *Lawrence* climbed to the highest rung on America's legal ladder.

The playing fields and the roles were switched.

Lambda Legal was the home team that knew the patrician justices and the terrain's subtleties. In fact, Lambda had scored judicial thumbs-up in this legal coliseum before.

On May 20, 1996, with Lambda attorneys as advocates, the U.S. Supreme Court in *Romer v. Evans* ruled that a Colorado-voter-approved, State constitutional amendment prohibiting protected status for homosexuals, was unconstitutional as a violation of the Equal Protection clause. Romer was governor of Colorado.

Suzanne B. Goldberg, the tall, intense, rail-thin, Harvard educated Lambda attorney who shepherded *Lawrence* initially in Houston, successfully masterminded *Romer* in Colorado.

Just as Goldberg and other skilled Lambda lawyers in 1996 left behind the conservative groups who bedeviled them in Colorado—in 2003, they left behind similar forces in Texas.

Although their public goal in 2003 was victory in *Lawrence*—their private hope, their private goal, was overturning the 1986 *Bowers v. Harwick* U.S. Supreme Court decision they hated with devoted passion. The ruling upheld the constitutionality of Georgia's law criminalizing consensual homosexual *and* heterosexual sodomy.

As they would acknowledge publicly later, *Lawrence* was the vehicle Lambda used to, in effect, re-litigate the sexual issues in *Bowers*.

My interviews with many of the participants in *Lawrence* revealed that oral and anal sodomy is the essential sexual intimacy that defines homosexuals' self-identity.

To proclaim consensual same-sex sodomy as criminal not only degraded their innermost sexual desires, but branded homosexuals *as* criminals—it affected their self-esteem, and their working or professional lives as well, Lambda felt.

"Down with *Bowers*" was the intellectual rallying cry.

But, ironically, after 1996, prospects for sodomy arrests dimmed as society became more accepting of gays.

Circumstances of a "genuine" arrest to test the constitutionality of Texas' 21.06 presented a legal conundrum—difficult without violating Fourth Amendment prohibitions on search and seizure. Without exigent circumstances, authorities wouldn't be able to invade a home's interior to prosecute a misdemeanor sodomy violation.

Since the sex act would be consensual and occur in private, logically one of the participants would have to summon police to invite the arrest. But if one of the same-sex participants invited police observers (*"We're having sex! Come on over!"*), or *complicit* third parties invited observers (*"They're having sex! Come on over!"*), that *invitation* would destroy claims of an expectation of privacy, thus precluding a constitutional challenge on privacy grounds.

So police would have to encounter a 21.06 violation after entering private premises for a legally defensible reason other than same-sex sodomy—and, ideally, under exigent circumstances (commission of a felony, immediate danger of death or serious bodily injury).

The factual circumstances—required for an arrest under 21.06 to be legally sufficient to use as a vehicle for a constitutional challenge—were so narrow as to almost eliminate happenstance.

Deliberately violating 21.06 required precise events, tailored exactly to the criminal misdemeanor statute.

Those exact events, in perfect order, occurred in the Lawrence and Garner arrests.

Addressing attendees of a *Lawrence* seminar at South Texas College of Law in Houston on February 14, 2004, Lambda's Suzanne Goldberg explained that as the years passed since 1986 *Bowers,* and 1996 *Romer*, with no suitable *criminal* case they could use, Lambda Legal became more and more desperate to find a case to test consensual sodomy law.

They were tired of waiting.

Fingers were drumming on tables.

Their patience was growing very, very thin.

They found themselves in the ironic position of hoping to be arrested and prosecuted under a Texas statute that, by its terms and history, almost precluded arrest. If Texas' law was struck down, all similar laws in other states would be negated as well, under U.S. Supreme Court precedent.

Lambda called a strategizing summit meeting of national homosexual organizations in early 1998.

By 1998, Justices Byron White, Warren Burger and Lewis Powell, who voted with the majority in the 1986 *Bowers* court, were dead. In 1998, when Lawrence and Garner were arrested, only two justices from the *Bowers* majority remained: Justices Sandra Day O'Connor and William H. Rehnquist.

With such a reconfigured legal playing field, Lambda's hope sprang high.

"I have to say my personal involvement with *Lawrence v. Texas* [began] even before, well before John [Lawrence] and Tyron [Garner] were arrested [September 17, 1998]," Goldberg revealed in her opening remarks to the February 2004 Houston seminar.

"After the *Romer* decision came down in 1996, the lawyers at Lambda Legal got together with the lawyers of the other national lesbian and gay legal groups. We talked about: 'What do we do with *Romer*? How do we make the *Romer* decision mean something beyond the scope of that particular Colorado amendment?' One of the places we immediately turned to was: 'We need to challenge sodomy laws. We need to challenge the [about] dozen or so remaining sodomy laws around the country.' Why?" Goldberg asked rhetorically.

"Because sodomy laws branded gay people as walking criminals. Maybe you weren't arrested yet, but if you were gay you were presumably violating a law that says engaging in oral or anal sex is prohibited. Lots of these laws were what we at Lambda finally called the equal opportunity laws. The laws for anybody. It meant most of the states that still had sodomy laws prohibited these acts to anybody," she told her Houston audience.

"So after *Romer* we [at the summit meeting of national homosexual organizations] said: "Now is the time. Now we have a way [with *Romer*] to go after sodomy laws," she continued. "Our thinking was: 'We are not going to blaze a path to full equality for lesbians and gay men in this country until we get rid of these laws that criminalize the sexual intimacy of lesbians and gay men.

"What does all that have to do with *Lawrence*? We will not advance towards full equality for gay people unless the laws that deem gay people's sexual intimacy [as] criminal are invalidated.

"So we started researching. We researched: 'OK, let's look at all of the states that have these laws. Let's figure out which ones we can challenge," Goldberg revealed.

Although Texas didn't realize it, in 1998, Lambda Legal—partnering with other national homosexual rights groups—fixed its crosshairs on the Lone Star State, taking careful, interested aim at an inviting legal target— 21.06.

"That [national strategy meeting] was in early 1998. Later in 1998, Mitchell [Katine] called and said: 'I have these two guys John Lawrence and Tyron Garner who have been arrested inside an [Houston, Texas] apartment and charged with violating the Homosexual Conduct law,'" Goldberg continued, returning to the topic of Texas.

In what she says was an amazing coincidence of timing, Lambda Legal was just minutes away from a legal department staff meeting on the very day Houston attorney Mitchell Katine phoned Goldberg at Lambda Legal's New York headquarters. Katine phoned to tell her of the Lawrence and Garner arrests, she said.

Neither she nor Katine, who keep meticulous records on all their activities, can recall the exact date on which Katine made the historic phone call, for which they had all waited for years. The phone call that, from their perspective, would free them from sexual tyranny.

"[*Lawrence*] was the perfect case," she said.

Although I spoke briefly with Goldberg in person in Houston that February day, she did not respond to subsequent e-mails from me or through Lambda, for a full interview.

Ruth E. Harlow, born in 1961 in the small, Midwestern company town of Midland, Michigan, served as Lambda Legal Director during most of the nearly five-year pendency of *Lawrence*. She is identified by all factions as THE architect of the historic legal victory.

Harlow earned an undergraduate degree from Stanford University, then graduated from Yale Law School.

"My late father was a lawyer for Dow Chemical, but he was more of a businessman than a lawyer," Harlow said. "My mother was a housewife. I was a curious and motivated child, the youngest in my family. I got to the point where I wanted to see a bigger world." She has two brothers and one sister. Her mother is still living.

"I convinced my parents to send me, at 14 years old, to boarding school in Andover, Massachusetts. My father was a big advocate of public schools, and didn't want to send me away. But once he visited Andover, he thought maybe this is a good idea. Andover is the place where I got my idealism and learned about civil rights. Andover is very rigorous academically. I love learning. It was a great thing for me." The flat, vaguely nasal tone of her voice reflects Harlow's Midwest past.

"At Stanford University I thought I wanted to be a chemist. But I took a seminar in my freshman year, taught by a woman named Lois Scheinfeld, on housing discrimination. She taught our group of college freshmen how to write briefs and do appellate argument. That fascinated me," Harlow explained in a July 31, 2004, telephone interview.

"Through a friend from Andover, I arranged a summer job in New York City after my freshman year, with John Doar, a former Justice Department attorney in the 1960s. He is a mild-mannered, quiet guy but he managed to have a big role in history. I found it inspirational. He had the biggest role in sending me off to be a civil rights lawyer," Harlow said. (Doar did not respond to an e-mail request for a comment about Ruth Harlow).

Doar congratulated her after the *Lawrence* decision. "He told me he was proud of me," Harlow said.

Although Ruth Harlow's public persona is serious and studious—her lodging choice of The Hotel Rouge for the defendants and top Lambda people when *Lawrence* was argued before the Supreme Court perhaps reveals her inapposite, playful alter ego.

The hotel, near Washington, D.C.'s downtown, is decorated almost entirely in red, and offers a signature drink "The Adultress." "If you're lucky, the hypnotiq girls will be there to give you free shots. *Tres tres debaucher*," writes one hotel reviewer. Reservations can be made only on the Internet.

"I picked the hotel. I wanted us to stay at a place that was fun and upbeat, not too expensive. It was a fun place to stay," Harlow remembered.

*The National Law Journal,* which selected Harlow as 2003 Attorney of the Year, wrote that her colleagues described her as "chief strategist, meticulous brief writer, brilliant and humble [who] shepherded to victory the most important gay rights case in a century, *Lawrence*."

"Ruth is really the person who guided (*Lawrence*) in its major years," Lambda Executive Director Kevin Cathcart said.

"So confident was Harlow that the [sodomy] law would be struck down that she planned to launch a new career after the justices ruled. She has since left law for architecture," the *Journal* wrote on December 22, 2003. But Harlow's architectural dalliance was short-lived. In July 2004 she joined the New York City-based law firm of White & Case.

Of the team that shepherded the *Lawrence* case, only attorneys Patricia Logue and Susan Sommer remained at Lambda after the Supreme Court's June 26, 2003, decision. Suzanne Goldberg teaches at Rutgers University Law School.

The four women—Goldberg, Harlow, Logue and Sommer—met in the gay rights movement. Susan Sommer, who is heterosexual, was Harlow's classmate at Yale Law School, Class of 1986, where she worked on law review.

Sommer, who in photos bears a vague resemblance to husky-voiced veteran actress Elizabeth Ashley, also received her bachelor's degree from Yale, where she graduated Phi Beta Kappa and summa cum laude. Like Harlow, she was born in 1961.

Susan Sommer and her husband, a health care attorney, have three children.

Born in New York City, Sommer said she "grew up in a liberal Jewish family, not observant. I grew up debating civil rights and other issues of the day." Right after law school, Sommer clerked in San Francisco for a federal judge, then joined a large New York City law firm. "I talked to Ruth [Harlow]," she said. "And the next thing I knew I began working at Lambda. Four years ago when I began working, there was one other lawyer who was not gay or lesbian. Now there are a few more. We are definitely in the minority."

Sommer said her job during the March 26, 2003, oral argument was to sit in the courtroom with John Lawrence. "We wanted to make sure he would not be bombarded by reporters or anybody. That wasn't what he wanted," she remembered. "When we got up to leave, to walk down the aisle, he took my hand. I held his hand as we walked out of the courtroom. It was a very moving time to make a connection over it. But also I think it was just that the courtroom was very crowded, to make sure we didn't lose each other to get out together. It was just an incredible day."

Patricia M. Logue, the fourth member of the Lambda Legal quartet working the *Lawrence* case, also has Yale in her background. Both her parents graduated from Yale, as did all her uncles. She was raised in a Roman Catholic family.

After earning her BA degree in 1981 from Ivy League Brown University, which she chose "because it wasn't Yale," Logue received her law degree, cum laude, in 1986 from Northwestern University, then worked in labor litigation at a Chicago law firm. She heads Lambda's Midwest office, opened in 1993 in Chicago.

"It [*Lawrence*] was the ultimate, clean case," Logue—who, in photos, resembles avant-garde artist Andy Warhol—is quoted.

Hiram Sasser, a young attorney who authored an *amicus* brief filed in the Supreme Court on behalf of a conservative organization, Liberty Legal, supporting retention of 21.06, was generous in praise of his opponents' legal acumen.

"They [Lambda] do a very good job of what they are doing. They are no slouches," Sasser said. "Their objective is to make sure that marriage is defined as whatever they want it to be defined as. If you don't like that idea, you will be shouted down so to speak, or you will be shut down. Your company will be forced to extend same-sex benefits

and all that kind of thing. It's basically a forced acknowl-
edgement and recognition that the gay lifestyle is OK.
Really to me that is what I perceive as their agenda."

To Sasser, and many other conservative observers,
*Lawrence* was never the main interest of the homosexual
community. *Lawrence* was a tool. Merely a means to an
end of unlatching the floodgates to the institution of
same-sex marriage.

*Bowers v. Hardwick* was always Lambda's real target,
Sasser said. Because as long as *Bowers* remained the
controlling precedent, the sexual acts implicit in marriage
were illegal.

"*Bowers* is the whole point of *Lawrence.* The whole
point of *Lawrence* was really about advancing the attack
on traditional marriage. The whole point of *Lawrence* was
to get another case under their belt in order for the gay
folks to be able to then attack the idea of traditional marriage only being between a man and a woman," Sasser
said.

Leaders in the homosexual community do not deny
that premise.

# Speaking for History:
# The U.S. Supreme Court

Tall, bespectacled attorney Paul M. Smith strode from the pale-green carpeted attorneys' lounge, down the white-columned hallway toward the United States Supreme Court courtroom on March 26, 2003. Friends, acquaintances, well-wishers and colleagues slapped him on the back, shook hands, and greeted him with the same high enthusiasm with which he greeted them.

For Smith, then 47, this was homecoming.

Smith, managing partner of the prestigious Jenner & Block law firm in Washington, D.C., had argued in the high court many previous times. Having clerked in 1980-81 for U.S. Supreme Court Justice Lewis F. Powell Jr., Smith understood not only the strict formality of the court's public face, but more importantly, was sensitive to the nuanced significance of day-to-day judicial life in chambers.

Like the Lambda attorney quartet, whom he said had "put me through the ringer" preparing him for March 26, Smith's platinum academic attainments matched those of the justices before whom he was about to appear.

Paul Smith was their credentialed, high-achiever mirror image, and they his.

A Brahmin addressing Brahmins.

Smith was born March 9, 1955, in Salt Lake City, Utah, then moved within a few months to California, his parents' home state. Smith said of his personal background, "We lived in Los Angeles, and then near San Jose, California, until I was 11, when we moved to the New York City suburb of Stamford, Connecticut. I attended public high school in Stamford, but graduated from the International School of Geneva, Switzerland, which I attended for one year when my father was transferred to France. All of these moves, after the move from Utah were transfers by IBM. My father has a PhD in math, and taught for two years before joining IBM. My mother was a teacher, and later, in business. My father's father was a lawyer."

After graduating summa cum laude in 1976 from Amherst College, Smith, like Justice Clarence Thomas, graduated from Yale Law School.

Smith, who graduated Phi Beta Kappa in 1979, served as editor in chief of the Yale Law Review. Being law review editor is considered one of the highest achievements at any law school. Highly visible to lawyers and judges living in Washington, D.C., as president and board member of the Washington Council of Lawyers, Smith was also a member of the steering committee of the District of Columbia Bar.

In colloquial terms, Smith knew the proper fork to use. He was an insider's insider.

Lambda head strategist Ruth Harlow—who ceded her opportunity for oral argument to him, handpicking Smith to argue *Lawrence*—had chosen legal talent both wisely and well.

"Paul [Smith] stood up there as an openly gay man, a former Supreme Court clerk, someone they were comfortable with. And he gave *gravitas* to what we were all saying," Harlow explained in the December 2003 *National Law Journal.*

"It was the most intensive preparation that I have ever done," Smith told the *Journal* about his interaction with Lambda's woodshedding foursome. "There weren't many legal or technical issues to address. It was more about how to talk to the court about the subject and how they would respond."

In his interview, Katine cut to the chase lawyer-style: "We were going to the United States Supreme Court to talk about sex."

As Smith entered a special side door of the high court, where the rising sun casts rays along the marbled sidewalk, he noticed devoted spectators who had camped out on the sidewalk for 24 hours, hoping to qualify for one of the limited seats in the small courtroom.

"I am always nervous. The feeling was unique here because of the historic importance of the case and because of the expectations of the huge crowd of very sophisticated onlookers, including many of the people most involved in promoting GLBT [gay-lesbian-bisexual-transgender] rights for the past decade or two," Smith said.

Among the onlookers was U.S. Representative Barney Frank, a Massachusetts Democrat, and the only openly gay legislator in the U.S. House. Frank did not respond to a written request for comments about the case.

Smith estimates he labored three weeks, full-time, preparing for the 30-minute presentation.

"I'd estimate I spent about 120-to-140 hours preparing. I had another Supreme Court argument that kept me busy until three weeks before [*Lawrence*]. Of course we [Lambda] had just completed the briefing. So the issues and case law were not unfamiliar," Smith indicated.

Two cases are heard each morning in the high court. March 26, 2003, a dry civil case was heard first—then *Lawrence.*

The Supreme Court chamber, flanked by 24 marble columns, is relatively small, measuring 82-by-91 feet, but rising 44 feet to a coffered ceiling of decorative, sunken square panels. The bench and furniture is mahogany.

Along the top of all four sides of the chamber, sculpted marble panels depict legal themes and famous lawgivers.

Light streams in from courtyards, through floor-to-ceiling windows on each side, filtered through old-fashioned venetian blinds, and tall, elaborate filigree brass screens.

The ambience exudes a message that this room is for serious matters.

The real deal.

The scene was five years and a world away from Justice of the Peace Court on Wallisville Road in Houston, Texas, where the case began with Judge Parrott, who is not an attorney.

A little known irony is that JP Court and the Supreme Court of the United States—the lowest and highest points of the tiered judicial system—are the only courts where there is no legal requirement that the judges be attorneys.

As participants and observers settled in, filling every available nook and cranny, Paul Smith lifted the white quill from his podium. The feather memento is traditionally provided to each attorney who argues before the court. Turning with a flourish, he presented the quill to Houston attorney Mitchell Katine, in recognition of Katine's devotion to the case.

Each speaker has exactly 30 minutes. Attorneys are instructed beforehand on the courtly, strict, formalistic language and behavior expected.

Smith, his red-blond hair accentuated in the lighting, stepped forward first.

The arguing attorney stands behind a wooden lectern directly in front of the Chief Justice. There are two lights on the podium. Additional lights, visible only to the speaker, are in front. When the white light goes on, the attorney has five remaining minutes to argue. When the red light goes on, argument is over. The attorney has used all the allotted time.

When court convenes at the crack of a gavel, everyone rises. The marshal chants:

> "The Honorable, the Chief Justice and the Associate Justices of the Supreme Court of the United States. Oyez! Oyez! Oyez! All persons having business before the Honorable, the Supreme Court of the United States are admonished to draw near and give their attention, for the Court is now sitting. God save the United States and this Honorable Court!"

Like great winged birds, the full sleeves of their black robes flapping, justices swoop into the high-ceilinged courtroom simultaneously, by three front entrances through a red curtain behind the bench. Chief Justice William Rehnquist and two senior associate justices enter through the center. Three other associate justices enter through each side, seating themselves in order of seniority. A clerk sits behind each, waiting any request.

The chief justice occupies the middle seat under a huge, round gold clock hanging from the ceiling. The others alternate left to right, ending with the most junior associate justice on the far right, as the speaker faces the nine jurists.

Everyone remains standing until the justices are seated.

"Mr. Chief Justice, and may it please the court," Smith began in perfect accordance with stringent court rules.

There would be no second chances. No excuses.

Like an Olympic race, this was it.

Hear the starter gun. Run as fast as you can.

Don't fall down.

All the years of work and preparation culminated in these relatively few moments in the unforgiving glare of an international spotlight.

Attorneys are warned that, as in lower appellate

courts, justices frequently interrupt the advocate with peppering questions. As a Supreme Court clerk himself, Smith had observed successful techniques for maintaining poise and equanimity under the barrage of inquiry.

After Smith uttered six sentences, Chief Justice Rehnquist fired the first question, challenging Smith on the length of the historical ban on sodomy.

> *Chief Justice Rehnquist:* "On your substantive due process, [what] we're talking about here has been banned for a long time. Now you point to a trend in the other direction, which would be fine if you're talking about the Eighth Amendment. But I think our case is like Glucksberg, say if you're talking about a right that is going to be sustained, it has to have been recognized for a long time. And that simply isn't so."

Masterfully employing successful political techniques, Smith eruditely responded to a justice's question, adroitly returning to "stay on message."

Thrust and parry. Verbally thrust and parry for 30 minutes exactly.

Then Smith sat down.

Lambda attorney Susan Sommer described Smith's presentation to the court as "eloquent and elegant, poised. Beautifully done. Not a missed step." Attorneys on both sides agreed. Smith's was a *bravura* performance.

After Harris County District Attorney Chuck Rosenthal used his 30 minutes of argument, Smith and the courtroom crowd emptied to a press conference on the gray-marble front steps of the august Supreme Court building. Photos show media mobbing Smith and Lambda principals.

Having thus worked up an appetite, Smith and the joyous entourage of national notables from homosexual communities across the U.S. convened to a preplanned luncheon about three blocks away at La Colline, one of Washington D.C.'s finest French restaurants.

On the clear, crisp, bright sunshiny day they collectively walked a victor's stride entering under the restaurant's long, green awning at 400 North Capitol Street, Northwest.

The U.S. Capitol's white dome is visible from the windows of the chic eatery, where *terrine de foie gras* is a house specialty. Participants estimate that as many as 100 people attended, among them Mitchell Katine, and defendant John Geddes Lawrence.

Ruth Harlow sat at the round table one seat away, to Paul Smith's left. Harlow's colleague Patricia Logue sat at her left. In photographs, Harlow had a smile that seemed incandescent, lighting her usually serious face.

How did Smith foresee what the high court might rule?

"I felt pretty optimistic, with some small concerns because Justices O'Connor and Kennedy had been uncharacteristically quiet," Smith said.

In about 90 days, the court would make public its decision.

# Muffing the Lines:
# The District Attorney Stumbles

There were no magna cum laude or Phi Beta Kappa academic laurels listed behind Charles A. Rosenthal Jr.'s 1976 graduation from South Texas College of Law in Houston.

Rosenthal, who began working in the Harris County District Attorney's Office right after being admitted to the Texas Bar in 1977, periodically attracted notoriety for his less intellectual—more earthy—escapades.

Locally, Rosenthal had garnered an eyebrow-raising reputation light years removed from patrician Paul Smith and the pedigreed justices of the Supreme Court of the United States.

Rosenthal's league wasn't Ivy.

"Chuck" or "Chuckie" as Rosenthal was called, was most infamous for two incidents, although there were omnifarious Rosenthal rogueries from which to choose.

In one incident, on February 1, 2000, it came to public light in the *Houston Chronicle* that over his years as an assistant district attorney, Rosenthal habitually compiled and distributed to the DA's office and to others, *his* list of judicial candidates and incumbents who merit the DA's office vote.

His 1998 list was the one that finally came to public attention.

Rosenthal proudly entitled his endorsements the "Bar Poll"—perhaps hoping that readers might conclude it was the genuine Bar Poll done by the Houston Bar Association, but adding his byline name to the right, to avoid any real confusion.

Although Rosenthal's 1998 list profanely trashed nearly all local judges including me, most publicly sensational were his comments maligning Judge Pam Derbyshire, whose chambers were next door to mine. Rosenthal's comments about her inferred anti-Semitism.

Judge Derbyshire is Jewish.

Because less than 30 percent of registered voters vote in party primaries locally, the block of 300-plus votes from the DA's office is significant enough to change election outcomes.

Demonstrating that he retained some sense of humor, retiring DA Holmes claimed in the *Chronicle* article that he knew absolutely nothing about Rosenthal's endorsement list for the 1998 election cycle, despite the fact that Rosenthal was a Holmes confidante for those many years of distributing the list throughout the DA's office.

According to the February 1 *Chronicle* article, many of Rosenthal's "recommendations" were too profane to print in a family newspaper.

In an earlier escapade, reported in the September 22, 1995 *Chronicle,* Rosenthal tossed firecrackers down the stairwell of the multistory district attorneys office building, frightening staff working late. Rosenthal was 49 years young at the time, and had worked at the DA's office for 18 years. He took some intra-office discipline for that middle-aged frolic.

When the Hotze-Harmon-Blakemore Republican political machine of Harris County put Chuckie forward in 1999 as its candidate to replace the retiring Holmes in the 2000 election, outsiders were puzzled. In the DA's office hierarchy, Rosenthal had climbed only as high as one of several chiefs of felony divisions. He was several promotional rungs down from First Assistant, the top prosecutor next to the DA. And, if even only some of the whisperings were true, Chuckie had a closetful of embarrassments.

But with machine backing, Rosenthal easily won the countywide election in 2000 to ascend Holmes' throne.

Insiders were not at all surprised at Rosenthal being the machine's DA designee.

Rosenthal perfectly fit the machine's preference to fill positions of genuine power with a pretentious, physically attractive, intellectual dim bulb who is politically and financially needy. A malleable candidate, subject to flattery, of weak character, who remembers, without being reminded, on which side his political bread is buttered

Born February 7, 1946, Rosenthal graduated from Houston's Lamar High School, as did Holmes. He received a BA degree in psychology from Baylor University, Waco, Texas. He is married to Cynthia Hoover, an FBI agent, his second marriage.

Chuckie reminded me of the vain, vacuous news anchor Ted Baxter on the popular, classic Mary Tyler Moore television-comedy ensemble cast—only a grumpy, unsmiling version.

After Smith spoke, Chuckie Rosenthal rose to speak on behalf of the State of Texas at the podium in front of the Supreme Court of the United States on March 26, 2003. The rest of the nation was about to see for themselves, firsthand, the dirty little secret the Harris County, Texas, legal community had whispered for years. Unfortunately for Rosenthal, the marshal's opening chant asking that God save the Court, had not included Chuck Rosenthal.

Rosenthal was like a pair of scuffed boots in a room of spit-shined wing tips.

*New York Times* reporter Linda Greenhouse, unfavorably comparing Rosenthal's groping presentation to Paul Smith's seamless perfection, sniffed: "The argument proved to be a mismatch of advocates to a degree rarely seen at the court."

"It was . . . shocking," exclaimed Suzanne Goldberg, visibly shuddering at the remembrance of Rosenthal's ineptitude.

Nine times during Rosenthal's presentation, the audience erupted in laughter, unprecedented in anyone's memory. "And most were laughing *at* Rosenthal, not with him," said Hiram Sasser.

"Early on, the justices smelled Rosenthal's blood in the water, so they toyed with him for their intellectual amusement, and the amusement of the audience," Sasser remembered.

"It was an embarrassing day to be from Texas," said Houston attorney John Nechman, a Katine friend who accompanied Katine and Lawrence to the capital.

"I didn't do as well as I'd like," Rosenthal told the *Chronicle.*

As national media swarmed around Smith and the Lambda *coterie* when the crowd adjourned to the courthouse steps, photos show Rosenthal and a lone companion descending the marble staircase along the side, unnoticed and unsought by the feverish national press. Rosenthal attracted no media suitors.

"Rosenthal stopped and stood off to the side for awhile, watching Smith and the reporters. No one was coming over to ask him anything. Finally, Rosenthal walked over to them. They asked him a few questions. It was kind of sad," remembered Nechman, who photographed the poignant scene.

Rosenthal took a taxi back to his hotel room, alone.

What was the mood on the flight back to Houston?

"I can't really speak for Chuck's mood. I was relieved

that it was over, and a little bit concerned about how the argument had gone," Assistant District Attorney Delmore said.

Could Delmore be more specific about how the argument had gone?

"No!" Delmore exclaimed emphatically, raising his voice slightly.

Early on, when the Supreme Court agreed to review *Lawrence*, Delmore faced the important issue of who would present the oral argument on behalf of Texas on a national stage. Conventional wisdom among attorneys is that although cases are rarely won on oral argument, cases *can* be lost on oral argument.

Delmore said early on he presented Rosenthal with three options: 1) Delmore or Assistant District Attorney Scott Durfee, both experienced in appellate appearances, could argue the case; 2) prosecutors could hire [or maybe get pro bono] an attorney experienced in arguing to the U.S. Supreme Court [as Lambda did]; or 3) Rosenthal could argue.

Rosenthal didn't hesitate long over his decision.

"I remember Chuck slept on it. He phoned me the day after I gave those three options. He said I'd like to do it myself," Delmore remembered.

Delmore said the prosecution never really investigated seeking expert outside help, because early on Rosenthal quickly expressed an interest in doing the argument. "There are probably a number of people who would have been willing to argue that case on fairly short notice," Delmore added.

One does not argue with one's boss.

Delmore said Rosenthal's entire preparation consisted of three sessions of a morning or an afternoon each.

"The first was about three weeks before March 26, 2003—an informal in-house here [in the office] just to get Chuck warmed up. Senior prosecutors at the DA's office acted as judges," Delmore recalled.

The second prep session was about a week later at South Texas College of Law in Houston.

Rosenthal's third and final prep session was Monday in D.C. before the Wednesday argument. "One of the amicus volunteered to set it up at a foundation in Washington. I do not remember the name of the foundation," Delmore said.

Tuesday, the morning before the argument, "we attended Supreme Court arguments (in other cases) to give Chuck a little familiarity with the courtroom itself, and the procedures and so forth. We also saw another argument the morning of the *Lawrence* case."

And Rosenthal's reaction to scathing criticism of his 30 minutes of international fame?

"I don't read that stuff," Rosenthal explained to the *Chronicle*.

# The Loyal Opposition:
# Hiram Sasser

Affable, tall, lanky, smiling, fresh-faced Hiram Sasser makes you think: Oklahoma cowboy. No doubt about it. Rope a calf? No problem, sir.

His buzz hair cut bespeaks military: United States Army Reserves.

Sasser, at 26, and just graduated from Oklahoma City University School of Law in 2002, authored a *Lawrence* amicus brief filed in the U.S. Supreme Court by Liberty Legal—a Dallas-based conservative organization funded privately. He serves as Litigation Director on a two-attorney staff.

Sasser's brief, entitled "Brief of Amici Curiae Texas Legislators, Representative Warren Chisum, et al., in Support of Respondent" was one of about a dozen amicus briefs extolling wide-ranging views on the issues, filed by various groups and individuals.

The 29-page brief is signed by 69 Texas state legislators, including six state senators.

Amicus briefs, are also known as friend of the court briefs, and may be filed in criminal and civil cases. In lay terms, amicus briefs, advocating one side of the case, are a sort of public lobbying effort by interested parties, presenting arguments and information to supplement briefs filed by the main litigants.

Liberty Legal's mission statement says:

> "Liberty Legal Institute, founded in 1997 by Chief Counsel Kelly Shackelford, fights to protect religious freedoms and First Amendment rights for individuals, groups and churches. Liberty Legal's assistance is provided free of charge to ensure all individuals and groups can thrive without the fear of governments restricting their freedoms.
>
> "Liberty Legal successfully battles in the courts for religious freedoms, student's [sic] rights, parental rights, the definition of family, and other freedoms.
>
> "The Institute offers its assistance pro bono. Attorneys across Texas donate their professional expertise and time to fight for these sacred freedoms.
>
> "Liberty Legal is headquartered in Plano, Texas with affiliate offices located in Dallas, Houston, Austin, Midland, Lubbock and San Antonio."

Liberty Legal has been described as the conservative counterpart to the American Civil Liberties Union (ACLU). The headquarters office is at 903 18th Street, in Plano, Texas, a Dallas suburb.

In a 2004 appearance before the appellate section of the Houston Bar Association (HBA), Sasser won the sophisticated audience's attention with careful timing and clever one-liners rivaling the skills of a professional comedian. He used his finely polished wit and sarcasm to keep the scholarly appellate attorneys laughing. Sasser is an outstanding public speaker.

Sasser told the HBA seminar that on the morning of March 26, 2003, the day of oral argument, he strained to retain his sense of humor as he trudged to the "ensuing debacle that was going to happen." Sasser did not retain much confidence that his side, which sought to uphold 21.06, would prevail.

*"Maybe the justices will be beamed away. Maybe space*

*aliens will swoop down, capture them, and speed off. Maybe a miracle will happen,"* Sasser, a devoted Star Trek fan, remembered thinking to himself as he walked into the high court that day.

"That was really the only way that I could perceive that Texas was going to win *Lawrence*—if you had a massive reconfiguration of the U.S. Supreme Court in about 10 minutes! Everybody knew which way this case was going to go. The Supreme Court was going to strike down the [consensual] sodomy law."

Weeks earlier, five minutes of observing DA Chuckie Rosenthal struggling to cope with legal argument clued Sasser that "it was really going to be bad." A national embarrassment in the making.

Well before March 26, Liberty Legal contacted Rosenthal offering free expertise on appellate argument styles, tactics, strategies, and presentation, in the form of moot court sessions. Moot court is a fancy name for practice court.

"I pretty much knew the first five minutes of the first moot that this was an uphill battle," Sasser remembered, sighing. "Doing appellate argument is a lot different than being in a trial. You could tell that Chuck Rosenthal had never done an appellate argument in his life. He never had. It was kind of frustrating to see that. That was the state of the situation. That's what you got to live with."

How does appellate argument differ from argument to a trial court jury?

"[In the appellate court] you are dealing with a much higher level of intellectual plane. You are talking to experienced legal jurists rather than a jury of your peers, so to speak. You're dealing with people that have a significant amount of experience handling the law. It's just a lot different [than a trial court jury]. You have to see them in action and know what the difference is and really get a feel for it," Sasser explained.

The aspect of *Lawrence* that concerned Sasser most was that because defendants pled no contest at every trial stage, there was no factual record except the 69-word, probable cause affidavit handwritten by Deputy Sheriff Quinn the arresting officer. And that was not stipulated to by either prosecution or defense.

"I have never heard of a Supreme Court Case that had no factual record [other than *Lawrence*]," Sasser said. "You have to have a factual record.

"Justice Kennedy wrote the opinion in *Lawrence* without a factual record, when that guts not only Supreme Court precedent, but even his own statements, quoted in my brief, that you have to have a factual record in order to decide a constitutional issue.

"The U.S. Supreme Court can do what they want to do. They don't really have any boundaries. So if they don't want a factual record, I guess they don't have to have one.

"In *Lawrence* it wouldn't have mattered if there was a record, or no record, or whatever else it was. At least six justices wanted to get rid of this [sodomy] law. [So] technical rules and the rule of law and that sort of thing is a minor inconvenience.

"[The Supreme Court] treated it like a gnat. They just said, well, we are not going to be bothered by those pesky rules and ways of conducting justice.

"We are just going to issue our advisory opinion and leave it at that," Sasser said.

Informed of the 2004 Jones-Katine, Lawrence-Garner coyness about whether the defendants were copulating, Sasser erupted in anger: "Now they are even equivocating on whether or not they had sex at all? It just shows what a farce of a case it was!

"It was a giant circus spectacle for the Supreme Court to impose its will on the country! That's all it was. The court doesn't care! If Garner and Lawrence weren't having sex, they never violated the law!"

"There is a maxim of constitutional law that if you don't have to decide the constitutional issue, then you don't. What the court should have done then, if Lawrence and Garner really did not engage in the sexual activities, the court should have said: 'You didn't violate the law! Therefore, your conviction is overturned!'" Sasser suggested angrily.

# Supreme Court Decision: Press Conferences, Parades

Mitchell Katine was sitting at his office desk in Houston, Texas on June 26, 2003.

Throughout May and June, the Supreme Court of the United States makes biweekly announcements of its decisions in cases presented during the previous months.

As each group of decisions filled the anxious weeks, the high court had announced nothing about *Lawrence v. Texas*. June 26 was the last day any remaining cases *could* be announced before the court recessed for the summer. The next couple of days were traditionally celebrated as Gay Pride days across the United States.

Today *had* to be the day.

Katine was surrounded by embanked photographers, reporters, and television cameras when the phone call came in. Breathless with anticipation, Katine picked up the phone.

After nearly five years of litigation, he expected someone on the other end would tell him what the Supreme Court ruled on *Lawrence v. Texas*.

"Mom?" Katine exclaimed, incredulous.

"You won, son! You won!" Loni Katine shouted into the receiver from her South Florida condo.

"But Mom, how do you know?"

"It's on CNN son. I just saw it on CNN!" she exclaimed.

"So that's how I found out. My mother told me!" Katine remembers, smiling.

Lambda's Ruth Harlow, Paul Smith and their supporters—attorneys Bill Hohengarten and Lawrence Tribe—were seated in the Supreme Court on June 26, 2003, to hear the ruling on *Lawrence v. Texas.*

"They had waited until the last possible day of the term to announce the decision. We knew it was going to be that day. I had been very confident about the outcome throughout our litigating it. But the fact that the court kept us waiting until the last possible day made some doubts creep in," Harlow remembered in a July 2004 telephone interview. "So I was very anxious to hear the outcome.

"When Justice Kennedy began reading the opinion, they don't tell you when they launch who won. You just have to wait until the justice has said enough that you understand which way the case is going.

"I remember sitting there and finally getting to the sentence that we believe that *Bowers v. Hardwick* must be revisited, or something like that. And once Justice Kennedy read that, I knew that we had won in a very big and fundamental way.

"It's really just hard to describe that emotion. I was ecstatic and overwhelmed really by the way that we had won. I didn't realize the court would go as far as they did in terms of apologizing for *Bowers* and making such a strong statement in the other direction.

"I think I definitely got choked up. I didn't actually start crying, but some of my colleagues did. Very emotional moment, absorbing the magnitude of what had happened."

Paul Smith said he did not get choked up. "Instead, I was relieved not to have lost the case! Several people asked me to sign a copy of the opinion," Smith said in a 2004 interview.

"That same day our firm won a big death penalty case in the Supreme Court. So we Jenner & Block folks came back to the office and had champagne for everyone in the conference room. Then the group that litigated *Lawrence* went out to lunch. I flew to New York and spoke briefly at a rally in the Village," Smith recalled.

For Ruth Harlow, the moments were much more emotional. "There was an incredible sense of euphoria. When you leave the Supreme Court, you need to maintain a certain amount of decorum until you get out the doors of the courtroom. People were doing that. But as soon as they got out the doors, they were hugging each other. Just a sense of disbelief at the change we had just accomplished," Harlow said. "There were big smiles and happiness."

Lamba's New York City staff was gathered around a radio and a computer on June 26, 2003, spilling out in front of attorney Susan Sommer's office, waiting for a call from Harlow on her cell phone.

"I was assigned to do a nationwide phone hookup for our members who could call in so I could give an account of the decision and its import," Sommer remembered in a 2004 phone interview. "When I heard that we had won and that *Bowers* was overruled, I surprised myself and found myself in tears. Then I quickly pulled myself together because immediately we needed to start speaking with reporters and doing all kinds of talking and celebrating,"

"I think that night I stumbled home to bed. It was nice to know that the message was getting out. That a young generation was learning a new way and a better way of thinking about gay people, and that this had come from the United States Supreme Court," Sommer added.

For all the participants—victors and vanquished—it had been a long, contentious battle way longer than the five years the case had pended in the courts.

A greater cultural war lay ahead.

But for a few days in the gay community, joyous delirium reigned.

Harris County Assistant District Attorney Bill Delmore avoids a direct answer when asked if he disagreed with the June 26 U.S. Supreme Court ruling.

He does not respond yes or no.

"Really, I'm still a little unclear as to why the historical approach that we thought that they committed themselves to using, was not used in the determination of whether there was a substantive due process right," Delmore said in a May 2004 interview.

Justice Don Wittig, who served on the Houston-based 14th Court of Appeals when *Lawrence v. Texas* traveled through, disagrees with the Supreme Court's ruling.

"I think it is an erosion of moral principles that this country was founded on, and that the Constitution was founded on," Wittig said. "I think the State has a huge interest in regulating abhorrent, abnormal behavior.

"[The decision] is a further undermining of basic moral tenets [saying] that the law cannot judge morality in the bedroom or living room or whatever. That's never been the case. It's always been of course the law can reach into the bedroom, and it does."

That the high court based its ruling on right to privacy "is really bad," according to Justice Wittig.

"There is no privacy right to murder, rape, mayhem, incest, statutory rape," Justice Wittig continued. "Right of privacy is very flimsy, man-made. I hate to call it a principle."

The 6-3 majority opinion of the U.S. Supreme Court,

written by Justice Anthony Kennedy, based on the Right to Privacy under the Due Process Clause of the Fourteenth Amendment—not only struck down Texas' 21.06, but it overruled the prior precedent in 1986 *Bowers*—saying *Bowers* "was not correct when it was decided, and not correct today."

The majority concluded that the Texas statute "furthered no legitimate state interest which can justify its intrusion into the personal and private life of an individual."

The blistering dissenting opinion, written by Justice Antonin Scalia, accused the majority justices of "signing on to the so-called homosexual agenda, by which I mean the agenda promoted by some homosexual activists directed at eliminating the moral opprobrium that has traditionally attached to homosexual conduct." Changes in the law are up to the democratic process through state legislatures, not the courts, Justice Scalia said.

Justice Scalia's dissent, joined by Justices Thomas and Rehnquist, raised questions about the future ripple effect of the majority's decision in *Lawrence.*

"Today's opinion dismantles the structure of constitutional law that has permitted a distinction to be made between heterosexual and homosexual unions, insofar as formal recognition in marriage is concerned," Justice Scalia wrote.

More than a year after the U.S. Supreme Court's 2003 decision, Katine asked Texas State Sen. John Whitmire, a Houston Democrat, when the high court's decision would be reflected statutorily in Texas. (Even though a court has struck down a law, and thus the law is unenforceable, it can remain on the books, so to speak, until removed by legislative action.)

"I asked him, 'Now that the Supreme Court has declared 21.06 unconstitutional, how long will it be before the Texas legislature removes 21.06 from the books?'

"And he said, 'Mitchell, it is going to take a long time.'"

# The Too Perfect Case: Was It a Setup?

Mitchell Katine suggested *Unintentional Heroes* as the title for this book. But among the judges, police officers, lawyers, activists, and others who were involved with or became interested in the landmark case Lawrence v. Texas, Katine's suggested title would be both praised and derided. There is wide divergence of opinion about whether subjective words like "unintentional" and "heroes" should be applied to the defendants in *Lawrence v. Texas.*

While some agree with Katine that the defendants were heroes, others disagree philosophically about how heroism is to be defined in the context of this controversial case.

Whether the events of September 17, 1998, were unintentional or intentional, attracts even stronger debate. Rumors of a setup began almost immediately after the arrests—not that the incidents were faked, but that the incidents were a prearrangement tailored to test 21.06.

That the case was just too, too perfect.

Was it a setup?

**MITCHELL KATINE, Houston attorney for Lawrence and Garner:**

How would Katine define "setup?"

"A setup would be something that would be planned by people with an ultimate objective to change the law. I know that nobody: Lawrence, Garner, me, Lane Lewis, planned for this to occur *in order to change the law.*"

Could it have been planned without Katine's knowledge?

"No."

Planned but never revealed to Katine?

"No. Why would we have our clients be regular, everyday guys who are not comfortable in the limelight, not comfortable with public speaking? If we were to set it up, we would do it differently."

How would Katine set it up?

"We would select professional-speaking type people who were prepared to handle the worldwide media attention, who were able to convey a lot of the principles relating to civil rights and equal justice, who didn't have any [criminal] records, who were willing to get a [criminal] record.

"For example when the group in Massachusetts [wanted to challenge] marriage statutes, they found six couples who had been together in monogamous relationships for 20 years, another couple that had three children, another couple who were very professionally established and respected, another couple who were sick, and the hardship of not being married could focus on that. That's a planned legal attack.

"You have people who would evoke sympathy, understanding, empathy and compassion. In our [case] what we have is ordinary guys who evoke those emotions because this demonstrates this [arrest] could have happened to anyone. Anyone who was in a same-sex sexual experience in private, as opposed to these other types of planned events.

"That is my explanation of how I would have done it, versus how it happened as a matter of fact.

"But I have a second prong, and that is: So what? How does that diminish it, if it was planned? It doesn't. It was planned in Massachusetts. It was planned in San Francisco."

If it was planned, does that change anything procedurally since the Supreme Court has already ruled?

"Absolutely not. I do discrimination matters all the time. You set those up by having black people go to an apartment complex. They don't get an apartment. Then the next day a white person comes and they get an apartment when they don't really want one. That's a setup."

Why didn't they set up a case to test 21.06? Have two men call the police and say: *"We're having sex! Come on over!"*

"I don't know that anybody really imagined that the police would really ever arrest someone."

They thought the police wouldn't come?

"[The police] wouldn't come. They wouldn't arrest them. Because arresting people is optional. Who knew what the police would do? And probably they also felt . . . I think they gave up on Texas. They probably didn't think they could win in Texas."

Is it possible that someone set it up and never told Katine?

"Absolutely not."

What would be his ethical obligation as an attorney if someone admitted to him privately that the whole incident was orchestrated, prearranged?

"I guess I would be more ambiguous in responding. I would say things like, 'Let's talk off the record.' I wouldn't be as adamant as I am. It's so hard when you know something is the truth, and people will tell you, 'Oh, I don't believe that. It had to be a setup!'

"What possible shred of evidence or even implication? Give me anything! These are my clients. What about them indicates that this was a setup? The third guy who you know was Eubanks—well they were friends with both of them. [Eubanks] was in a relationship with Garner. That wasn't known before and it's probably not widely known. I don't know if that changes things.

"If people will know that Garner or Lawrence and Eubanks were friends for 20 years, then Lawrence and Garner were together and lived together. That puts a little more meat on the story that quite frankly, not many people know at this point because we didn't share any of that."

What if Katine now were to admit: "Yes! It was a setup!" What effect would that have nationally?

"None. Nobody has ever said that if *Lawrence* was a setup, it would be a less compelling case," Katine concluded.

## GARY POLLAND, Attorney and former Harris County Republican Chair:

Does Polland have any evidence of his allegations made to the media that the events comprising *Lawrence v. Texas* were a preplanned setup?

"No I don't have any independent evidence. I wasn't there. It was based on my understanding of the facts, which were that there was a complaint by someone unnamed about a disturbance in a house. So police went to the scene to check on the disturbance. They go in to find out what is going on. Instead of finding a disturbance, they find two men copulating, OK?

"But no one ever appears to be the person who made the complaint. So I thought it was just too convenient that the call is made, and when the police show up, these guys are going at it. So I drew the conclusion that this was a setup, a plan by gay rights activists to test Texas' sodomy statute.

"It was just . . . I think it was a logical connection. The other thing is, of course we know how few sodomy cases are ever made, and unheard of in someone's private home. Unheard of! I mean yeah, if you are sodomizing someone at the park, yeah you can get arrested! But unheard of to happen there [in a private home]. So you almost . . . it just has that feel. It is kind of like you know..."

How does Polland think it went down? Did gay rights organizations pay someone to make the complaint?

"Oh I don't think they were paid.

"I think they got together and said: 'We need to have a test case on sodomy and we need to have it in the privacy of someone's home.' They found people who were willing to do it, then made the phone call.

"And the police did what you would expect them to do, which is to check out the disturbance, find that men are sodomizing themselves in front of the police, which is—it *was* illegal except for the legislative courts—and then get arrested. Thus, the beginning of the [legal] challenge!"

Suppose it was a setup. Would that change anything?

"Assuming it was a setup, it means that the whole effort was an orchestrated attempt to reach the issue of same-sex marriage. You have to say they have been real successful!"

Is that the direction they were moving in?

"I think that was the plan all along," Polland theorized.

Does Polland think they knew Lawrence and Garner, and Lawrence and Garner agreed to it?

"I think the men were recruited. They were told: 'You do this, you will be the one to help liberate us from oppression. Your names will become famous. We have good lawyers who are ready to handle this case.' And they did. Mitchell Katine is a gay rights activist, and he is a good lawyer. These guys would not have been able to hire Mitchell Katine! Wouldn't have happened!  I wonder if David Jones will tell you the truth it was a setup?"

Did David Jones have something to do with a setup?

"I don't think Jones had anything to do with the setup. I think Jones was brought in after, to help. To advise on the criminal aspect. So I think that the fact they had Katine representing them tells you."

Suppose the United States Supreme Court justices find out it was a setup. Would that change their 2003 *Lawrence v. Texas* ruling?

"I don't know. From a judicial standpoint, how would you feel if you were a judge and you were asked to make a constitutional ruling on an issue, and then you find out it is just a setup? It is all orchestrated. It wasn't even real. Even if I was a liberal, I would be ticked off," Polland fumed.

How would that go over? Wouldn't the law (21.06) be (struck down) in the same manner as it was?

"Maybe if something had been done to dig up and make it more that it was bogus on the front end, it may not have gone anywhere. But hey, the 14th Court of Appeals ruled on it too!"

Does Polland know anybody else who thinks it was a setup?

"The prosecutors think it."

### ANGELA BEAVERS, Prosecutor:

"I never did think it was a setup. And I read the offense report. I just never got that feeling at all."

Why not?

"From what I remember in the offense report, there were details that rang true. There were just too many things that happened as far as minute details that would lead me to believe that this was something that just happened. It wasn't a setup or anything like that."

If it was prearranged, so what?

"I think I even heard that later, after the plea was already done [on December 22, 1998]. There is no time during the time that I dealt with the case that I ever thought that. If I did think that, I probably would have mentioned it to Mitchell [Katine] or whoever," Beavers said.

### BILL DELMORE, Appellate Prosecutor:

How would Delmore define setup?

"Some sort of organized effort to create a vehicle for litigation."

Was *Lawrence v. Texas* a setup?

"I believed it very likely that it was a setup early on in the case. Because frankly I just couldn't imagine how the police officer could be in a situation where there was sexual conduct continuing, and he would be so offended by it that he would actually go to a JP Court and file a complaint. A lot of police officers told me that their inclination would be to ignore it, and get on with the investigation."

Does Delmore think if there was a setup that it involved the police?

"That was one reason I wasn't clear on that. I didn't understand why the police officer would take that step—that other officers were telling me that they would not be inclined to take. But the fact that any setup would apparently necessitate either the officer being a part of the deal or them engaging..." Delmore's voice trails off.

"...Another option is they [Lawrence and Garner] continuing to engage in the conduct to the point where the officer would be offended and outraged by it. Those were two possibilities. I couldn't decide which it was. I later realized from doing a search in the *Chronicle* archives that the individual, one of the plaintiffs in *Lawrence*, I believe was charged with Class C assault for an altercation in a hotel involving a third party [Eubanks] that had made the false phone call that brought police to the apartment.

"When I learned that, I started believing that this was not a setup."

Why?

"Because it all seemed to fit. It seemed like the chances that this really was fueled by jealousy rather than some organized effort to get a vehicle for a Supreme Court challenge seemed much more likely," Delmore reasoned.

"We all did speculate that it was a setup to create a vehicle for the litigation, but the fact that the officer would have to have been part of it was the flaw in that. And was the reason why we ultimately decided not to make that claim or accusation," Delmore explained.

"I don't think I ever discussed with Chuck [Rosenthal] the possibility that it was all a setup," Delmore added.

**HIRAM SASSER, Attorney for Liberty Legal:**

"There is no doubt that it was a setup. Even Mitchell Katine told me [in 2004]: 'Every day I learn new facts about what happened.' I hope that's not really the way he actually operates his cases, and discusses issues with his clients . . . that [Katine] doesn't uncover all the facts from the very beginning. I think [Katine] is a much better lawyer than that," Sasser said.

Is Katine being disingenuous?

"I don't know if [Katine] was being disingenuous. He was trying to explain what his client Lawrence just told me [in 2004] when I asked [Lawrence], 'Who was the guy who [called the cops]?' [Katine] said the person who filed the false report [Eubanks], then led [police] to the room, was actually an ex-lover of [defendant] Tyrone Garner. And that being the case, [Katine said] it was a jealousy motive.

"Which is interesting that [Katine] actually knew who it was, and the client knew who it was—but in the [U.S. Supreme Court] brief, [Katine identified [the male who phoned police] as an unknown person. So the client[s] [Lawrence and Garner] knew who the person was! And then supposedly [Katine] is just now [in 2004] learning this?" Sasser continued, outrage building in his voice.

"Who knows if the lawyers knew it was a setup or not? Or maybe they suspected it or whatever. I can smell a setup when I see it. But hey! It doesn't really matter now. I'm not complaining about it. It's just really sour grapes now. I mean, kudos to them [Katine and Lambda] for recognizing that the U.S. Supreme Court wouldn't care," Sasser added.

## JOHN GEDDES LAWRENCE and TYRON GARNER, Defendants :

"Was it staged? No. I would not have subjected myself to this stuff because of that. No way," Lawrence said.

Subjected himself to what?

"To the abuse by the cops, to being dragged down my stairs, with people out at the swimming pool, in my underwear, barefooted in the cold of the night, huddled in a cop car. No. If I would have staged something, it would have been a lot less dramatic," Lawrence said.

Does Garner have any idea why all the rumors of a setup?

"I don't know," Garner responded.

Was it a setup?

"No," Garner said.

"See, that is the same thing that Jose in radiology says: 'It was all a big setup,'" Lawrence interjected.

Someone at Lawrence's job said that?

"Someone I know that works in the hospital," Lawrence explained in an April 2004 interview, as Katine silently shook his head negatively, signaling Lawrence to shut up.

Lawrence then changed his prior reference: "People in my office have never said anything. But I have heard people talking and that is the gist of the situation. In fact I called [Katine] the first time I heard it."

Has he heard that more than once?

"Yeah," Lawrence said.

## DEPUTY JOSEPH RICHARD QUINN,
### Arresting Officer:

"Initially, I didn't think it was a setup.

"Then as days passed, I heard the rumors around the courthouse. I began thinking about it. I came to believe it was a setup."

Why?

"Several reasons. The back bedroom door was open. [Lawrence and Garner] wanted to make it easy for us to find them in there. If you are going to have sex, and there are people around, as there were that night, you'd usually close the bedroom door.

"And, [Lawrence and Garner] weren't surprised when two uniformed deputies entered the bedroom where they were having sex, while they were having sex. They just looked at us blankly when we entered in uniform with drawn guns. Most people having sex would look surprised to see two deputies. They weren't.

"Also they *kept* having sex while we were standing there! Most people would try to cover up, or look embarrassed. I had to physically separate them, or they would have continued!

"Then when Lawrence started verbal abuse, Lawrence used legal terminology—about privacy of his home, constitutional rights, those types of phrases. Lawrence told us: 'You have no right to be here. You are violating the privacy of my home, plus a string of profanities.' I guess, looking back, Lawrence's use of legal terms attracted my attention a bit even then."

"It [the arrest] was something the defendants wanted to happen," Deputy Quinn concluded.

Other factors he considered retrospectively were "the immediate *nolo contendere* plea, and simultaneous appeal. There was also the nearly overnight response by the various legal counsels, and gay and lesbian associations, to join the cause, even though there was little media coverage until the day [November 20, 1998] in Judge Parrott's court," Deputy Quinn added.

"If I had a chance to do it again, I would take the same action," Deputy Quinn volunteered.

## RUTH HARLOW, Lead Lambda Attorney:

"It wasn't a setup. I think there are a couple of reasons people might have tried to put that information out there. One of the men who put that rumor out there was a Republican who wanted to undermine the legitimacy of our claims. Another reason is just amazement that the State of Texas really did have the power they had, and that something like this could happen. That they would just [act on] a mistaken report, burst into someone's apartment. And if they interrupted them having sex, instead of saying we are so sorry, apologizing and leaving, that the State would have the power to haul them off to jail," Harlow said in a July 31, 2004, phone interview.

She faults the prosecution equally.

"And then there were repeated times when the State could have dropped the charges. No one was in control at that time except the State, and so at anytime the prosecution could have said: 'This isn't a good idea. This is a mistake. We really don't want to take this seriously.' But every step of the way the State actually prosecuted them, then defended the law!" she added.

But if the State hadn't prosecuted, then Harlow and Lambda wouldn't have had their *Lawrence* victory, correct?

"Well, that is true. But I am responding to the idea that we somehow controlled the whole thing. Yes, we were victorious. So it played out in a way that was very positive. There is no way that we could have set this up," she concluded.

(I did not inform Ms. Harlow that in 2004, Katine, Jones, Lewis, and the defendants themselves implied Lawrence and Garner were not engaged in sex when the deputies arrived September 17, 1998.)

### MIKE PARROTT, Justice of the Peace:

Were the events of September 17 preplanned by the defendants in order to be arrested to have standing to challenge Texas' consensual sodomy law?

"I don't know ... Deputy Quinn is a big guy, with a big-g-g-g voice. It's hard to imagine that the defendants didn't hear him," Judge Parrott observed.

### DAVID ALLAN JONES, Katine's Co-Counsel for the Defendants:

"A lot of people have said that this case was a setup. I have heard that from lots of people."

*Was* it a set up?

"No. I don't know where anybody could get that we could put this kind of thing together. You certainly would have picked more astute clients if you were going to set anything like this up."

If it was a setup, so what? Would that change anything?

"Probably not now."

Since the Supreme Court has already ruled, what would be the procedural consequences?

"I don't know. Another hearing."

## ANNISE PARKER, Houston City Controller and Lesbian Activist:

"As *Lawrence* was working it's way up, I would hear a lot: 'Well, you guys set this up.'"

"No. If we had set it up, it wouldn't have been the two gentlemen who actually ... they were not activists. They were not the kind of poster children that you could go out and raise money from the gay community."

Did Lane Lewis set this up and not tell Parker?

"No."

Why not?

"I don't believe anybody can keep a secret like that," Parker concluded.

## DEPUTY WILLIAM DARNELL LILLY, Arresting Officer:

"A setup? No... I never have heard any rumors about that," said Deputy Lilly. "There's nothing I can think of to indicate that it was a setup, except that [Lawrence and Garner] continued to have sex while we were standing there in uniform!"

## SUSAN SOMMER, Lambda Attorney:

"There is no truth to those allegations. There is nothing really more to say. It's not true."

## SHERYL ROPPOLO, JP Chief Clerk:

Roppolo does not believe the incident was a setup. She also does not believe Deputy Quinn, her Channelview High School classmate.

"Have you seen the complaint? Deputy Quinn said they entered and announced 'Police!' He claims to have actually observed them in the act! You know, strangers coming into your house! From what I understand from one of the other officers that was there, that he kicked the door! So it wasn't like they didn't make a lot of noise going in there! It just made no sense to me whatsoever or anybody else that read it," she fumed.

"I don't care if you're heterosexual or homosexual. The door gets kicked, somebody hollers 'Police!' They walk from that room to another room. Hey! It's over! I don't care what your sexual preference is—you stop!" she continued indignantly.

So she doesn't believe Deputy Quinn?

"I did not believe that he observed them in the act," she concluded.

### DEPUTY DONALD WAYNE TIPPS, Arresting Officer:

"I had not heard the rumors about a setup. There was nothing to indicate that. But I believe that homosexual sodomy is wrong," he said.

### DEPUTY KENNETH LANDRY, Arresting Officer:

"I've never heard of the setup allegations. I don't think so, based on the totality of the situation," he said.

### SERGEANT KENNETH OLLIVER ADAMS, Supervising Officer:

"I didn't know about the setup allegations. Well, if it was a setup, they got what they wanted!"

### NATHAN PAUL BROUSSARD, Assistant to JP Chief Clerk Sheryl Roppolo:

Did not consent to an interview.

### ROBERT ROYCE EUBANKS, Witness, who directed officers to Lawrence and Garner:

Beaten to death on or about October 11, 2000. Houston Police Department homicide case remains unsolved.

# Connecting the Dots:
# "Thin Slicing"

L ogistically, at least five participants were needed to execute a flawless violation of 21.06: start with two to
have sex, and one to meet the cops—to ensure deputies
arrived at the correct apartment, at the correct time,
through an unlocked front door.

Since two would be busy having sex, and one busy
funneling the cops to discover the sex behind yet another
unlocked door, the bedroom door—a fourth man was
needed as a coordinator inside Lawrence's apartment, receiving telephoned instructions from one or more monitors outside who could see the events unfolding, but, in
the shadowy darkness and commotion, not *be* seen.

Neither Garner nor Lawrence expressed ordinary
human surprise when, during their sexual activity, two
uniformed deputies charged in with guns drawn. Perhaps
they were *expecting* that audience.

The fourth man was on the kitchen phone, nearest the
back bedroom where Lawrence and Garner were copulating, within voice range of the bedroom *and* within sight
range of the front door, to *inform* Lawrence and Garner

the exact moment the deputies would be arriving so the lovers could time their sex act to coincide perfectly.

When the man on the kitchen phone, who identified himself as Ramon Pelayo Velez, saw four uniformed deputies with guns drawn on him, he did not look surprised. Instead, he continued talking on the phone until ordered to drop the phone and show deputies his hands.

In 2004 interviews, Garner and Lawrence vacillated on what the fourth man Velez was doing in Lawrence's five-room apartment, and whether they even knew him. Garner said Velez arrived about 15 minutes before the deputies, and began using the kitchen phone. In 2004, Lawrence said Lawrence was "getting ready to watch the news and go to bed" during that time frame. So if Lawrence wasn't having sex, it is unlikely, in such small quarters, that Lawrence didn't know about a stranger in his kitchen for 15 minutes talking on the phone.

Particularly since Velez obviously knew where Lawrence and Garner were.

Velez pointed to the back bedroom, directing the deputies there.

Thus Velez joined Eubanks on September 17, 1998, as participant number four, and the second person to help-fully channel the deputies at crucial points—directing them closer and closer toward locating Lawrence and Garner having sex.

Velez' equanimity gives rise to the suspicion that he was on the phone with someone—a fifth participant—who, from outside Lawrence's apartment had watched the deputies arrive, watched them talk to Eubanks, then watched them begin creeping up the outside stairs. A monitor or advisors who could direct the night's activities, relaying all the outside unfolding events to the apartment occupants, instructing the four men on procedures as the dutiful deputies arrived. The monitor(s) would be extremely knowledgeable in criminal procedure.

There was always the risk that Velez wouldn't be able to exit Lawrence's apartment before deputies arrived. Or maybe the monitors wanted Velez present as an observer when deputies did arrive. Whoever it was outside knew that in either eventuality, there was nothing with which Velez could be charged. Knowing that, it was probable the cops, as they did, would let Velez walk away.

To continue talking on a phone in view of four uniformed deputies with guns drawn, Velez had to be speaking with someone whose authority over him, whose connection with him transcended, exponentially, the authority exhibited by police.

Or, perhaps for Velez, the element of surprise was missing. Velez *knew* the four deputies were creeping up the outside stairs. Someone was telling him that on the phone.

Of even more significance is the timing of Velez' arrival at Lawrence's apartment just 15 minutes before the deputies—around the time the phone call to the Sheriff's Department was made.

Lawrence's apartment was in a huge complex. If Velez was a stranger to Lawrence and Garner as they claimed, how did Velez find his way unerringly to Lawrence's apartment during the narrow, few-minutes window of time while deputies were racing in patrol cars to the scene—then, according to Garner, almost immediately begin using Lawrence's kitchen phone?

By what transportation did Velez arrive? Did someone who knew Lawrence, Garner and Eubanks transport Velez to the scene with perfect timing?

"You have no right to invade my home! You are violating my right to privacy! Jackbooted Nazis!" John Lawrence shouted in his verbal barrage. It seemed Lawrence was reading aloud from the table of contents in a constitutional law book. The words most defendants hurl when arrest is imminent, are usually confined to phrases beginning with "mother."

Who was the fourth man in Lawrence's apartment who called himself Velez?

I wasn't surprised when the investigator I hired couldn't find Velez. I always thought the fourth man provided false identification.

Learning Velez' true identity might be a "smoking gun" proving whether the case was a pre-scripted performance.

A 2004 nonfiction book entitled *Blink* by Malcolm Gladwell, terms this type of thinking process "thin-slicing." Boiled to its essence, to paraphrase Gladwell's theme: "The kind of thinking that happens in the blink of an eye ... what goes on in that first two seconds is perfectly rational ... those instant conclusions that we reach are really powerful and really important and, occasionally, really good ..."

"I think that this is the way that our unconscious works, that when we leap to a decision, or have a hunch, our unconscious is ... sifting through the situation in front of us looking for a pattern, and throwing out all that is irrelevant and zeroing in on what really matters. And the truth is that it's really good at this, to the point where thin-slicing often delivers a better answer than more deliberate and exhaustive ways of thinking," Gladwell writes in *Blink*.

The man deputies described as Velez seemed to be someone I had seen.

Someone I had seen recently.

I kept turning the physical description of Velez over and over in my mind.

In researching *Lawrence*, I spent as much time thinking—trying to figure how pieces fit together—as I did interviewing and writing.

One day in March I remembered where I had seen a similar man.

But I needed a photo of that man. Ideally a photo that wouldn't depict only him. A photo that would include others, to eliminate the power of suggestion when I showed the photo to witnesses.

Obtaining a photo of the man, in time to show it to the next arresting deputy I was to interview, was nip and tuck.

Showing photos to a witness for the purpose of seeing whether the witness can make an identification must be carefully done. A police officer, for instance, can't show a witness one photo and suggest: "Is this Fred Smith who robbed you?" Ideally, several photos should be shown to avoid suggestion. Also, a neutral question should be asked, such as: "Do you recognize anyone?"

Katine always insisted that I accept many of his photos about the case.

He e-mailed photos to me, he showed photos to me when I visited his office, he loaned photos to me to copy. Katine seemingly photographed *everything*.

So on March 16, 2004, when I drove to interview Deputy William Darnell Lilly, I took along many of Katine's photos documenting *Lawrence* and related events.

Since *Lawrence*, Deputy Lilly, an African American, had been promoted to detective in the Sheriff's Child Abuse Investigation Unit, which has an office in a strip shopping center. Deputy Lilly ushered my husband and me into a small, windowless interview room where we sat at a table. Deputy Lilly's demeanor is very serious, very professional. He is strictly business. The interview, mainly about his role in the arrests of September 17, 1998, lasted about 45 minutes. During the interview, I asked Deputy Lilly about the setup theories. He said he hadn't heard those rumors.

"There's nothing I can think of to indicate that it was a setup, except that [Lawrence and Garner] continued to have sex while we were standing there in uniform!" Deputy Lilly said at that point in our interview.

Then I got out a folder of Katine's photos, most made on a color printer.

Photos of the man I thought might be Velez were among them, but I didn't tell Deputy Lilly that. I asked Deputy Lilly to tell me if he saw Velez in any of the photos.

I showed him Katine's photos taken in Washington, D.C., the day the case was argued, photos of the Gay Pride Parade in Houston, photos of the defendants standing with Katine in a yard—on and on, handing them to Deputy Lilly in groups. I deliberately did not first show him the photos I speculated could include Velez.

Although Deputy Lilly politely studied each photo I handed him, he was getting bored.

"If I saw him in one of the pictures, I really couldn't say. Is this the Supreme Court? Press conference afterward?" Deputy Lilly asked me as he shuffled through Katine's photos.

I want to show you some more photos, I said, pulling some from my stack.

"Will the photos [he just looked at] be in your book?"

Maybe. I don't know. They were given to me by Mr. Katine.

"Have you thought of a title?"

I don't know, I said.

I handed Deputy Lilly the photos depicting the man I thought was probably Velez, but of course I didn't *say* that!

Do you see anybody in these pictures you recognize? I asked him, trying not to indicate by any facial expression of my own that these photos were any different than the others.

I wish I had had a video camera record of what happened next.

It was among the three or four, true, real, electrifying moments of high, high drama in my 24 years of practicing criminal law. Those years cover a *lot* of very high drama.

Just writing about March 16, 2004, remembering that moment with Deputy Lilly, gives me chills.

"Who is this here?" Deputy Lilly asked, instantly jabbing his fingertip on a man in one of the photos. Deputy

Lilly's reaction was instantaneous with my putting the photos down on the desk. Simultaneously, he came alive.

His boredom vanished.

He sat bolt upright, staring me full in my face—in complete, absolute astonishment.

Deputy W.D. Lilly looked at me as if I had just stepped out of a spaceship.

How could this woman he had never met, bring him a photo of the man who had been on the phone in Lawrence's kitchen when the deputies arrived the night of September 17, 1998?

You tell *me* who it is, I responded, not wanting to put words into his mouth.

"It could have been the guy! I remember the black hair!" he exclaimed, fully animated, completely engaged in the moment—looking back and forth at me, then the photo. "*Is* that him [Velez]?" Deputy Lilly asked me.

I sat quietly, trying not to react in an excited manner to his identification.

I don't know at this point, I said.

"It very well could have been him!" Deputy Lilly repeated. He still seemed in a state of shock at his own recognition of the man in the photo.

"If so, who *is* he? I know he's got to be a significant figure," Deputy Lilly said.

I looked at my husband, who had not known anything about this in advance. I had not told him, fearing that he might inadvertently derail any identification. I could tell that my husband, also an attorney, wanted to know more too.

I paused. The small room was absolutely silent as Deputy Lilly and my husband stared at me, awaiting my answer.

He is Mr. Katine's partner, I said.

Deputy Lilly jerked back in his chair, perhaps much the way Deputy Quinn described Deputy Lilly jerking backward when he saw Lawrence and Garner copulating the night of the arrest.

"No! Really?" he exclaimed, raising his voice even

more. His mental gears where whirling at high speed, at cop speed.

"In other words, if that's the guy [Velez], then there's some validity to the setup?" Deputy Lilly asked rhetorically, leaning toward me. He had a slight nervous laugh.

Then he just sat at the desk for a few moments, putting both hands, elbows akimbo, at his sides. He seemed emotionally overwhelmed at the concepts racing through his psyche.

Deputy Lilly kept looking at the photo of Katine with his partner-lover Walter Domingo Avila—Avila, whom Deputy Lilly had just identified as Velez, the fourth participant in the flawless violation of 21.06.

"This is wild!!!" Deputy Lilly exclaimed.

I wish I could re-create on paper the way he expressed it. Texans are known for a certain kind of shouting. It's defined as "whooping," which means great exultation.

Deputy Lilly whooped.

You zeroed right in on that, didn't you? I confirmed.

"Yes! Yes!! This is wild!!!" he kept repeating.

Would you agree I didn't suggest it to you? I asked Deputy Lilly.

"No! No you didn't!" He laughed nervously, the way people do who are trying to release their own emotional tension.

"This is wild!" he exclaimed again.

On his own, Deputy Lilly began examining several other photos of Katine and his lover-partner Walter. Walter Domingo Avila looked slightly different in each photo, depending on the lighting, position of Avila's face, hairstyle, and so on.

"Is this him?" Deputy Lilly asked me, quickly pointing to Katine's partner Walter Domingo Avila again, in another photo.

Deputy Lilly's ability to point out Avila a second time was an important bolstering of his first identification, demonstrating the deputy continued to ID Avila despite slight changes in Avila's appearance, position, and so forth.

It's the same guy you just pointed out. Yeah, I responded.

"That really could be him!"

Could be? How sure are you in terms of more than 50 percent? I asked Deputy Lilly.

"You know, I would almost have to say probably about 75 percent," he said.

OK.

Although the deputy *said* 75 percent, his body language said "100 percent."

"Is this the . . . who is this guy?" Deputy Lilly asked, pointing to Katine who was with Avila in several of the photos.

That's the attorney [Katine]. The same guy you've been seeing in the other photos.

"Is the attorney [Katine] gay?" Deputy Lilly asked me.

Yes.

The photos of Katine and Avila were with their adopted boy and girl.

"Who are the kids?"

They adopted those children.

"So they [Katine and Avila] are lovers?" Deputy Lilly continued.

Yes.

For the second time in the last few minutes, Deputy Lilly, a veteran cop, just sat there silently for some time. He seemed to think through the momentous implications, become overwhelmed by the obvious conclusions of his identification, then submit the equation back through his brain again and again—coming up with the same inevitable conclusion every run—then trying to absorb the result.

"Man! So we're thinking *he* set the whole thing up?"

I can't accuse anybody of that, because I don't have any proof at this time. But your identification is very interesting, I told him.

"Well, it's . . ." Deputy Lilly said. He still seemed to be mentally reeling.

It (Lilly's identification of Avila) fits the description that you gave me, before I showed you the pictures.

"Yes ma'am!"

In the interview portion of our conversation, I used a defense attorney technique of first locking a witness into a specific description before showing any photos. Then, later, the witness can't wiggle out of any discrepancies between the description they gave, and the photo they then identified.

So you're about 75 percent? I reiterated.

"I'm about 75 percent," Deputy Lilly confirmed. I think Lilly was much more certain than he said. Based on his physical reactions, I think Lilly was 100 percent *positive.* I kept thinking of that old song with a line about saying "no-no" with your lips, and "yes-yes" with your eyes.

Just for the record, as soon as I showed you the pictures, right away you identified Avila? Almost instantly? I asked.

"Yes ma'am! I did!" Deputy Lilly again seemed lost in thought, trying to get his mental bearings around the magnitude of what just happened in this small room.

"This *is* interesting! It's almost a suspense..." his voice drifted off. I think he was starting to say "novel. "

Yes.

"Let me ask you a question. Who was it that suggested that the whole thing [arrest] was a setup?" Deputy Lilly inquired.

Gary Polland. P-o-l-l-a-n-d. He at that time was chairman of the Republican Party in Harris County. He's the only person I know who publicly suggested that. Other people suggested that privately. But [Polland] was quoted in the newspaper saying that, I explained.

"And he [Polland] feels like the attorney [Katine] and this guy [Walter Domingo Avila] set it up?" Deputy Lilly asked.

Polland had no specifics, and still doesn't, I explained.

❖

That same date, March 16, 2004, I had an evening interview at a local restaurant with Sheriff's Deputy Donald Wayne Tipps, another one of the five deputies who arrived at the scene at Lawrence's apartment on September 17, 1998.

Deputy Tipps came with his very beautiful wife and their adorable baby. We sat in the restaurant's outdoor patio.

Of course I did not tell Tipps anything about Deputy Lilly's identification of photos.

With Deputy Tipps, I followed much the same procedure as I had with Deputy Lilly. I did the interview, locking Deputy Tipps into a description of the man Velez on the phone in Lawrence's kitchen the night of the arrests.

Then toward the end, I showed Tipps lots of photos, the same photos I had shown Lilly: of Katine in D.C., the Houston Gay Pride parade, the defendants and so on.

As with Deputy Lilly, Deputy Tipps seemed quickly to become bored, recognizing no one in those photos.

Then I handed him the photos of Katine and Katine's lover partner Walter Domingo Avila.

Here are some more pictures. Look at them carefully. Tell me if you recognize anybody in these pictures, I directed him.

Like Deputy Lilly, Deputy Tipps immediately zeroed in on Avila. Instantaneous like Deputy Lilly. But Deputy Tipps' identification was much weaker.

Deputy Tipps pointed to Avila.

"That Hispanic guy looks familiar. But I'm not sure who he is."

OK. How does he look familiar do you think? I asked.

"Aw, I just, he just looks familiar to me."

Do you think you've seen him before? I continued.

"Possible."

There are some pictures of him...other shots, I added, handing him more photos.

"Am I correct in assuming that these are coupled with kids?" Tipps asked me, referring to Katine and Avila.

Yes. They adopted the children, I explained. Do you think you might have seen the Hispanic guy before?

"The Hispanic guy looks familiar. But I can't say 100 percent for sure if I know him or not. Or if I've seen him, or if he's just one of those faces I go 'God that guy looks familiar, you know?'" he explained.

I adopted my practiced, neutral judicial face.

Deputy Tipps handed the photos back to me.

Nearly two weeks later, on March 29, I interviewed Sergeant Ken Adams, and showed him the photos in the same manner. He did not recognize anyone.

April 1, I interviewed Deputy Ken Landry who did not recognize anyone.

When I interviewed Deputy Lilly, I had already interviewed Deputy Quinn on March 6. So I mailed Deputy Quinn the photos. I do not know in what manner he viewed them. But Deputy Quinn said he did not recognize the man who identified himself as Velez in any of the photos.

April 2, when I interviewed Katine, I asked him if his partner Walter Domingo Avila had any role in the events of *Lawrence*.

"No." Katine said.

I did not tell Katine about the deputies' identification, nor did I share identification information among the deputies.

Weeks later I mailed all the deputies a color photo of Clovis Lane Lewis, which I printed from Lewis' Web site. All contacted me saying they did not recognize Lewis. Deputy Quinn added that Lewis was not the man on the phone in Lawrence's kitchen.

In his book *Blink*, author Gladwell explains the process of intuition. "We have some experiences. We think them through. We develop a theory, and then we finally put two and two together."

That's how I came up with the possibility that Velez and Walter Domingo Avila are the same person.

If the man on the phone in the kitchen was receiving instructions from monitors, the man had to be reliable. Someone who the monitor(s)/director(s) of the arrests trusted absolutely—because the role played by "Velez" was essential. The man on the kitchen phone couldn't be someone of the caliber of Eubanks—a loose-canon drinker who talked too much. Eubanks, though, was handy as a felon who didn't mind taking a misdemeanor arrest for false report. Garner and Lawrence wouldn't do, because they would be busy having sex.

Because he did not immediately drop the phone, whoever "Velez" was talking with on the phone had to be someone who commanded from "Velez" a loyalty so profound, it would be greater than his fear of four uniformed deputies with drawn guns a few feet away.

That type of loyalty usually has a deep emotional base.

"Velez" was extremely close to whoever he was speaking.

"Velez" also had to be someone who, in the years after the arrests, could still be controlled by whoever directed the September 17 scenario. Someone close to the director(s)/monitor(s) so the director could ensure that the secret of what really happened before the arrests, could be kept a secret. Someone who would want to help the monitor(s) because of personal affections, and who would want to keep the secret for the same reasons. Again, not someone like Eubanks, who wasn't beholden to anybody.

Avila fit that profile exactly.

We couldn't locate "Velez" because—maybe he was hiding in plain sight.

Further, Katine was extremely insistent that I not use Walter's last name Avila, even though Katine had already used it many, many times in Katine's regular e-mailings to a long list of recipients.

But my suspicions were triggered even more by Katine's pullback when I tried to obtain photos of Avila.

My research assistant Suzanne Testa and I were in Katine's office February 17, 2004. Katine was to provide answers to my written questions to the defendants—answers Katine said he had obtained. But Katine refused to just give me the information on the phone or via e-mail. He insisted we come to his office to hear him read from his notes.

After his pronouncements, he pulled out some photos of Walter. I had been wondering what Walter Domingo Avila looked like. Katine's ego was obliging. He and Walter had been to Katine's home ground in South Florida for Katine's appearance on a local television program. There were seemingly endless photos of their children and Walter in Miami.

Katine had captured Walter's face in great detail, close up, and from many different angles. The photos were excellent. Weeks later I mentally connected those photos with the descriptions deputies gave of "Velez."

Usually Katine gave me photos, e-mailed me photos, many and often, but he had not transmitted these excellent, clear photos of Walter in Miami. Only shown them to Suzanne and me that day in his office. I needed Katine to e-mail me at least some of the Miami photos. Since many had been with their children, I said something about wanting photos of Katine and Avila as parents.

To my surprise, Katine said I couldn't have copies of those Miami photos. He said he would send something else. Katine withholding any photos was an extreme departure from his usual enthusiasms.

I held my breath figuratively for several days, waiting. I worried that Katine had somehow picked up on *my* theory: that "Velez" and Walter might be the same person.

Did Katine sense my suspicions?

Usually I played cat to Katine's mouse. This time Katine played cat.

In a few days, Katine e-mailed me photos that were more interesting for what he left out. Katine had selected photos of Walter from occasions other than Miami. The man in those photos was clearly Walter, but at such odd angles and lighting as to make his features more vague. The excellent close-up photos of Walter in Miami were not included. Maybe Katine wasn't taking any chances, just in case I might have connected the dots. Two of the photos were from those taken in Miami. But Katine chose shots where Walter's face was in the distant background, or nearly obscured by a child.

That nuanced departure from Katine's usual modus operandi convinced me—my intuition was right on. So, in a way, Deputy Lilly's identification and Deputy Tipps' recognition of Walter didn't surprise me.

I played a thin-slicing hunch, and got lucky.

When I had basically concluded my research about *Lawrence*, I began thinking about a conversation in 2000 with a prosecutor in my court. Perhaps his remarks had nothing to do with *Lawrence,* but the information was intriguing. I mentally hopped along this rabbit trail, just to conceptualize how it might play out, if it was related to the *Lawrence* puzzle.

In late 2000, a prosecutor who used to be a lieutenant in the Houston Police Department was assigned to my court. Like Eubanks, the prosecutor liked to talk. I dug around in my notes until I found my entry for December 22, 2000.

I wrote: This morning my Number 2 prosecutor Earl Musick again wandered up to the bench in a mood to chat. (The holidays are often a less busy time in criminal court). I had not raised this particular topic Musick discussed. Musick is just a friendly guy who likes to tell war stories from his days as a lieutenant of police in the Houston Police Department. After he retired, his daughter was going to law school, so he joined her. They served as father-daughter assistant district attorneys.

Musick, tall and still handsome, with a booming voice, launched into one of his entertaining stories within full listening range of my staff, clerks, attorneys and courtroom spectators. Although I was sitting on the bench, it was not a private conversation, nor did I initiate it.

He began regaling us with how, when he was an HPD officer, he was in charge of security during the August 1992 Republican National Convention in Houston.

"We tried to keep the demonstrators from disrupting the Republican convention," said Musick. "One group of demonstrators were homosexuals. Before the convention began, I went to another police agency to ask if they had a confidential informant who could infiltrate the homosexual group who planned to demonstrate.

"We got a CI (confidential informant) who told us in advance when all their demonstrations would occur!" Lieutenant Musick revealed triumphantly.

"So District Attorney Johnny Holmes, me and Assistant District Attorney Don Stricklin [now a felony court judge] were sitting in a car a few feet away from this homosexual group called ACT UP when they began demonstrating. We had police officers on horses who could twirl the horses around in a circle to disperse demonstrators better than any method, without harming anyone," Musick explained to us.

"Our confidential informant was so good we knew in advance exactly what ACT UP would do—and when they would do it!" Lieutenant Musick proudly told my courtroom spectators and me.

Even though Lieutenant Musick spilled the beans eight years after the convention events, HPD would probably not be happy with his public disclosure. But there the information was, voluntarily published in open court by one of their high-ranking retired officers.

If *Lawrence* was a manufactured case, as I argue it probably was, it's brilliance and perfection of execution was impressive. It was not put together by amateurs.

Some observers, including at first Assistant District Attorney Bill Delmore, thought the arresting deputies might have been complicit in any setup. ADA Delmore later decided they were not.

After meeting and interviewing all five arresting deputy

sheriffs, my opinion is that the deputies were dutiful professionals not involved whatsoever in any setup.

But at least in 1992, there was a CI operative in the homosexual community. Presumably, that person shared the homosexuals' goal of wanting a case to test 21.06 up through the courts to eliminate sodomy as a criminal act.

Teasing that thought out, was it possible that a CI, either the 1992 CI or another CI, organized the arrest events? Organized the arrests independently, as a rogue CI—or at the behest of handlers who wanted to get rid of 21.06?

The possibilities raised intriguing mental trails to explore.

I kept thinking of the photo on Annise Parker's office wall of the HPD officers. Could there be some clue there? But at this writing, I could not definitively link Lieutenant Musick's disclosures to *Lawrence* events.

I learned long ago that in criminal law, absolutely nothing is too shocking, outlandish or improbable that it couldn't actually happen. As Deputy Joe Quinn said: "You could tell me that . . . there's a guy walking down the street with his head in his hand, and I would believe it."

That's what made every day I spent in court for 24 years, fascinating.

If the arrests were scripted in order to test the constitutionality of 21.06, which I argue they were, how *did* that prearrangement come about? How high up did it go? That is, who knew about it, and when did they know it?

Assuming the arrests were a setup, there are infinite possibilities including:

1) Lane Lewis conceived the idea on his own, recruited the participants, and carried out the plan alone.

2) Lane Lewis along with others—perhaps Broussard, Katine, Jones, or anyone of the "cast"—conceived the idea and joined in meticulous planning and organization required for the perfect case.

3) Katine knew about the arrests in advance, or Katine suspected the planned arrests were about to occur, and after they did, followed a Don't Ask, Don't Tell protocol. Deputy Lilly's ID of Katine's partner Walter as "Velez," and Deputy Tipps' much weaker recognition of Walter, are of course, fascinating. If the identifications are correct, then Katine was involved in orchestrating the arrests.

4) Lambda Legal may or may not have known in advance about the arrests. And, after the arrests, although they suspected a setup, may also have adopted a Don't Ask, Don't Tell posture.

5) Other persons, whose names have not yet surfaced, participated in the planning and execution of the arrests.

There are other nearly endless permutations.

Houston City Controller Annise Parker quotes Katine as saying early on, "I'm going to document this [case], and someday I will be famous."

Clearly, Katine was and is someone who sought, loved, and continues to love the limelight around the *Lawrence* case. But did Katine and/or his protégé, the in-your-face Lewis, make the case happen?

As a lawyer myself, I noted Katine's careful, lawyerly language: "I know nobody Lawrence, Garner, me, Lane Lewis planned for this to occur *in order to change the law.*"

Katine did not put a period after "occur."

Although he is not an attorney, Lewis had much the same lawyerly response as his mentor Katine: "If there was anything I could say as far as my part in this, *it was never my intention to simply change the law.*"

Another lawyerism Katine spoke near the beginning of our April interview attracted my attention: "I believe that people are telling me the truth," Katine said.

Was Katine—as a good lawyer would—doing advance preparation for a defense of: "I believed him/them when they told me,"....whatever?

Katine's public challenges for anyone to bring him a shred of evidence that the case was staged, rings hollow in view of Katine's continued iron-grip control of interviews with the defendants almost five years after the

Supreme Court ruled.

Katine's position is analogous to saying: There is *no* pot of gold, but you absolutely, positively can't ever search for it in my backyard!

As a real estate attorney, Katine lacked the extremely sophisticated knowledge of criminal law required to put together a case that would withstand years on the appeal road to the Supreme Court. The arrests were probably in the planning stage for weeks. If there were dress rehearsals too, that would not surprise me.

David Jones, who downplays his own role, would have that knowledge of criminal law. So would another local attorney, whose name Katine dropped fleetingly in one of our conversations. Ironically, the attorney—a brilliant legal strategist— is someone who, not long after I began my research, I thought of as possibly involved with *Lawrence.*

Someone, like Jones and Katine, who craves the public limelight.

Only the participants know how it went down.

And while in 2004 they seemed to be changing their story to say the defendants weren't even having sex, the principles continue to maintain that the case wasn't a setup.

Subpoenas for phone records and bank records from during the time frame before and after the events of *Lawrence* would resolve many questions. But I lack the authority to issue such subpoenas.

All the attorneys and scholars with whom I spoke cannot think of any "crime" the participants committed if *Lawrence* was a planned arrest. Although certainly, judges and the court system are not amused by such manufactured cases.

Apparently even if the participants now admitted: "Yes, we did it, and here's how!"—they did not violate any laws.

# Uneasy Stirrings in the Grave: Whodunit?

Until I saw a photograph of Robert Royce Eubanks, I had difficulty writing *Sex Appealed.*

I don't know, consciously, why that was.

I had heard the cops' physical description of Eubanks. I saw his physical description on paperwork from his prior criminal history. I read lengthy clinical descriptions of his multiple injuries catalogued on the report of the autopsy on his body. From the medical examiner's graphic report listing Eubanks' death as a homicide, it was possible for even a layperson to conclude—his violent demise was the result of a horrific beating by one or more persons.

When I served as a state court, felony-division chief prosecutor in Florida, murders were always my favorite cases. I used to beg the homicide division to assign me their "dog" (weak evidence) murder and manslaughter cases to try to a jury, just to get experience. Impressed with my eagerness to volunteer for extra work, veteran homicide prosecutors Kelly Hancock, Tom Kern, and others, graciously shared their expertise.

Murders fascinate juries and television viewers too. My prosecutor colleagues said that's because few jurors can imagine themselves robbing a 7-11 at gunpoint or dealing drugs. But nearly everyone can imagine that, under specific circumstances, he or she could end the life of another human being.

As a former prosecutor, I had read many autopsy reports of stabbings, and shootings, but never a beating death—merciless blows struck again and again, even after the victim was clearly helpless, unable to defend himself.

Until I could obtain a photo of Robert Royce Eubanks, I felt mentally stalled on writing about the *Lawrence* case.

When Eubanks' police mug shot, taken September 17, 1998, clattered out of my printer weeks after I began research, I sat at my desk staring at Eubanks' photo quite awhile.

As a judge and a lawyer, I had seen many a Robert Royce Eubanks.

I hadn't seen Eubanks specifically of course, but so many defendants like him processed through the federal and state criminal systems.

Stumbling past in endless streams.

He had a felony record and had served prison time. But from the perspective of veterans of years in criminal court, Eubanks' criminal record wasn't that bad: an arson, a theft.

Everything is relative after you've worked in criminal courts awhile.

In what was to be his final police mug shot, Eubanks has a crooked smile, and that sort of goofy, dazed, unkempt look that comes from starting young on too many drugs, and too much alcohol, for too many years. Eubanks looked as I had anticipated he would look: a pest, a nuisance, an aggravation to everyone he ever met—but a comparatively harmless pest, nuisance and aggravation.

Not a cold-eyed, heartless, menacing thug, or a sharp-eyed cunning manipulator. More the 10-year-old annoying brother you wish would just go away, please. Then you finally give him 25 cents to go away. He keeps the money, and stays, realizing he's onto something potentially profitable.

Eubanks had that smirky attitude rooted in a basic self-eroded intelligence. Street smart, loud, boastful, an adventuresome con, probably a talker. Deputy Quinn said Eubanks talked nonstop in the back of the patrol car on September 17, 1998.

Someone who never shut up.

A blabber with inside knowledge.

A drunk who had nothing to lose.

Was his homicide the act of strangers? Or had Eubanks become inconvenient to one or more persons? Did Eubanks, as Annise Parker said Lane Lewis did, begin wanting money? Did Eubanks try blackmail?

To solve Eubanks' murder—the "why" would indicate who.

After I saw Eubanks' photo, whatever feelings blocked my writing, lifted.

I first met attorney Mitchell Katine on January 15, 2004, in Houston when he lectured about the Lawrence case to the Federal Bar Association. I chatted with him briefly to arrange a later appointment.

My husband and I then spoke with Katine in his office January 19, 2004, about my serious attempt to begin writing a nonfiction book detailing the *Lawrence* case.

From the moment I began conversation with Mitchell Katine on January 19, even before Katine told me, I sensed that Robert Royce Eubanks was dead. Sitting opposite Katine in his law office conference room January 19, I just felt that very, very strongly.

So when Katine, in response to my January 19 question asking what happened to Eubanks, said, "I *think* he's dead!" his answer confirmed what I somehow already knew. Not knew in *fact* yet, but just knew from 24 years of practicing criminal law.

Speculation was unnecessary. Eubanks was dead. I felt certain of that.

I don't know if my intuitive analysis was the result of my years toiling in criminal prosecution and criminal defense, or if my feelings would have existed independently of my legal background.

The fact that Katine said "I *think* he's dead!" attracted my attention. After we left Katine's office, my husband remarked too about Katine's use of the word "think."

I felt that Katine *knew* Eubanks was dead. It wasn't speculation on Katine's part. I felt that even though I had no facts then to support my feeling. Why had Katine equivocated with the word *think*?

Eubanks was one of the major characters in *Lawrence*. For almost five years, Katine kept in frequent contact with Eubanks' close friends Lawrence and Garner—why wouldn't Katine know for *sure* whether Eubanks was dead?

Then there was Katine's tone when he spoke the word *dead*—derisive.

Not a tone of voice I ever heard Katine use in any other context.

Katine's emotion about Eubanks is puzzling. It seems jarringly disproportionate to the degree of contact Katine said he had with Eubanks. If Katine's contact with Eubanks was limited to Eubanks' initial appearance October 12, 1998, in Katine's office, why Katine's depth of negative feeling even five years later?

Katine's subsequent similar references to Eubanks were Katine's only departure from the upbeat, professional persona he routinely displayed.

But Katine wasn't alone in exhibiting noteworthy disconnect or seemingly incongruous reaction when asked about the ending of Eubanks' life. Other *Lawrence* players verbally distanced themselves too.

David Jones, Katine co-counsel for *Lawrence*, was even more disingenuous about Eubanks.

I asked Jones in our March 18, 2004, interview, what happened to Eubanks.

"I don't know," Jones responded.

"Do you know where Eubanks is?" I persisted.

"No." Jones answered.

Garner and HPD Homicide Sergeant Williamson both confirmed that Jones represented Garner regarding the Grand Jury investigation into Eubanks' homicide!

Lane Lewis, who said he babysat Eubanks for months after the September 17 arrests, claimed he didn't know Eubanks was dead until June 26, 2003, the day the Supreme Court issued its decision.

"[Lawrence] told me," Lewis said.

How did Lawrence say Eubanks died? I asked Lewis.

"I had asked [Lawrence], 'Whatever happened to Robert [Eubanks]?' And I think [Lawrence] said, 'Eubanks passed away several years ago' or something," Lewis said.

Do you know how Eubanks died? I asked Lewis in April 2004.

"I'm sure it was AIDS. I didn't ask. I just assumed," Lewis said.

Though their interlocking friendships spanned 23 years, neither Lawrence nor Garner visited Eubanks in the hospital as he lay dying. Because hospital personnel found Lawrence's name in Eubanks' effects as the person Eubanks wanted contacted in emergencies, Lawrence had been informed quickly of Eubanks' critical condition. In our April 2004 interview, Lawrence and Garner evinced apparent indifference to his death.

Eubanks' homicide seemed *the* topic that metaphorically emptied the room of those involved with *Lawrence*.

When Eubanks' autopsy report churned out of my printer, confirming his October 10, 2000, homicide—I was not surprised.

I received the autopsy report long before I received his photo.

Manner of death: homicide

Cause of death: blunt force head injuries.

Cause of death wasn't a surprise either. I had been thinking beaten to death would be the method and means.

Homicide detectives know that certain kinds of death indicate that the murderer probably knew the victim: stabbing, strangulation, beating. To perpetrate those acts, the killer must get very physically close to the victim, interact in the most intimate of ways, touch the victim, see their suffering, have the victim see them, often be covered with the victim's bodily fluids—up close, and very, very personal. Not like shooting with a gun where there is physical distance, a certain anonymity—the murderer and victim are not as likely to know each other personally—like someone shooting the clerk at a convenience store.

Robert Eubanks probably did not die at the hands of a stranger.

Cops know too that a beating death often indicates the murderers" extreme anger toward the victim—inflicting a message with every blow. It is not usually a killing with a financial or ideological motive. It is one of the most challenging types of murder for police to solve. No convenient bullet to match with a gun, or fingerprints on a knife. Usually there is no "weapon" to trace.

A really savvy murderer would realize that, in choosing a method of death.

David Jones, the experienced criminal law practitioner in Katine's law firm who worked on *Lawrence* with Katine, also seemed to go out of his way to disparage Eubanks' credibility at any opportunity, particularly to portray Eubanks as a liar.

So did Katine, Lewis and Lawrence.

Only Garner, ironically, remembered some positive things about his friend. In June 2004, at the Lambda breakfast, when I asked Garner how he remembered Eubanks, Garner said Eubanks was loving and kind.

After the events of *Lawrence*, when Garner was arrested for assaulting Eubanks and for violating a protective order Eubanks had against Garner, Jones was quoted in a November 24, 1999, Houston Chronicle article: "No one should be surprised that there is some tension between the two. He [Eubanks] wrongfully put them in jail. I am very suspicious of anything that comes out of the mouth of that guy [Eubanks]."

In my interview with Jones, he again referred to Eubanks as a liar in a derisive tone strikingly similar to Katine's tone.

Katine said that when Eubanks accompanied Lawrence, Garner, and Lewis to Katine's office, Katine took one look at Eubanks and immediately ordered Eubanks to wait in the reception area. "I didn't want that guy [Eubanks] around," Katine said, without being specific as to why.

If Eubanks' involvement with the case ended September 21, 1998, when he pled guilty to the misdemeanor of Filing a False Police Report, why did Katine and Jones seem to go out of their way to create an image of Eubanks as unworthy of belief? Wasn't Eubanks out of the picture September 22?

Why would it matter whether Eubanks was believed?

Believed [credible] about what?

I spoke with Katine many times during my research, but our formal interview was April 2, 2004. By then I had Eubanks' autopsy report and photo.

I asked Katine again, much as I had on January 19, 2004: Where is Eubanks?

"He's dead. I understand him to be dead. I don't know that for sure, but that's what I have heard is he is dead," Katine responded.

Does Katine have any knowledge about the circumstances of Eubanks' death?

"No."

What makes Katine think Eubanks is dead?

"That is what I have been told."

Did Katine know that Eubanks death was ruled a homicide?

"No."

Did Katine know Tyron Garner was subpoenaed before a Harris County Grand Jury in connection with Eubanks' homicide?

"No."

Did Katine represent Garner in that regard?

"No. What did the Grand Jury decide?" Katine asked.

I did not know, since, in Texas, Grand Jury proceedings are secret. However, logically, since Garner has not been charged with Eubanks' murder, the Grand Jury must have decided, for unknown reasons, not to indict Garner at that time.

"I would imagine the Grand Jury never indicted [Garner]. I have visited with him and to my knowledge there is no arrest warrant issued for him, and he was not charged with that crime. I'm just guessing. I don't know where [Garner] is right now. He is out and about," Katine said.

Did Katine know that [Eubanks' death] had been ruled a homicide?

"I had heard some rumors about things like that."

Does Katine know anything about the homicide?

"No I don't. I don't know any of the circumstances or how he died—if he was shot or stabbed or run over. I have no idea," Katine said.

Eubanks was apparently beaten to death I said.

Katine, usually never at a loss for words, paused as if he were thinking not only what to say next, but how to say it.

"Oh my goodness. OK. Was it with an instrument?" he asked.

Apparently, I responded.

"OK. I don't know anything about that," Katine said.

Lawrence and Katine were in contact in October 2000 when Eubanks was murdered, because the sodomy case was pending a decision before the *en banc* 14th Court of Appeals.

Is it logical that Lawrence didn't mention Eubanks' homicide to Katine?

If Katine knew since October 2000 that Eubanks was dead, why would Katine continue to evince uncertainty in January 2004?

"Boy! It's been a long time since I've seen that face!" Lane Lewis exclaimed during our April 2004 interview when I handed him Eubanks' police mug shot. Despite Lewis' statement, Lewis seemed uncomfortable looking at the photo.

When is the last time Lewis saw Robert Eubanks?

It was the only time during a nearly 2-hour interview that take-no-prisoners Lewis broke eye contact.

"I don't remember," Lewis said, looking down.

Who was Robert Royce Eubanks? I asked Lawrence.

"[Eubanks] was from Conroe, Texas. His parents . . . I have to get this story straight. I think he was in illegitimate child. He had been put up for adoption. A professor in Conroe and his wife adopted Royce and his sister. The mother later lived in Kansas and remarried. Royce somehow or another found out about her and had gotten in contact with her," said Lawrence, who refers to Eubanks by his middle name Royce.

Eubanks' biological mother?

"Yes. From what I understand, he had a very troubled childhood. He had moved to Houston early on by himself. I don't know all the details, but I know that he had lived here in Houston. He had worked at several motels. La Quinta," Lawrence continued.

What work did he do at the motels?

"Night clerk. Stuff like that."

Did Eubanks have a high school education?

"Yeah."

Did he have any college education?

"I don't know," Lawrence said.

Did either Lawrence or Garner ever meet any of Eubanks' family members?

"I had talked with his mother a couple of times because she would call to find out where he was," Lawrence said.

His biological mother or adoptive mother?

"I think it was his biological mother. His adoptive parents didn't want anything to do with him. His sister is still ... I don't know if she is still in this area or if she is back in Bryan-College Station. She used to live there," Lawrence remembered.

Lane Lewis knew Eubanks well. What kind of person was Eubanks?

"Alcoholic. Rowdy and good ol' boy. In and out of jail. Trouble with jail," Lewis said.

How would Lewis describe Eubanks?

"Think Gilley's but gay," Lewis summarized.

Gilley's, where portions of the John Travolta movie "Urban Cowboy" were filmed, was a notorious country western bar that burned to the ground several years ago in Pasadena, Texas.

Eubanks' mother was completely unaware of Eubanks' role in the *Lawrence* case. She wasn't sure if she had received a copy of the autopsy report.

"Robert grew up partly in Texas, partly in Arkansas, partly in Copenhagen, Denmark, partly in Pennsylvania," his mother explained in a 2004 telephone interview.

Military service did not bring the family to Denmark, but Eubanks' mother was reluctant to explain why Eubanks had lived in Europe.

Is she aware of any investigation into Eubanks' death?

"I don't know. I don't think there is an investigation," she said.

She said she was at the hospital in Houston when her son died. Was Eubanks ever able to speak or did he remain unconscious?

"No, he was ... by the time they found him, he was virtually already gone."

Was he an only child?

"He has a sister."

What kind of person was Eubanks?

"I just think it would take a very long-drawn-out time. I'm not ready to go into this," Eubanks' mother said.

Robert Royce Eubanks is buried in Mount Pleasant— a small town in northeast Texas. There was no funeral to mark Eubanks' passing, only a brief graveside ceremony on October 18, 2000, according to funeral home records. Survivors are listed as his sister, his mother, and his stepfather. The small rural cemetery of modest head-stones is on Farm-to-Market Road 1000 outside town.

There seems to be no active investigation of his murder.

Eubanks was a homosexual, but there is no call to in-vestigate his killing as a hate crime against homosexuals under any of Texas' applicable hate crime statutes.

Although without Eubanks, there would have been no case for Lambda to spend $750,000 championing all the way to the Supreme Court of the United States, Lambda is not stepping forward to fund an investigation into Eubanks' death, nor to offer a reward for information about his killers.

The silence of Robert Royce Eubanks' grave among the East Texas pine trees is absolute for the individual with-out whom *Lawrence v. Texas* would never have happened.

Annise Parker said the events of *Lawrence v. Texas* couldn't have been a setup, because "no one could keep a secret that long."

When Parker said that, I remembered how she re-vealed that the homosexual community successfully kept the arrests off media radar for as long as they chose.

I also remembered an old prosecution saying: Two people can keep a secret only if one of them is dead.

# Epilogue

$I$ mailed a letter to all nine justices of the Supreme Court of the United States, telling them my background and that I was writing a nonfiction book about *Lawrence v. Texas*. I asked each:

1) Over your years on the court, what percentage of cases would you estimate come before the court, as did Lawrence with no underlying facts other than the probable cause affidavit?
2) Purely hypothetically, were "setup" allegations later found to have some basis, what would be the procedural effect, if any, since the case is long closed?
3) In the history of the court, as far as anyone knows, has a situation as in (2) above ever occurred?

Two of the nine justices responded.

Only Justice Clarence Thomas responded personally:

"Dear Judge Law,

I am in receipt of your letter of May 6, 2004 in which you set forth several questions regarding *Lawrence v. Texas*. However, I am unable to provide you with the information that you requested.

Sincerely,
Clarence Thomas"

Justice David H. Souter responded through his secretary Michele Blincoe:

"Dear Judge Law,

Your letter dated May 6th to Justice Souter has been

received. I must ask you, however, to excuse the Justice from contributing to your research for your potential book about *Lawrence v. Texas*. It would be inappropriate for the Justice to comment on cases or issues that may present themselves before this Court. I hope you will understand.

> Yours sincerely,
> Michele Blincoe
> Secretary"

Justice Ruth Bader Ginsburg did not respond to my letter.

However, in August 2004, while channel surfing, my husband and I happened to tune in just as a tape replay aired of Justice Ginsburg's March 12, 2004, address to students and faculty at the University of Connecticut School of Law. She mentioned *Lawrence v. Texas*!

We quickly scribbled notes on that portion of her remarks. But we wanted, if possible, to get a transcript of only that section. So I contacted *University of Connecticut Law Review* Editor in Chief Thomas Farris, who referred us to the Summer 2004, Volume 36 edition, which he said featured a transcript of Justice Ginsburg's March 12, 2004, remarks.

But when I examined the "transcript" in the *UC Law Review*, it differed considerably from the notes my husband and I had made. I sent an e-mail asking if the *UC Law Review*'s "transcript" had possibly been edited?

Yes, it was edited, by Justice Ginsburg herself, Farris responded.

"We had her remarks transcribed, and sent them to her for her review. She edited them," Farris explained. Although the introduction on the UC article identified the "transcript" of the question-and-answer session as an "edited transcript," the article did not identify her main remarks as having been edited.

"Our faculty advisor, and former clerk to Justice Ginsburg, Professor Paul Berman told me that he doesn't think the Justice intended any substantive difference between her spoken and printed remarks," Farris added.

❈

This is what Justice Ginsburg actually said, according to the *unedited* transcript:

"The problem with constitutional adjudication is that there is no higher court, apart from the amending process, and amending our Constitution is very difficult. Sometimes that's a heartening thing. So if the court has gotten it really wrong—think of *Plessy v. Ferguson* that introduced the separate but equal doctrine—could any court say, "Oh stare decisis is so important that we must adhere to that precedent?"

"And the court concluded in the *Lawrence* case that *Bowers v. Harwick* was a very wrong decision and inconsistent with what we have regarded as the due process guarantee to every human of essential equal dignity.

"So of course the Court thought it was a so wrong decision and no one else could right it for us, that would overturn *Bowers v. Hardwick*."

This is how Justice Ginsburg edited her remarks:

"For constitutional adjudication, in contrast, there is no higher court apart from the amending process, and amending our Constitution is very difficult. One can be glad for that, but it does indicate that if the Court has gotten it really wrong, there is something of an obligation to correct ourselves. Think of *Plessy v. Ferguson* which introduced the separate but equal doctrine. Could a late 20th century Court tolerably say: "Go away, stare decisis is so important, we must adhere to that precedent?"

"The court concluded in the *Lawrence* case that *Bowers v. Hardwick* was so wrong, and that no other decisionmaker was likely to correct us. So the Court overturned the precedent."

*Stare decisis*, meaning "let the decision stand," is a legal principle that, barring extenuating circumstances, courts should be guided by prior decisions.

Justice Ginsburg's remarks offer an extraordinary insight into the mental processes of members of the U.S. Supreme Court in considering *Lawrence v. Texas.*

Although attorneys could argue other interpretations, it would appear from both versions of Justice Ginsburg's remarks that she saw the majority in *Lawrence* (herself included) as activist judges who had a predetermined goal of righting or "correcting" what they felt was a 1986 wrong in *Bowers.*

Activist judges—judges who have a social policy agenda such as Justice Ginsburg describes—incite conservatives and the religious right into a veritable fury. Conservatives feel that judges should confine themselves to interpreting the law, not acting as zealous missionaries for a cause.

Justice Ginsburg seems to admit that issues of the constitutionality of 21.06 were brushed aside in the Court's eagerness to act for legislative bodies that might be unwilling or unable to amend the Constitution to fit the majority Court's idea of what is "right" sexually and/or socially.

For those who feel that the Constitutional doctrine of separation of powers provides needed checks and balances among legislative, executive, and judicial powers, Justice Ginsburg's characterization of the *Lawrence* majority as eager to substitute its authority for legislative authority, would be blasphemous.

If one is liberal, her remarks might be comforting.

If one is conservative, her remarks might be alarming.

Her remarks could also be interpreted as indicating that the Court was willing to issue a ruling based only on a 69-word probable cause affidavit because they didn't really care what the facts were in *Lawrence.*

Justice Ginsburg's March 12, 2004, televised revelation of what she feels was the majority court's motivation in *Lawrence*, might appear to validate the statement made by conservative attorney Hiram Sasser of Liberty Legal Institute: "For this particular case, apparently some of the justices wanted to help reshape America. So they just decided to do it however they needed to do it."

# Acknowledgments

**Special acknowledgments** to my publisher, Eakin Press of Austin, Texas; my husband Donald O. Jansen, senior partner at Fulbright & Jaworski LLP; Nanette Primeaux who transcribed all the interview tapes; Suzanne Testa my researcher; and Ronald Wright, MD, JD, of Fort Lauderdale, who graciously analyzed Eubanks' autopsy without charge.

**Acknowledgments** to the following for their friendship: Linda Addison, Houston; Charles Alcorn, Houston; Bucky Allshouse, Houston; Dr. Marie Appling, Houston; Hon. Bill Archer, Washington, D.C.; Hon. Susan Baker, Texas; Linda and John Barrett, Houston; Patricia Barrow, Houston; Robert L. Beals, Florida; Hon. Paul Bettencourt, Houston; Ron Bliss, Houston; Gretchen Bonhert, Houston; Hon. George Brescher, Fort Lauderdale; Richard and Joyce Briggs, Indiana; Joan Brookwell, Fort Lauderdale; Hon. Diane Bull, Houston; John and Penny Butler, Houston; Don Carlson, Washington, D.C.; Hon. Maria Casanova, Houston; Ed Claflin, New York; Posey Manuel Clinton, Houston; Bruce Dice, Houston; Marcus Dobbs, Houston; Craig Driskell, Fort Worth; Jane Dystel, New York; Sherry Eastwood, Palm Beach; Alice Falconer, San Francisco; Edward B. Fiske, North Carolina; Marie Flickinger, Houston; Miriam Goderich, New York; Roger and Sherry Haagenson, Fort Lauderdale; Barbara Hauser, Houston; Hon. Joe Hayes, Michigan; Yvonne McRoberts

265

Hooker, Arizona; Dr. Steve Hotze, Houston; Ann L. Jones, Virginia; Kathryn Kelber, Houston; Rod and Mary Koenig, Houston; Hon. Jan Krocker, Houston; Margaret Lavender, Fort Lauderdale; Hon. Tony Lindsay, Houston, Mr. Terry Lowry, Houston; Louis and Mary Ann Macey, Houston; Paul and Betty Martin, Houston; George McEvoy, Florida; Betty Medsger, New York; George Mickelis, Houston; Rob Mosbacher, Houston; Suzanne O'Malley, New York; Dick Ostling, New York; Patrick Oxford, Houston; Hon. Ted Poe, Washington, D.C.; Veronica Phillips, Houston; Hon. Paul Pressler III, Houston; Ralph Ray Jr., Fort Lauderdale; Kenny Rodgers, Houston; Judy Safern, Los Angeles; Jim Sales, Houston; Charles and Betti Saunders, Houston; Hon. Mark Speiser, Fort Lauderdale; Heber Taylor, Galveston; Hon. Olen Underwood, Houston; Michael Wallace, Houston; Dr. Hiley Ward, Pennsylvania; Lisa Cavanaugh Weise, Houston; Hon. John Wildenthal, Houston; Walter P. Zivley, Houston.

# Time Line

**1860**  Texas adopts a law prohibiting sodomy, applicable to males and females.

**1943**  Texas adopts a law prohibiting oral sex, applicable to males and females.

**1973**  Texas repeals prior sex laws, adopting 21.06 prohibiting same-sex oral and anal sex.

**1986**  U.S. Supreme Court upholds Georgia sodomy law prohibiting sodomy for same- and opposite-sex couplings.

**1994**  Texas Supreme Court dismisses civil suit *State v. Morales*, which sought to eliminate 21.06

**1996**  U.S. Supreme Court strikes down voter-approved amendment to Colorado constitution, which sought to exclude homosexuals from constitutional protections afforded heterosexuals.

**September 17, 1998**  John Lawrence and Tyron Garner are arrested under 21.06 with a fine-only misdemeanor. Katine, Jones and Lambda Legal accept case, vow to proceed up appeal court ladder.

**September 21, 1998**  Robert Royce Eubanks, who led police to Lawrence and Garner copulating, pleads guilty to False Report, sentenced to 30 days in jail.

267

**November 20, 1998** Lawrence and Garner plead no contest in Justice of the Peace Court, appeal up to County Criminal Court #5.

**December 18, 1998** Judge signs order transferring case from Court #5 to Court #10. Reason given: Agreement of the parties.

**December 22, 1998** Lawrence and Garner plead no contest in County Criminal Court #10. File appeal to Houston-based 14th Court of Appeals.

**June 8, 2000** Three-judge panel of 14th court votes 3-2 to overturn convictions, and throws out 21.06. But their ruling applies only to the 14-county area around Houston, and not to the entire State of Texas.

**June 28, 2000** State files motion requesting that entire 14th court (*en banc*) review the three-judge panel decision.

**September 13, 2000** 14th Court grants State's motion for rehearing *en banc*.

**On or about October 11, 2000** Robert Royce Eubanks is beaten to death. Medical examiner rules death a homicide.

**March 15, 2001** 14th court votes 7-2 to reinstate Lawrence-Garner convictions, upholds 21.06, overrules three-judge panel opinion.

**April 13, 2001** Defense files appeal, called Petition for Discretionary Review, in Texas' Court of Criminal Appeals.

**April 19, 2002** Texas Court of Criminal Appeals refuses to review case.

**July 16, 2002** Appeal, called Petition for Writ of Certiorari, filed in Supreme Court of the United States.

**December 2, 2002** U.S. Supreme Court agrees to consider the case.

**March 26, 2003** Oral argument in Supreme Court of the United States

**June 26, 2003** By a 6-3 vote, U.S. Supreme Court strikes down Texas 21.06 as an unconstitutional violation of Right to Privacy.

**June 28** Traditional Gay Pride celebration day across U.S.

# About the Author

While Judge Janice Law was still basking in the glow of being judge-elect in Harris County, Texas, Criminal Court Number 5—two misdemeanor cases charging the male defendants with Homosexual Conduct were assigned to her court. Harris County includes Houston, the fourth largest city in the United States.

Beginning judges hope for an uneventful grace period while learning the ropes of a new position. The two high-profile sex cases came into her court preceded by weeks of national and international publicity, and a fervent commitment by attorneys of Lambda Legal, a New York-based homosexual rights organization, to take the Houston cases to the U.S. Supreme Court as a challenge to the constitutionality of Texas' 119-year-old law (Texas Penal Code Section 21.06) criminalizing consensual, same -sex sodomy.

There is an eight-week lag between the time a judge is elected and the time she actually takes office. Her judicial predecessor transferred the high-profile cases to another court on a Friday afternoon, thirteen days before Judge Law took the bench on January 1, 1999. The unusual transfer, coupled with persistent rumors that the arrests were staged for the purpose of litigation, stirred her investigative journalist instincts, which she had honed years earlier as a newspaper reporter.

Five years later, when she became a visiting judge, and the U.S. Supreme Court had ruled, Judge Law reactivated her journalist persona. She decided to investigate the *Lawrence* case.

Stanford University journalism professor, the late Dr. William L. Rivers, in his book *The Mass Media* (Harper & Row, 1975) wrote of Janice Law's investigative journalist ability: "Law's stories make it clear that she is among the ablest fact gatherers in American journalism, fully capable of teaching many other journalists how to root out fact, how to bring to light hidden significances. Law reported facts as a perceptive political reporter does..."

Janice Law was born in Flint, Michigan. Her father, Willis, had an eighth-grade education, and worked as a machinist at AC Spark Plug, a General Motors factory. Her mother Elizabeth worked as a cashier at the Purple Cow restaurant in the Durant Hotel in Flint. When Law graduated in 1963 from the University of Michigan, Ann Arbor, with a BA degree in English and Journalism, she was the second person ever—in all generations on both sides of her family—to receive an undergraduate college degree.

For the next 14 years, she worked as a reporter for various newspapers across the United States, while her first husband served as a United States Air Force officer. Some of her journalistic work is included in *Professional Newswriting*, by Dr. Hiley Ward (Harcourt, Brace Jovanovich, Inc., 1985); *The Mass Media* by Dr. William L. Rivers (Harper & Row, 1975); and *The Effete Conspiracy and Other Crimes by the Press* by Ben H. Bagdikian (Harper & Row, 1972).

In 1976 she entered Nova Law School in Fort

Lauderdale, Florida, working the night police desk as a reporter at the *Fort Lauderdale News* to support herself during the first year of law school, until she could get student loans. Marking another personal milestone, she was the first person on both sides of her family ever to receive a professional college degree.

After graduating in 1979, she worked as a state prosecutor in Florida until 1985 when she moved to Houston, Texas. She served as staff attorney for the federal judges in the Southern District of Texas from 1985-1988, processing prisoner complaints filed under federal Civil Rights Act, Section 1983. From 1988, she worked in the litigation section of the City of Houston Legal Department. In 1990, she moved to McAllen, Texas, on the Texas-Mexico border, to serve as an Assistant United States Attorney. From 1991-1994 she worked in Houston as a criminal defense attorney for the indigent, until appointed by the mayor as an Associate Municipal Judge for the City of Houston. In 1998, she was elected as judge in Harris County, Texas, County Criminal Court Number 5.

She now serves as a visiting judge for Texas judges who are vacationing, ill, or absent.

Judge Law may be contacted on her web site: www.JudgeJaniceLaw.com.